®

✔ KT-167-596

Swedish
phrase book

Berlitz Publishing Company, Inc.

Princeton   Mexico City   Dublin   Eschborn   Singapore

Contents

Pronunciation

This section is designed to familiarize you with the sounds of Swedish using our simplified phonetic transcription. You'll find the pronunciation of the Swedish letters and sounds explained below, together with their "imitated" equivalents. To use this system, found throughout the phrase book, simply read the pronunciation as if it were English, noting any special rules below.

The Swedish language

Sweden is the largest of the three Scandinavian countries. It is about the size of California and has a population of around 8 million people, a figure which is comparable to the population of London, England.

Swedish is spoken in almost all of Sweden, apart from parts of Lapland in the far north, where there are Lapp – **Samiska** – and Finnish-speaking areas. Swedish is also spoken in the coastal regions of Finland and Estonia. Although there are characteristic spoken dialects in the various regions, written Swedish has been standardized.

Before the Vikings ruled the seas of northern Europe, the Nordic countries spoke more or less the same language, Old Norse. This language gradually grew into what, today, is Danish, Icelandic, Norwegian, and Swedish. Danes, Norwegians, and Swedes can understand one another (if they speak slowly), but because Iceland is so isolated, the language has retained its closeness to the original Old Norse.

Pronunciation

Swedish has very consistent rules as far as the sounding of individual letters is concerned. However, the pronunciation of words and phrases is made more complex because of the importance of rhythm to indicate meaning. The language has a so-called "musical accent;" the intonation moves up and down and it sounds a bit like music. For example: the word **anden** means either "spirit" or "duck" depending on the rhythm.

The most important thing to remember when pronouncing Swedish is that all the individual letters should be pronounced distinctly, even vowels and consonants at the ends of words.

The Swedish alphabet has 29 letters, the last three of which are the vowels **å**, **ä**, and **ö**. Unlike English, the letter **y** is always a vowel. This means that Swedish has nine vowels. However, Swedish vowels are pure vowel sounds, not a combination of two sounds (diphthongs) as they often are in English. Diphthongs only occur in dialects such as Gotländska (spoken on the island of Gotland), Skånska (spoken in the southern province), and Dalmål (spoken in Dalarna, a province roughly in the middle of the country.)

Although radio and television are contributing to a "leveling out" of Swedish, dialects are alive and are encouraged, adding a richness to the language.

Consonants

Letter	Approximate pronunciation	Symbol	Example	Pron.
b, d, f, h, l, m, n, p, t, v, x	approximately as in English			
c	like *s* in *s*it	s	**cykel**	*sewkel*
ck	pronounced as in English ti*ck*	ck	**flicka**	*flicka*
g	1. hard, like *g* in *g*et	g	**gata**	*gaatah*
	2. soft, like *y* in *y*et	y	**get**	*yeht*
	3. after *r* and *l* pronounced as part of that letter	l'/r'	**borg**	*bor'*
j	1. soft, like *y* in *y*et	y	**jag**	*yaag*
	2. after *r* and *l* pronounced as part of that letter	l'/r'	**familj**	*faamil'*
k	1. like *k* in *k*eep	k	**katt**	*kat*
	2. like *ch* in *ch*urch with a slight *t* sound preceding	ch	**köpa**	*churpa*
q	like *k* in *k*eep	k	**Blomquist**	*bloomkvist*
r	pronounced more strongly than English *r*; rolled	r	**röd**	*rurd*
s	like *s* in *s*ee	s	**sitta**	*sitah*
w	like *v* in *v*ery	v	**wennergren**	*vennegrehn*
z	like *s* in *s*ee	s	**zon**	*soon*

Vowels

Swedish vowels are divided into two groups: hard and soft. **a**, **o**, **u**, and **å** are hard vowels; **e**, **i**, **y**, **ä**, and **ö** are soft. Vowels can also be pronounced either "long" or "short."

Letter	Approximate pronunciation	Symbol	Example	Pron.
a	1. when long, like *a* in c*a*r	*aa*	**dag**	*daag*
	2. when short, between the *a* in c*a*t and *u* in b*u*t	*a* or *u*	**taxi/tack**	*taxi/tuck*
e	1. when long, like *é* in pâté	*eh*	**vet**	*veht*
	2. when short, like *e* in m*e*n	*e*	**vett**	*vet*
i	1. when long, like *ee* in b*ee*	*ee*	**bil**	*beel*
	2. when short, like *i* in b*i*t	*i*	**mitt**	*mit*
o	1. when long, like *oo* in b*oo*t or like *aw* in r*aw*	*oo* or *aw*	**sko** **son**	*skoo* *sawn*
	2. when short, like *o* in f*o*nt	*o*	**font**	*font*
u	like *ou* in m*ou*sse;			
	a) pronounced long before a single consonant and at the end of a word	*eu*	**ruta**	*reuta*
	b) pronounced short before a double consonant	*eu*	**rutt**	*reutt*
y	similar to *ew* in n*ew* with lips tightly rounded;			
	a) pronounced long before a single consonant and at the end of a word	*ew*	**byta**	*bewta*
	b) pronounced short before a double consonant	*ew*	**bytt**	*bewtt*
å	1. when long, like *aw* in l*aw*	*aw*	**gå**	*gaw*
	2. when short, like *o* in h*o*t	*o*	**sång**	*song*
ä	1. when long, like *ai* in *ai*r	*ai(r)*	**här**	*hair*
	2. when short, like *e* in s*e*t	*e*	**säng**	*seng*
ö	like *u* in f*u*r;			
	a) pronounced long before a single consonant and at the end of a word	*ur*	**smör**	*smur*
	b) pronounced short before a double consonant	*ur*	**rött**	*rurt*

Stress

Swedish words are pronounced with even stress on all syllables, with a few exceptions. For those words, the stressed syllable has been marked in the phonetic transcription with an underline.

Pronunciation of the Swedish alphabet

A	aa		**P**	pe
B	beh		**Q**	ku
C	seh		**R**	airr
D	deh		**S**	ess
E	eh		**T**	te
F	eff		**U**	ew
G	geh		**V**	ve
H	haw		**W**	deubbelve
I	ee		**X**	eks
J	jee		**Y**	ew
K	kaw		**Z**	sairta
L	ell		**Å**	aw
M	em		**Ä**	ai
N	en		**Ö**	ur
O	oo			

9

Basic Expressions

ESSENTIAL

Yes.	**Ja.** *yaa*
No.	**Nej.** *nay*
Okay.	**Okej.** *awkay*
Please.	**... tack.** *... tuck*
Thank you.	**Tack.** *tuck*
Thank you very much.	**Tack så mycket.** *tuck saw mewcket*

Greetings/Apologies
Hälsningsfraser/Att be om ursäkt

Hello./Hi!	**Hej./Hejsan!** *hay/haysun*
Good morning/afternoon.	**God morgon/middag.** *goo morron/middag*
Good evening/night.	**God afton/natt.** *goo afton/nut*
Good-bye.	**Adjö/Hej då.** *ayur/hay daw*
Excuse me! *(getting attention)*	**Ursäkta!** *eurshekta*
Excuse me. *(May I get past?)*	**Ursäkta mig.** *eurshekta may*
Excuse me!/Sorry!	**Förlåt mig!** *furlawt may*
Don't mention it.	**Ingen orsak.** *ingen oorshaak*
Never mind.	**Det spelar ingen roll.** *det spehlar ingen rol*

Communication difficulties
Kommunikationssvårigheter

Do you speak English?	**Talar ni engelska?** *taalar nee engelska*
Does anyone here speak English?	**Kan någon här tala engelska?** *kun nawgon hair taala engelska*
I don't speak Swedish.	**Jag talar inte svenska.** *yaag taalar inteh svenska*
Could you speak more slowly?	**Kan ni tala lite långsammare?** *kun nee taala leeteh longsammare*
Could you repeat that?	**Kan ni upprepa det?** *kun nee eupp-rehpa det*
Excuse me? [Pardon?]	**Förlåt.** *furlawt*
What was that?	**Vad var det?** *vaad vaar det*
Could you spell it?	**Kan ni stava det?** *kun nee staava det*
Please write it down.	**Kan ni skriva det, tack.** *kun nee skreeva det tuck*
Can you translate this for me?	**Kan ni översätta det?** *kun nee urver-setta det*
What does this/that mean?	**Vad betyder det här/det där?** *vaad betewder det hair/det dair*
Please point to the phrase in the book.	**Kan ni peka på uttrycket i boken.** *kun nee pehka paw eut-trewcket ee booken*
I understand/don't understand.	**Jag förstår/förstår inte.** *yaag furstawr/furstawr inteh*
Do you understand?	**Förstår ni?** *furstawr nee*

– *Det blir fyrtiofyra kronor och sjuttio öre.*
(That's 44 kronor and 70 öre.)

– Jag förstår inte. (I don't understand.)

– *Det blir fyrtiofyra kronor och sjuttio öre.*
(That's 44 kronor and 70 öre.)

– Kan ni skriva det, tack. ... "Forty-four kronor
and seventy öre." Var så god.
(Please write it down. ... Ah, "forty-four
kronor seventy öre." Here you are.)

Questions Frågor

In Swedish, questions are formed:

1. by reversing the order of the subject and the verb so that the verb starts the sentence:

John är här.	**Är John här?**
John is here.	Is John here?

2. by using a question word, e.g., **vad** (what), followed by the verb and then the subject:

Vad heter du?	**Vad sysslar du med?**
What is your name?	What do you do?

Where? Var/Vart?

Where is it?	**Var ligger det?**	*vaar ligger det*
Where are you going?	**Vart ska du gå?**	*vart skaa deu gaw*
across the road	**över gatan**	*urver gaatan*
around the town	**runt stan**	*reunt staan*
at the meeting place [point]	**vid mötesplatsen**	*veed murtes-platsen*
far from here	**långt härifrån**	*longt haireefrawn*
from the U.S.	**från USA**	*frawn eu es aa*
here	**hit**	*heet*
in Sweden	**i Sverige**	*ee svairr-yeh*
in the car	**i bilen**	*ee beelen*
inside	**inne i**	*inneh ee*
near the bank	**nära banken**	*naira bunken*
next to the post office	**intill posten**	*intil posten*
opposite the market	**mitt emot torget**	*mit emoot tor-yet*
on the left/right	**till vänster/höger**	*til venster/hurger*
on the sidewalk [pavement]	**på trottoaren**	*paw trootooaaren*
outside the café	**utanför kaféet**	*eutanfur kafehet*
there	**dit**	*deet*
to the hotel	**till hotellet**	*til hootelet*
towards Stockholm	**mot Stockholm**	*moot stockholm*
up to the traffic light	**fram till trafikljusen**	*fram til trafeek-yeusen*

When? När?

When does the museum open?	**När öppnar museet?**
	nair urpnar meusehet
When does the train arrive?	**När kommer tåget?**
	nair commer tawget
10 minutes ago	**för tio minuter sedan**
	fur teeoo mineuter sehdan
after lunch	**efter lunch** *efter leunsh*
always	**alltid** *alteed*
around midnight	**omkring midnatt** *omkring meed-nut*
at 7 o'clock	**klockan sju** *klockan sheu*
before Friday	**innan fredag** *innan frehdag*
by tomorrow	**i morgon** *ee morron*
every week	**varje vecka** *varyeh vecka*
for 2 hours	**i två timmar** *ee tvaw timmar*
from 9 a.m. to 6 p.m.	**från klockan nio till klockan arton**
	frawn klockan neeoo til klockan aarton
in 20 minutes	**om tjugo minuter** *om cheugoo mineuter*
never	**aldrig** *aldrig*
not yet	**inte ännu** *inteh enneu*
now	**nu** *neu*
often	**ofta** *ofta*
on March 8	**den åttonde mars** *den ottonde mush*
on weekdays	**på veckodagar**
	paw veckoo-daagar
sometimes	**ibland** *eebland*
soon	**snart** *snaart*
then	**då** *daw*
within 2 days	**om två dagar** *om tvaw daagar*

GRAMMAR

Swedish nouns are either "common gender" or "neuter gender" ➤ 15. Most words for living things are common gender, while many "inanimate objects" are neuter gender. Unfortunately, there are no simple rules to indicate which gender is which.

What sort of …? Vad för slags …?

I'd like something …	**Jag skulle vilja ha …** *yaag skeulleh vilya haa*
It's …	**Den/Det är …** *den/det air*
beautiful/ugly	**vacker/ful** *vacker/feul*
better/worse	**bättre/sämre** *betreh/semreh*
big/small	**stor/liten** *stoor/leeten*
cheap/expensive	**dyr/billig** *deur/billig*
clean/dirty	**ren/smutsig** *rehn/smeutsig*
dark/light	**mörk/ljus** *murk/yeus*
delicious/revolting	**härlig/äcklig** *hairlig/ecklig*
early/late	**tidig/sen** *teedig/sehn*
easy/difficult	**lätt/svår** *let/svawr*
empty/full	**tom/full** *toom/feull*
good/bad	**bra/dålig** *braa/dawlig*
heavy/light	**tung/lätt** *teung/let*
hot/warm/cold	**het/varm/kall** *heht/varm/kal*
narrow/wide	**smal/bred** *smaal/brehd*
next/last	**nästa/sista** *nesta/sista*
old/new	**gammal/ny** *gammal/new*
open/shut	**öppen/stängd** *urpen/stengd*
pleasant/nice/unpleasant	**angenäm/trevlig/otrevlig** *anyeh-nairm/trehvlig/ootrehvlig*
quick/slow	**snabb/långsam** *snub/longsam*
quiet/noisy	**tyst/störande** *tewst/sturrandeh*
right/wrong	**rätt/fel** *ret/fehl*
tall/short	**lång/kort** *long/kort*
thick/thin	**tjock/tunn** *chock/teunn*
vacant/occupied	**ledig/upptagen** *lehdig/euppttaagen*
young/old	**ung/gammal** *eung/gammal*

How much/many? Hur mycket/många?

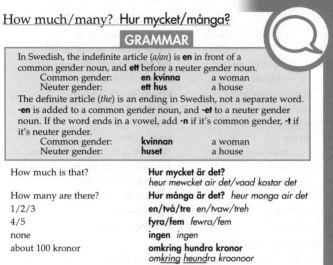

> In Swedish, the indefinite article (*a/an*) is **en** in front of a
> common gender noun, and **ett** before a neuter gender noun.
>
> | | | |
> |---|---|---|
> | Common gender: | **en kvinna** | a woman |
> | Neuter gender: | **ett hus** | a house |
>
> The definite article (*the*) is an ending in Swedish, not a separate word.
> **-en** is added to a common gender noun, and **-et** to a neuter gender
> noun. If the word ends in a vowel, add **-n** if it's common gender, **-t** if
> it's neuter gender.
>
> | | | |
> |---|---|---|
> | Common gender: | **kvinnan** | a woman |
> | Neuter gender: | **huset** | a house |

How much is that?	**Hur mycket är det?** *heur mewcket air det/vaad kostar det*
How many are there?	**Hur många är det?** *heur monga air det*
1/2/3	**en/två/tre** *en/tvaw/treh*
4/5	**fyra/fem** *fewra/fem*
none	**ingen** *ingen*
about 100 kronor	**omkring hundra kronor** *om<u>kring</u> <u>heun</u>dra kroonoor*
a little	**lite** *leeteh*
a lot of traffic	**mycket trafik** *mewcket tra<u>feek</u>*
enough	**tillräckligt** *<u>til</u>reckligt*
few/a few of them	**få/några** *faw/<u>naw</u>gra*
more than that	**mer än så** *mehr en saw*
less than that	**mindre än så** *<u>mind</u>reh en saw*
much more	**mycket mera** *mewcket <u>meh</u>ra*
nothing else	**inget annat** *inget anat*
too much	**för mycket** *fur mewcket*

Why? Varför?

Why is that?	**Hur kommer det sig?** *<u>var</u>fur/heur <u>kom</u>mer det say*
Why not?	**Varför inte?** *<u>var</u>fur inteh*
It's because of the weather.	**Det är på grund av vädret.** *det air paw greund aav <u>vaid</u>ret*
It's because I'm in a hurry.	**Det är därför att jag har bråttom.** *det air <u>dair</u>fur at yaag haar brottom*
I don't know why.	**Jag vet inte varför.** *yaag veht inteh <u>var</u>fur*

Who?/Which? Vem?/Vilken?

Who's there?	**Vem är det?**	*vem air det*
Who is it for?	**Vem är det till?**	*vem air det til*
(for) her/him	**(till) henne/honom**	*(til) heneh/honom*
(for) me	**(till) mig**	*(til) may*
(for) you *(sing./plur.)*	**(till) dig/er**	*(til) day/ehr*
(for) them	**(till) dem**	*(til) dem*
someone	**någon**	*nawgon*
no one	**ingen**	*ingen*
Which one do you want?	**Vilken vill ni ha?**	*vilken vil nee haa*
this one/that one	**den här/den där**	*den hair/den dair*
one like that	**en sån där**	*en son dair*
not that one	**inte den där**	*inteh den dair*
something	**något**	*nawgot*
nothing	**ingenting**	*ingenting*

Whose? Vems?

Whose is that?	**Vems är det?**	*vems air det*
It's …	**Det är …**	*det air*
mine/ours/yours *(sing./plur.)*	**min/vår/din/er**	*min/vawr/din/ehr*
his/hers/theirs	**hans/hennes/deras**	*hans/henes/dehras*
It's … turn.	**Det är … tur.**	*det air … teur*
my/our/your *(sing./plur.)*	**min/vår/din/er**	*min/vawr/din/ehr*

GRAMMAR

Possession is formed by adding **–s** (singular and plural) to the noun:

Kvinnans kappa	the woman's coat
Husets tak	the roof of the house

Possessive adjectives agree in gender and number with the thing possessed and not the possessor:

	common	neuter	plural		common	neuter	plural
my	**min**	**mitt**	**mina**	its	**sin**	**sitt**	**sina**
your	**din**	**ditt**	**dina**	our	**vår**	**vårt**	**våra**
his	**sin**	**sitt**	**sina**	your	**er**	**ert**	**era**
her	**sin**	**sitt**	**sina**	their	**sin**	**sitt**	**sina**

How? Hur?

How would you like to pay?	**Hur vill ni betala?** *heur vil nee betaala*
by cash	**kontant** *kontant*
by credit card	**med kreditkort** *mehd kredeet-koort*
How are you getting here?	**Hur ska ni komma hit?** *heur skaa nee komma heet*
by car/bus/train	**med bil/buss/tåg** *mehd beel/beuss/tawg*
on foot	**till fots** *til foots*
quickly	**snabbt** *snubt*
slowly	**sakta/långsamt** *sakta/longsamt*
too fast	**för fort** *fur foort*
very	**mycket** *mewcket*
with a friend	**med en vän** *mehd en ven*
without a passport	**utan pass** *eutan pus*

Is it …?/Are there …? Är det …?/Finns det …?

Is it free of charge?	**Är det gratis?** *air det graatis*
It isn't ready.	**Det är inte färdigt.** *det air inteh fairdigt*
Is there a shower in the room?	**Finns det dusch på rummet?** *fins det deush paw reummet*
Is there a bus into town?	**Finns det buss till stan?** *fins det beuss til staan*
There aren't any towels in my room.	**Det finns inga handdukar på mitt rum.** *det fins inga hand-deukar paw mit reumm*
Here it is/they are.	**Här är det./Här är de.** *hair air det/hair air deh*
There it is/they are.	**Där är det./Där är de.** *dair air det/dair air deh*

17

Can/May? Kan?

Can I …?	**Kan jag …?** *kun yaag*
May we …?	**Får vi …?** *fawr vee*
Can you show me …?	**Kan ni visa mig …?** *kun nee veesa may*
Can you tell me …?	**Kan ni säga mig …?** *kun nee saya may*
Can you help me?	**Kan ni hjälpa mig?** *kun nee yelpa may*
May I help you?	**Kan jag hjälpa er?** *kun yaag yelpa ehr*
Can you direct me to …?	**Kan ni visa mig vägen till …?** *kun nee veesa may <u>vair</u>gen til*
I can't.	**Det kan jag inte.** *det kun yaag inteh*

What do you want? Vad önskar ni?

I'd like …	**Jag skulle vilja …** *yaag skeulleh vilya*
Could I have …?	**Kan jag få …?** *kun yaag faw*
We'd like …	**Vi skulle vilja …** *vee skeulleh vilya*
Give me …	**Ge mig …** *yeh may*
I'm looking for …	**Jag letar efter …** *yaag lehtar efter*
I need to …	**Jag behöver …** *yaag be<u>hur</u>ver*
go …	**gå …** *gaw*
find …	**hitta …** *hitta*
see …	**titta på …** *titta paw*
speak to …	**tala med …** *taala mehd*

– Ursäkta mig. (Excuse me.)

– *Javisst, kan jag hjälpa er?*
(Yes, can I help you?)

– Jag skulle vilja tala med Johan Berggren.
(Can I speak to Johan Berggren?)

– *Ett ögonblick, tack.*
(Just a moment, please.)

Swedish has two forms for "you": the formal **ni**, used only for people not known to you, and the informal **du**, used in all other situations.

Pronouns

	subject	object	possessive		subject	object	possessive
	(I)	(me)	(mine)		(we)	(us)	(ours)
e.g.							
I	**jag**	**mig**	**min/mitt**	it	**den/det**	**den/det**	**dess**
you	**du/ni**	**dig/er**	**din/ditt**	we	**vi**	**oss**	**vår/vårt**
he	**han**	**honom**	**hans**	you	**ni**	**er**	**er/ert**
she	**hon**	**henne**	**hennes**	they	**de**	**dem**	**deras**

Other useful words Andra användbara ord

fortunately	**lyckligtvis** *lewckligtvees*
hopefully	**förhoppningsvis** *furhopningsvees*
of course	**naturligtvis** *nateurligtvees*
perhaps	**kanske** *kansheh*
unfortunately	**tyvärr** *tew<u>vairr</u>*
also/but	**också/men** *ocksaw/men*
and/or	**och/eller** *ock/eller*

Exclamations Utrop

At last!	**Äntligen!** <u>*entligen*</u>
Go on.	**Fortsätt.** *foortset*
Nonsense!	**Dumheter!** <u>*deum*</u>*-hehter*
That's true!	**Det är sant!** *det air sant*
No way!	**Uteslutet!** *euteh-<u>sleut</u>et*
How are things?	**Hur är det?** *heur air det*
great/terrific	**bra/fantastiskt** *braa/fan<u>tas</u>tiskt*
very good	**utmärkt** *eutmairkt*
fine/okay	**fint/okej** *feent/awkay*
not bad	**inte dåligt** *inteh dawligt*
not good	**inte bra** *inteh braa*
fairly bad	**inget vidare** *inget <u>veed</u>are*
terrible	**dåligt/hemskt** *dawligt/hemskt*

Accommodations

All types of accommodations, from hotels to campsites, can be found through the Swedish tourist office in your country, and in Sweden at the Swedish Tourist Club (**Svenska Turistföreningen – STF**) and tourist information offices (**Turistbyrå**) in most towns. If you plan on visiting during the summer, book in advance.

Hotell *hootel*
First-class and deluxe hotels, found in big towns and cities. Prices and facilities vary, but standards are always high. Breakfast is usually included.

Familjehotell *fahmilyer-hootel*
Hotels offering special rates for families with children sharing the same room (three to six beds); operate during the summer only.

Turisthotell/Pensionat *tewrist-hootel/pahnshoonaat*
Clean and comfortable, these tourist hotels and guest houses are found in summer resorts and winter sports centers. They usually offer an all-inclusive package deal.

Sommarhotell *sommahr-hootel*
In Stockholm, Göteborg, and Lund student dormitories are opened to tourists in the summer. They are a good choice if you are traveling with a group.

Motell *mootel*
Reasonably priced accommodations for motorists, with a restaurant and car-friendly facilities.

Privatrum *privaatreum*
Bed and breakfasts. The tourist office gives recommendations.

Stugor/Lägenheter *steugoor/laigenhehter*
Wooden chalets or apartments, rented by the week via tourist offices during the summer.

Vandrarhem *vahndrahrhehm*
Youth hostels. Located all over Sweden, they are comfortable and a good value.

Reservations Reservationer

In advance På förhand

Can you recommend
a hotel in …?
**Kan ni rekommendera ett
hotel i …?** *kun nee
rekomen<u>deh</u>ra et hoo<u>tel</u> ee*

Is it near the center of town?
Ligger det nära centrum?
ligger det naira sentreum

How much is it per night?
Vad kostar det per natt?
vaad kostar det pairr nut

Do you have a cheaper room?
Har ni ett billigare rum?
haar nee et <u>billig</u>areh reumm

Could you reserve me a
room there, please?
Kan ni reservera mig ett rum där, tack?
kun nee reser<u>veh</u>ra may et reumm dair tuck

How do I get there?
Hur kommer jag dit?
heur <u>kom</u>mer yaag deet

At the hotel På hotellet

Do you have a room?
Har ni ett ledigt rum?
haar nee et lehdigt reumm

I'm sorry. We're full.
Tyvärr, det är fullbelagt.
tew<u>vairr</u> det air <u>feull</u>-belagt

Is there another hotel nearby?
Finns det ett annat hotell i närheten?
fins det et anat hoo<u>tel</u> ee <u>nair</u>hehten

I'd like a single/double room.
**Jag skulle vilja ha ett enkelrum/ett
dubbelrum.** *yaag skeulleh vilya haa et
enkel-reumm/et deubbel-reumm*

I'd like a room with …
Jag skulle vilja ha ett rum med …
yaag skeulleh vilya haa et reumm mehd

a double bed/twin beds
en dubbelsäng/två sängar
en deubbel-seng/tvaw sengar

a bath/shower
bad/dusch *baad/deush*

– Har ni ett ledigt rum? (Do you have a room?)

– Tyvärr, det är fullbelagt. (I'm sorry. We're full.)

– Jaså. Finns det ett annat hotell i närheten?
(Oh. Is there another hotel nearby?)

– Javisst, hotell Ambassadör ligger här intill.
(Yes, madam/sir. The Ambassador is very near.)

Reception Receptionen

I have a reservation.	**Jag har beställt rum.**	*yaag har bestelt reumm*
My name is …	**Mitt namn är …** *mit namn air*	
We've reserved a double and a single room.	**Vi har beställt ett dubbelrum och ett enkelrum.** *vee haar bestelt et deubbel-reumm ock et enkel-reumm*	
I've reserved a room for two nights.	**Jag har beställt ett rum för två nätter.** *yaag haar bestelt et reumm fur tvaw netter*	
I confirmed my reservation by mail.	**Jag har bekräftat min beställning per post.** *yaag haar bekreftat min bestelning pairr post*	
Could we have adjoining rooms?	**Kan vi få angränsande rum?** *kun vee faw ungrensande reumm*	

Amenities and facilities Bekvämligheter

Is there (a) … in the room?	**Finns det (en/ett) … på rummet?** *fins det (en/et) … paw reummet*	
air conditioning	**luftkonditionering** *leuft-kondishonehring*	
TV/telephone	**TV/telefon** *teh-veh/telefawn*	
Does the hotel have (a/an) …?	**Finns det … på hotellet?** *fins det … paw hootelet*	
fax	**fax** *fax*	
laundry service	**tvättservice** *tvet-service*	
satellite TV	**satellit TV** *satteleet-tehveh*	
sauna	**bastu** *busteu*	
swimming pool	**simbassäng** *simbasseng*	
Could you put … in the room?	**Kan ni ställa … på rummet?** *kun nee stella … paw reummet*	
an extra bed	**en extra säng** *en extra seng*	
a crib [child's cot]?	**en barnsäng** *en baarnseng*	
Do you have facilities for children/the disabled?	**Kan ni ta emot barn/rörelsehindrade?** *kun nee taa emoot baarn/rurrelseh-hindrade*	

How long …? Hur länge …?

We'll be staying …	**Vi kommer att stanna …**
	vee kommer at stanna
overnight only	**över natten** *urver nutten*
a few days	**ett par dagar** *et paar daagar*
a week (at least)	**en vecka (minst)** *en vecka (minst)*
I'd like to stay an extra night.	**Jag skulle vilja stanna en extra natt.**
	yaag skeulleh vilya stanna en extra nut

– Hej, jag har beställt ett rum. Mitt namn är John Newton.
(Hello. I have a reservation. My name's John Newton.)

– *God middag, Mr. Newton.*
(Hello, Mr. Newton.)

– Jag har beställt ett rum för två nätter.
(I've reserved a room for two nights.)

– *Det går bra. Kan ni fylla i den här inskrivningsblanketten, tack.*
(Very good. Please fill out this registration form.)

Kan jag få se ert pass, tack?	May I see your passport, please?
Kan ni fylla i den här blanketten/skriva under här.	Please fill out this form/sign here.
Vad står det på bilens nummerskylt?	What is your license plate [registration] number?

ENDAST RUMMET SEK …	room only … kronor
FRUKOST INGÅR	breakfast included
MÅLTIDER SERVERAS	meals available
EFTERNAMN/FÖRNAMN	last name/first name
ADRESS/GATA/NUMMER	home address/street/number
NATIONALITET/YRKE	nationality/profession
FÖDELSEDATUM/FÖDELSEORT	date/place of birth
PASSNUMMER	passport number
BILENS NUMMERSKYLT	license plate [registration] number
DATUM/ORT	place/date (of signature)
UNDERSKRIFT	signature

Price Priser

How much is it …?	**Hur mycket kostar det …?** *heur mewcket kostar det*
per night/week	**per natt/vecka** *pairr nut/vecka*
for bed and breakfast	**för ett rum med frukost** *fur et reumm mehd freukost*
excluding meals	**exklusive måltider** *exkleuseeveh mawlteeder*
for full board (American Plan [A.P.])	**för helpension** *fur hehl-pangshoon*
for half board (Modified American Plan [M.A.P.])	**för halvpension** *fur halv-pangshoon*
Does the price include …?	**Ingår … i priset?** *ingawr … ee preeset*
breakfast	**frukost** *freukost*
sales tax [VAT]	**MOMS** *moms*
Do I have to pay a deposit?	**Behöver jag betala handpenning?** *behurver yaag betaala hand-penning*
Is there a reduction for children?	**Finns det rabatt för barn?** *fins det rabatt fur baarn*

Decisions Beslut

May I see the room?	**Kan jag få se på rummet?** *kun yaag faw seh paw reummet*
That's fine. I'll take it.	**Det är bra. Jag tar det.** *det air braa. yaag taar det*
It's too …	**Det är för …** *det air fur*
dark/small	**mörkt/litet** *murkt/leetet*
noisy	**mycket buller** *mewcket beuller*
Do you have anything …?	**Har ni något …?** *haar nee nawgot*
bigger/cheaper	**större/billigare** *sturreh/billigareh*
quieter/warmer	**tystare/varmare** *tewstareh/varmareh*
No, I won't take it.	**Nej tack, jag tar det inte.** *nay tuck yaag taar det inteh*

Problems Problem

The … doesn't work.	**… fungerar inte.** *… feungehrar inteh*
air conditioning	**luftkonditioneringen** *leuft-kondishoonehringen*
fan	**fläkten** *flekten*
heating	**värmen** *vairmen*
light	**ljuset** *yeuset*
I can't turn the heat [heating] on/off.	**Jag kan inte sätta på/stänga av värmen.** *yaag kun inteh setta paw/stenga aav vairmen*
There is no hot water/ toilet paper.	**Det finns inget varmvatten/toalettpapper.** *det fins inget varm-vatten/tooalet-papper*
The faucet [tap] is dripping.	**Kranen droppar.** *kraanen droppar*
The sink/toilet is blocked.	**Det är stopp i handfatet/toaletten.** *det air stop ee handfaatet/tooaletten*
The window/door is jammed.	**Fönstret/dörren sitter fast.** *furnstret/durren sitter fast*
My room has not been made up.	**Mitt rum har inte städats.** *mit reumm haar inteh stairdats*
The … is/are broken.	**… är trasig.** *… air traasig*
blinds/shutters	**rullgardinen** *reull-gardeenen*
lamp	**lampan** *lampan*
lock	**låset** *lawset*
There are insects in our room.	**Det finns insekter i vårt rum.** *det fins insekter ee vawrt reumm*

Action Vidta åtgärder

Could you have that seen to?	**Kan ni sköta om det där?** *kun nee shurta om det dair*
I'd like to move to another room.	**Jag skulle vilja flytta till ett annat rum.** *yaag skeulleh vilya flewtta til et anat reumm*
I'd like to speak to the manager.	**Jag skulle vilja tala med direktören.** *yaag skeulleh vilya taala med direkturren*

25

Requirements Förfrågningar

Throughout Sweden the current is 220-volt, 50-cycle AC. If you bring your own electrical appliances, buy a Continental adapter plug (round pins) before leaving home. You may also need a transformer appropriate to the wattage of the appliance.

About the hotel Om hotellet

Where's the …?	**Var är …?** *vaar air*
bar	**baren** *baaren*
bathroom [toilet]	**toaletten** *tooaletten*
dining room	**matsalen** *maatsaalen*
elevator [lift]	**hissen** *hissen*
parking lot [car park]	**parkeringsplatsen** *parkehrings-platsen*
shower room	**duschrummet** *deush-reummet*
swimming pool	**simbassängen** *simbassengen*
tour operator's bulletin board	**reseledarens anslagstavla** *rehse-lehdarens anslaags-tavla*
Does the hotel have a garage?	**Har hotellet något garage?** *haar hootellet nawgot garaash*
Can I use this adapter here?	**Kan jag använda den här adaptern här?** *kun yaag anvenda den hair adaptern hair*

ENDAST RAKAPPARATER	razors [shavers] only
NÖDUTGÅNG	emergency exit
BRANDDÖRR	fire door
VAR GOD STÖR EJ	do not disturb
SLÅ … TILL LINJEN	dial … for an outside line
SLÅ … TILL RECEPTIONEN	dial … for reception
AVLÄGSNA INTE HANDDUKARNA FRÅN RUMMET	don't remove towels from room

Personal needs Personliga önskningar

The key to room ..., please.
Nyckeln till rum ..., tack.
newckeln til reumm ... tack

I've lost my key.
Jag har tappat min nyckel.
yaag haar tappat min newckel

I've locked myself out of my room.
Jag har låst ut mig ur rummet.
yaag haar lawst eut may eur reummet

Could you wake me at ...?
Kan ni väcka mig klockan ...?
kun nee vecka may klockan

I'd like breakfast in my room.
Jag skulle vilja ha frukost på rummet.
yaag skeulleh vilya haa freukost paw reummet

Can I leave this in the safe?
Kan jag lämna detta i kassaskåpet?
kun yaag lemna detta ee kassa-skawpet

Could I have my things from the safe?
Kan jag få mina saker från kassaskåpet?
kun yaag faw meena saaker frawn kassa-skawpet

Where can I find (a) ...?
Var kan jag få tag på ...?
vaar kun yaag faw taag paw

maid
en städerska *en staírdeska*

our tour guide
vår reseledare *vawr rehse-lehdare*

May I have (an) extra ...?
Kan jag få ... till?
kun yaag faw ... til

bath towel
en badhandduk *en baad-handdeuk*

blanket
ett täcke *et teckeh*

hangers
en hängare *en hengareh*

pillow
en kudde *en keuddeh*

soap
en tvål *en tvawl*

Is there any mail for me?
Finns det någon post till mig?
fins det nawgon post til may

Are there any messages for me?
Finns det något meddelande till mig?
fins det nawgot mehd-dehlande til may

Could you mail this for me, please?
Kan ni posta det här åt mig, tack?
kun nee posta det hair awt may tuck

BREAKFAST ➤ 43; CHANGING MONEY ➤ 138

Renting Hyra

We've reserved an apartment/cottage in the name of …	**Vi har hyrt en lägenhet/stuga under namnet …** vee haar hewrt en _lairgen_-heht/steuga _eunder_ _namn_et
Where do we pick up the keys?	**Var kan vi hämta nycklarna?** vaar kun vee hemta _newc_klarna
Where is the …?	**Var är …?** vaar air
electric [electricity] meter	**elmätaren** _ehl_-mairtaren
fuse box	**säkringarna** _sairk_ringarna
valve [stopcock]	**avstängningskranen** _aavstengnings_-_kraan_en
water heater	**varmvattenberedaren** _varmvat_ten-_berehd_aren
Are there any spare …?	**Finns det några extra …?** fins det nawgra extra
fuses	**säkringar** _sairk_ringar
gas bottles	**gascylindrar** gaas-sew_lind_rar
sheets	**lakan** _laak_an
Which day does the maid come?	**Vilken dag kommer städerskan?** vilken daag kommer _stair_derskan
When do I put out the trash [rubbish]?	**När ska jag ställa ut soporna?** nair skaa yaag stella eut _soo_poorna

Problems Problem

Where can I contact you?	**Var kan jag kontakta er?** vaar kun yaag kon_takt_a ehr
How does the stove [cooker]/water heater work?	**Hur fungerar spisen/varmvattenberedaren?** heur feung_ehr_ar _spees_en/_varmvat_ten-_berehd_aren
The … is/are dirty.	**… är smutsig(a).** … air smeutsig(a)
The … has broken down.	**… har gått sönder.** … haar got _surn_der
We accidentally broke/lost …	**Vi har råkat slå sönder/förlorat …** vee haar rawkat slå _surn_der/fur_loor_at
That was already damaged when we arrived.	**Det var redan trasigt när vi anlände.** det vaar rehdan _traas_igt nair vee _un_lendeh

Useful terms Användbara termer

boiler	**panna** *panna*
dishes [crockery]	**porslin** *poshleen*
freezer	**frys** *frews*
frying pan	**stekpanna** *stehkpanna*
kettle	**vattenkokare** *vatten-kookare*
lamp	**lampa** *lampa*
refrigerator	**kylskåp** *chewl-skawp*
saucepan	**kastrull** *kastreull*
stove [cooker]	**spis** *spees*
utensils [cutlery]	**matbestick** *maatbestik*
washing machine	**tvättmaskin** *tvet-masheen*

Rooms Rum

balcony	**balkong** *balkong*
bathroom	**badrum** *baad-reumm*
bedroom	**sovrum** *sawv-reumm*
dining room	**matsal/matrum** *maat-saal/mat-reumm*
kitchen	**kök** *churk*
living room	**vardagsrum** *vaardax-reumm*
toilet	**toalett** *tooalet*

Youth hostel Vandrarhem

Do you have any places left for tonight?	**Finns det några lediga platser ikväll?** *fins det nawgra lehdiga platser ee kvel*
Do you rent out bedding?	**Kan man hyra sängkläder?** *kun man hewra seng-klairder*
What time are the doors locked?	**När stängs ytterdörrarna?** *nair stengs ewtter-durrarna*
I have an International Student Card.	**Jag har ett internationellt studentkort.** *yaag haar et inter-nashonelt steudent-koort*

REQUIREMENTS ➤ 26; CAMPING ➤ 30

Camping Camping

Camping is extremely popular and well organized in Sweden. There are 750 sites, often by a lake or the sea, offering boating, canoeing, biking, and miniature golf. Many sites also offer two- to six-bed log cabins, which are fully equipped, except for bedding. Unless you have an International Camping Card, you will need a local camping card. You can camp for one night anywhere, but after that you have to ask permission if you are on private property. Ask at a tourist office for information.

Reservations Bokningar

Is there a campsite near here?	**Finns det en campingplats i närheten?** *fins det en kamping-plats ee nairhehten*
Do you have space for a tent/ trailer [caravan]?	**Har ni plats för ett tält/en husvagn?** *haar nee plats fur et telt/en heus-vangn*
What's the charge …?	**Vad kostar det …?** *vaad kostar det*
per day/week	**per dag/vecka** *pairr daag/vecka*
for a tent/car	**för ett tält/en bil** *fur et telt/en beel*
for a trailer [caravan]	**för en husvagn** *fur en heus-vangn*

Facilities Bekvämligheter

Are there cooking facilities on site?	**Finns det kokmöjligheter här?** *fins det kook-mur'lig-hehter hair*
Are there any electrical outlets [power points]?	**Finns det några nätuttag här?** *fins det nawgra nairt-eut-taag hair*
Where is/are the …?	**Var finns …?** *vaar finns*
drinking water	**dricksvatten** *drix-vatten*
trash cans [dustbins]	**soptunnor** *soop-teunnor*
laundry facilities	**tvättmöjligheter** *tvet-mur'lig-hehter*
showers	**duschar** *deushar*
Where can I get some butane gas?	**Var kan jag få tag på butangas?** *vaar kun yaag faw taag paw butaangaas*

INGEN CAMPING	no camping
DRICKSVATTEN	drinking water
INGEN ÖPPEN ELD/GRILLNING	no fires/barbecues

Complaints Klagomål

It's too sunny here.
Det är för soligt här.
det air fur sooligt hair

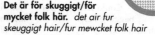

It's too shady/crowded here.
Det är för skuggigt/för mycket folk här. *det air fur skuggigt hair/fur mewcket folk hair*

The ground's too hard/uneven.
Marken är för hård/ojämn.
marken air fur hawrd/ooyemn

Do you have a more level spot?
Finns det en jämnare plats?
fins det en yemnare plats

You can't camp here.
Ni kan inte campa här.
nee kun inteh kampa hair

Camping equipment Campingutrustning

butane gas
butangas *beutaangaas*

campbed
tältsäng *telt-seng*

charcoal
grillkol *grillkawl*

flashlight [torch]
ficklampa *fick-lampa*

groundcloth [groundsheet]
tältunderlag *telt-eunderlaag*

guy rope
tältlina *telt-leena*

hammer
hammare *hammare*

kerosene [primus] stove
primuskök *preemeus-churk*

knapsack
ryggsäck *rewgg-seck*

mallet
trähammare *trair-hammare*

matches
tändstickor *tend-stickoor*

(air) mattress
luftmadrass *leuft-madrass*

paraffin
paraffin *parafeen*

sleeping bag
sovsäck *sawv-seck*

tent
tält *telt*

tent pegs
tältpinnar *telt-pinnar*

tent pole
tältstake *telt-staakeh*

Checking out Avresa

What time do we have to check out by?	**När måste vi checka ut?** *nair mosteh vee checka eut*
Could we leave our baggage here until ... p.m.?	**Kan vi lämna vårt bagage här till klockan ...?** *kun vee lemna vawrt bagaash hair til klockan*
I'm leaving now.	**Jag reser nu.** *yaag rehser neu*
Could you order me a taxi, please?	**Kan ni skaffa mig en taxi, tack?** *kun nee skaffa may en taxi tuck*
It's been a very enjoyable stay.	**Det har varit en mycket trevlig vistelse.** *det haar vaarit en mewcket trehvlig vistelseh*

Paying Betala räkningen

A service charge is included in hotel and restaurant bills, but you are expected to round up a restaurant bill to the nearest SEK10. Tipping is generally not expected, but it's always appreciated if the service has been exceptionally good. It is customary to give a small tip to hairdressers/barbers, taxi drivers, and porters.

May I have my bill, please?	**Kan jag få räkningen, tack?** *kun yaag faw rairkningen tuck*
How much is my telephone bill?	**Hur mycket är telefonräkningen på?** *heur mewcket air telefawn-rairkningen paw*
I think there's a mistake in this bill.	**Jag tror det är fel på den här räkningen.** *yaag troor det air fehl paw den hair rairkningen*
I've made ... telephone calls.	**Jag har ringt ... telefonsamtal.** *yaag haar ringt ... telefawn-samtaal*
I've taken ... from the mini-bar.	**Jag har tagit ... från mini-baren.** *yaag haar taagit ... frawn mini-baaren*
Can I have an itemized bill?	**Kan jag få en specificerad räkning?** *kun yaag faw en spesifisehrad rairkning*
Could I have a receipt, please?	**Kan jag få ett kvitto, tack?** *kun yaag faw et kvittoo tuck*

Eating Out

Restaurants Restauranger

Cocktail bar kocktailbaar
These "bars," found only in hotels in large towns and cities, serve canapés and other small snacks.

Dansrestaurang dansresteurang
Restaurants offering dining and dancing, found in large towns and cities.

Fiskrestaurang feeskresteurang
Fish and seafood restaurants.

Gatukök gaateuchurk
"Kitchen on the street," serving quick snacks such as sausages, hamburgers, mashed potatoes, French fries, and soft drinks.

Grillbar grilbar
Self-service restaurants offering hamburgers, steaks, French fries, beer, and soft drinks.

Gästgivargård yestyeevargord
Old country inns, with rustic décor and excellent cuisine.
A good choice for a **smörgåsbord** ➤ 46.

Kafé kaffeh
Coffee shops serving hot drinks, soft drinks, and small snacks.

Konditori kondeetoree
Coffee shops serving hot drinks, soft drinks, and a mouthwatering selection of pastries and cakes. Often also serve sandwiches and small snacks.

Korvstånd _koorvstond_
Hot-dog stands, sometimes selling hamburgers and French fries, too.

Kvarterskrog/Lunchrestaurang
kvaartehrskroog/leunschresteurang
Small neighborhood restaurants with good, inexpensive food, and beer and wine. For a good value, try the **dagens rätt** (the specialty of the day.)

Restaurang/Restaurant _resteurang_
There is no official rating system for restaurants. They can be anything from the classically elegant to the more informal. When in Stockholm, don't miss a memorable meal on a boat taking you out into the archipelago.

Stekhus _stehkheus_
Steak houses.

Värdshus _vairdsheus_
Old inns in smaller towns, often offering local specialties such as reindeer, moose, and poultry.

Meal times När äter man?
Frukost _freukost_
Breakfast is usually served from 7 to 10 a.m. Hotels and guest houses offer a large buffet selection of cheeses, cold meats, bread, toast, egg dishes, and cereals, and breakfast is generally included in the room price.

Lunch _leunsch_
Lunch is served from as early as 11 a.m. Although many Swedes have a cooked one-course meal at lunchtime, some opt for a sandwich or a salad. This is the best time to try the **dagens rätt** (specialty of the day.)

Middag _middah_
Dinner is normally eaten early, around 6 or 7 p.m., although restaurants continue serving until late, especially on the weekend.

Swedish cuisine Det svenska köket

Most visitors and tourists equate Swedish food with the **smörgåsbord** ➤ 46. Whereas the **smörgåsbord** does indeed represent a great many delicacies from Swedish cuisine, there are many other excellent Swedish dishes (not always found at a **smörgåsbord**) that visitors should sample. Swedes are fish lovers and some of their favorite seafood dishes include marinated herrings (**sill**), shrimps in their shells, some opt for **gravlax** (marinated salmon), and **kräftor** (crayfish, available in August) – all eaten with new potatoes, boiled with dill. For your main course, do not miss the opportunity to sample venison, moose or reindeer, served with rowanberry or wild cranberry jam. In the countryside, you will find desserts made with fresh **smultron** (wild strawberries) and **blåbär** (blueberries, bilberries).

A table for ..., please.	**Kan jag få ett bord för ...,** **tack.** *kun yaag faw et boord fur ... tuck*
1/2/3/4 (people)	**en/två/tre/fyra** *en/tvaw/treh/fewra*
Thank you.	**Tack.** *tuck*
The bill, please.	**Kan jag få räkningen, tack.** *kun yaag faw <u>rairk</u>ningen tuck*

Finding a place to eat
Att hitta någonstans att äta

Can you recommend a good restaurant?	**Kan ni rekommendera en bra restaurang?** *kun nee rekomen<u>deh</u>ra en braa resteu<u>rang</u>*
Is there a(n) ... near here?	**Finns det någon ... i närheten?** *fins det nawgon ... ee <u>nair</u>hehten*
Chinese restaurant	**kinesisk restaurant** *chi<u>neh</u>sisk resteu<u>rang</u>*
fish restaurant	**fiskrestaurant** *fiskresteu<u>rang</u>*
inexpensive restaurant	**billigare restaurant** *<u>bil</u>ligareh resteu<u>rang</u>*
Italian restaurant	**italiensk restaurant** *ital-<u>yensk</u> resteu<u>rang</u>*
traditional local restaurant	**värdshus** *vairds-heus*
vegetarian restaurant	**vegetariansk restaurant** *vegetaree-<u>ansk</u> resteu<u>rang</u>*
Where can I find a(n) ...?	**Var finns ...** *vaar fins*
burger stand	**ett korvstånd** *et korv-stond*
café	**ett kafé** *et ka<u>feh</u>*
with a terrace/garden	**med terrass/trädgård** *mehd te<u>rass</u>/traird-gawrd*
fast-food restaurant	**en grillbar** *en gril-baar*
ice-cream parlor	**ett glasstånd** *et glas-stond*
pizzeria	**en pizzeria** *en pitser<u>eea</u>*
steak house	**ett stekhus** *et stehk-heus*
coffee/pastry shop	**konditori** *kon<u>dee</u>-tor<u>ee</u>*

DIRECTIONS ➤ 94

Reserving a table Reservera bord

I'd like to reserve a table …	**Jag skulle vilja reservera ett bord …** *yaag skeulleh vilya reser<u>veh</u>ra et boord*
for two	**för två** fur tvaw
for this evening/ tomorrow at …	**till ikväll/imorgon klockan …** *til eekvell/eemorron klockan*
We'll come at 8:00.	**Vi kommer klockan åtta.** *vee <u>kommer</u> klockan otta*
A table for two, please.	**Ett bord for två, tack.** *et boord fur tvaw tuck*
We have a reservation.	**Vi har reserverat ett bord.** *vee haar reser<u>veh</u>rat et boord*

Till vilken tid?	For what time?
Vad är namnet, tack?	What's the name, please?
Tyvärr, det är fullbokat.	I'm sorry. We're very busy/full.
Vi har ett bord ledigt om … minuter.	We'll have a free table in … minutes.
Var snäll och kom tillbaka om … minuter.	Please come back in … minutes.

Where to sit Lämpligt bord

Could we sit …?	**Kan vi sitta …?** *kun vee sitta*
over there	**där borta** *dair borta*
outside	**ute** *euteh*
in a non-smoking area	**vid bord för icke-rökare** *veed boord fur ickeh-rurkareh*
by the window	**vid fönstret** *veed <u>furn</u>stret*
Smoking or non-smoking?	**Rökare eller icke-rökare?** *rurkareh eller ickeh-rurkareh*

> – Jag skulle vilja reservera ett bord till ikväll.
> (I'd like to reserve a table for this evening.)
> – Hur många blir ni? (For how many people?)
> – Vi blir fyra. (Four.)
> – Till vilken tid? (For what time?)
> – Vi kommer klockan åtta.
> (We'll come at eight o'clock.)
> – Vad är namnet? (And what's the name, please?)
> – Smith. (Smith.)
> – Det går bra. Välkomna! (That's fine. See you then.)

Ordering Beställa

Waiter!/Waitress!	**Ursäkta.** *eurshekta*
May I see the wine list, please?	**Kan jag få se vinlistan?** *kun yaag faw seh veen-listan*
Do you have a set menu?	**Har ni en meny?** *haar nee en menew*
Can you recommend some typical local dishes?	**Kan ni rekommendera några typiska rätter från den här regionen?** *kun nee rekomendehra nawgra tewpiska retter frawn den hair regeeoonen*
Could you tell me what … is?	**Kan ni tala om vad … är?** *kun nee taala om vaad … air*
What's in it?	**Vad är det i den?** *vaad air det ee den*
What kind of … do you have?	**Vad för slags … har ni?** *vaad fur slax … har nee*
I'd like …/I'll have …	**Jag skulle vilja ha …/Jag tar …** *yaag skeulleh vilya haa/yaag taar*
a bottle/glass/carafe of …	**en flaska/ett glas/en karaff …** *en flaska/et glaas/en karaff*

Vill ni beställa?	Are you ready to order?
Vad vill ni beställa?	What would you like?
Vill ni beställa drinkar först?	Would you like to order drinks first?
Jag kan rekommendera …	I recommend …
Vi har inte …	We don't have …
Det kommer att ta … minuter.	That will take … minutes.
Smaklig måltid.	Enjoy your meal.

– *Vill ni beställa? (Are you ready to order?)*
– Kan ni rekommendera en rätt från den här regionen?
(Can you recommend a typical local dish?)
– *Ja, jag kan rekommendera älgsteken.*
(Yes. I recommend the moose.)
– OK, då tar jag den. (OK. I'll have that, please.)
– *Tack, och vad vill ni dricka?*
(Certainly. And what would you like to drink?)
– En karaff rött vin, tack.
(A carafe of red wine, please.)
– *Tack. (Certainly.)*

DRINKS ➤ 49; MENU READER ➤ 52

Accompaniments Tillbehör

Could I have … without the …?	**Kan jag få … utan …?** *kun yaag faw … eutan*
With a side order of …	**Med en liten extra portion …** *mehd en leeten extra potshoon*
Could I have a salad instead of vegetables, please?	**Kan jag få sallad istället för grönsaker?** *kun yaag faw salad ee stellet fur grurn-saaker*
Does the meal come with …?	**Inkluderar varmrätten …?** *inkleudehrar varm-retten*
vegetables/potatoes	**grönsaker/potatis** *grurn-saaker/pootaatis*
rice/pasta	**ris/pasta** *rees/pasta*
Do you have …?	**Har ni …?** *haar nee*
any ketchup	**någon ketchup** *nawgon ketchup*
any mayonnaise	**någon majonäs** *nawgon mayoonairs*
I'd like … with that.	**Jag skulle vilja ha … till.** *yaag skeulleh vilya haa … til*
vegetables/salad	**grönsaker/sallad** *grurn-saaker/salad*
potatoes/French fries	**potatis/pommes frites** *pootaatis/pom frit*
sauce	**sås** *saws*
ice	**is** *ees*
May I have some …?	**Kan jag få lite …?** *kun yaag faw leeteh*
bread	**bröd** *brurd*
butter	**smör** *smur*
lemon	**citron** *seetroon*
mustard	**senap** *sehnap*
pepper	**peppar** *peppar*
salt	**salt** *salt*
oil and vinegar	**olja och vinäger** *olya ock vinairger*
sugar	**socker** *socker*
artificial sweetener	**sötningsmedel** *surtnings-mehdel*
vinaigrette [French dressing]	**vinaigrettesås** *vinnegret-saws*

MENU READER ➤ 52

General requests
Allmänna förfrågningar

Could I/we have a(n) ..., please?
Kan jag/vi få ..., tack?
kun yaag/vee faw ... tuck

ashtray
en askkopp *en ask-kop*

cup/glass
en kopp/ett glas *en kop/et glaas*

fork/knife
en gaffel/en kniv *en gaffel/en kneev*

plate/spoon
en tallrik/en sked *en tallrik/en shehd*

napkin
en servett *en servett*

I'd like some more ..., please.
Jag skulle vilja ha lite mer ..., tack.
yaag skeulleh vilya haa leeteh mehr ... tuck

That's all, thanks.
Det var allt, tack. *det vaar alt tuck*

Where are the bathrooms [toilets]?
Var är toaletten?
vaar air tooaletten

Special requirements Speciella önskemål

I can't eat food containing ...
Jag kan inte äta mat som innehåller ...
yaag kun inteh airta maat som inneholler

salt/sugar
salt/socker
salt/socker

Do you have any dishes/drinks for diabetics?
Har ni några rätter/drinkar för diabetiker?
haar nee nawgra retter/drinkar fur deeaabehtiker

Do you have vegetarian dishes?
Har ni vegetarianska rätter?
haar nee vegetaree-anska retter

For the children För barn

Do you have a children's menu?
Har ni en barnmeny?
haar nee en baarn-menew

Could you bring a child's seat, please?
Kan jag få en barnstol, tack?
kun yaag faw en baarn-stool tuck

Where can I change the baby?
Var kan jag byta på babyn?
vaar kun yaag bewta paw baybin

Where can I feed the baby?
Var kan jag mata babyn?
vaar kun yaag maata baybin

CHILDREN ➤ 113

Fast food/Café
Gatukök/Kafé

Something to drink Något att dricka

I'd like (a) …	**Jag skulle vilja ha …** *yaag skeulleh vilya haa*
tea/coffee	**thé/kaffe** *teh/kaffeh*
black/with milk	**utan/med mjölk** *eutan/mehd myulk*
(hot) chocolate	**(varm) choklad** *(varm) shooklaad*
cola/lemonade	**cola/sockerdricka** *kawla/socker-dricka*
fruit juice	**fruktjuice** *freukt-yoos*
orange/pineapple/tomato juice	**apelsin-/ananas-/tomat-juice** *apelseen-/ananas-/toomaat-yoos*

And to eat Och att äta

A piece/slice of …, please.	**En bit/skiva …, tack.** *en beet/sheeva … tuck*
I'd like two of those.	**Jag skulle vilja ha två av dem.** *yaag skeulleh vilya haa tvaw ahv dem*
burger/fries	**hamburgare/pommes frites** *hambur-yaareh/pom frit*
omelet/pizza	**omelett/pizza** *omelet/pitsa*
sandwich/cake	**smörgås/kaka** *smurgaws/kaaka*
ice cream	**glass** *glas*
chocolate/strawberry/vanilla	**chocklad/jordgubbs/vanilj** *shooklad/yoord-geubbs/vanil'*
A … portion, please.	**En portion …, tack.** *en potshoon … tuck*
small	**liten** *leeten*
regular [medium]	**vanlig** *vaanlig*
large	**stor** *stoor*
It's to go [take away].	**Jag ska ta den med mig.** *yaag skaa taa den mehd may*
That's all, thanks.	**Det var allt, tack.** *det vaar alt tuck*

– Vad vill ni beställa? (What would you like?)
– Två kaffe, tack. (Two coffees, please.)
– Svart eller med mjölk? (Black or with milk?)
– Med mjölk, tack. (With milk, please.)
– Någonting att äta? (Anything to eat?)
– Nej tack, det är allt. (No, that's all, thanks.)

Complaints Klagomål

I have no knife/fork/spoon.	**Jag har ingen kniv/gaffel/sked.** *yaag haar ingen kneev/<u>gaffel</u>/shehd*
There must be some mistake.	**Det måste vara ett misstag.** *det mosteh vaara et mistaag*
That's not what I ordered.	**Det här har jag inte beställt.** *det hair haar yaag inteh bestelt*
I asked for …	**Jag beställde …** *yaag besteldeh*
I can't eat this.	**Jag kan inte äta det här.** *yaag kun inteh airta det hair*
The meat is …	**Köttet är …** *churtet air*
overdone	**för mycket stekt** *fur mewcket stehkt*
underdone	**inte genomstekt** *inteh yehnom-stehkt*
too tough	**för segt** *fur sehgt*
This is too …	**Det här är för …** *det hair air fur*
bitter/sour	**beskt/surt** *beskt/seurt*
The food is cold.	**Maten är kall.** *maaten air kal*
This isn't fresh.	**Det här är inte färskt.** *det hair air inteh fairskt*
How much longer will our food be?	**Hur länge till behöver vi vänta?** *heur lengeh til be<u>hur</u>ver vee venta*
We can't wait any longer. We're leaving.	**Vi kan inte vänta längre. Vi går nu.** *vee kun inteh venta lengreh. vee gawr neu*
This isn't clean.	**Det här är inte rent.** *det hair air inteh rehnt*
I'd like to speak to the head waiter/manager.	**Jag vill tala med hovmästaren/chefen.** *yaag vil taala mehd <u>hawv</u>-mestaren/ <u>sheh</u>fen*

Paying Betala notan

I'd like to pay.	**Jag vill betala.** *yaag vil betaala*
The bill, please.	**Kan jag få notan, tack.** *kun yaag faw nootan tuck*
We'd like to pay separately.	**Vi vill betala var för sig.** *vee vil betaala vaar fur say*
It's all together.	**Allt tillsammans.** *alt til-sammans tuck*
I think there's a mistake in this bill.	**Jag tror det måste vara fel på notan.** *yaag troor det mosteh vaara fehl paw nootan*
What's this amount for?	**Vad står den här summan för?** *vaad stawr den hair seumman fur*
I didn't have that. I had …	**Jag åt inte det. Jag åt …** *yaag awt inteh det. yaag awt*
Is service included?	**Är serveringsavgiften inräknad?** *air servehrings-aavyiften inrairknad*
Can I pay with this credit card?	**Kan jag betala med det här kreditkortet?** *kun yaag betaala mehd det hair kredeet-koortet*
I forgot my wallet.	**Jag har glömt min plånbok.** *yaag haar glurmt min plawn-book*
I don't have enough cash.	**Jag har inte tillräckligt med kontanter.** *yaag haar inteh tilreckligt mehd kontanter*
Could I have a receipt, please?	**Kan jag få ett kvitto, tack?** *kun yaag faw et kvittoo tuck*
That was a very good meal.	**Det var en mycket god måltid.** *det vaar en mewcket good mawl-teed*

– Ursäkta, kan jag få notan, tack. (Waiter! The bill, please?)

    – Javisst, varsågod. (Certainly. Here you are.)

      – Är serveringsavgiften inräknad?
       (Is service included?)

    – Ja, det är den. (Yes, it is.)

   – Kan jag betala med det här kreditkortet?
    (Can I pay with this credit card?)

    – Ja, naturligtvis. (Yes, of course.)

    – Tack. Det var en mycket god måltid.
    (Thank you. That was a very good meal.)

Course by course Rätt efter rätt

Breakfast Frukost

Most hotels and guest houses offer a buffet breakfast, including
the items listed below and also cold meats, cereals, and cheeses.
Since the average Swede starts work at 8 a.m., breakfast is usually a
cup of coffee with an open-faced sandwich or a bowl of porridge (**gröt**) or
cereal. For a special treat, try Swedish yogurt, **filmjölk**, with your cereal.

I'd like …	**Jag skulle vilja ha …** *yaag skeulleh vilya haa*
bread/butter	**bröd/smör** *brurd/smur*
eggs	**ägg** *egg*
boiled/fried/scrambled	**kokt/stekt/äggröra** *kookt/stehkt/<u>e</u>gg-rurra*
fruit juice	**fruktjuice** *freukt-yoos*
grapefruit/orange	**grapefrukt/apelsin** *grape-freukt/apel<u>seen</u>*
honey	**honung** <u>*hawneung*</u>
jam/marmalade	**sylt/marmelad** *sewlt/marme<u>laad</u>*
milk	**mjölk** *myulk*
rolls/toast	**småbröd/rostat bröd** *smaw-brurd/rostat brurd*

Appetizers/Starters Förrätter

smoked salmon	**rökt lax** *rurkt lax*
marinated salmon	**gravlax** *graavlax*
variety of marinated herrings	**sillbricka** *<u>sil</u>-bricka*
game paté	**viltpaté** *vilt-<u>pateh</u>*

Färska räkor *fairska rairkor*
Unshelled shrimp [prawns]. You shell the shrimps and eat them with
toast, butter, and mayonnaise.

S.O.S. (smör, ost och sill) *es oo es (smur oost ock sil)*
A small plate of marinated herring, bread and butter, and cheese.

Toast skagen *toast skaagen*
Toast with chopped shrimp in mayonnaise, topped with bleak* roe.

Löjrom *lur'-rom*
Bleak* roe. Served with chopped, raw onions and sour cream and eaten
on toast.

* *Bleak* is a small silvery fish belonging to the carp family.

Soups Soppor

Soups are traditionally eaten in fall [autumn] and winter, and many are a meal in their own right. **Spenatsoppa** (spinach soup) and **ärtsoppa** (pea soup) are Swedish specialties, so do give them a try.

buljong	*beull-yong*	broth/consommé
fisksoppa	*fisk-soppa*	fish soup
grönsakssoppa	*grurnsaaks-soppa*	vegetable soup
kycklingsoppa	*chewkling-soppa*	chicken soup
löksoppa	*lurk-soppa*	onion soup
oxsvanssoppa	*ooxsvans-soppa*	oxtail soup
potatissoppa	*pootaatis-soppa*	potato soup
sparrissoppa	*sparris-soppa*	asparagus soup

Ärtsoppa *airt-soppa*
This pea soup is made from dried yellow peas and served with lightly salted pork or pork knuckle. It is traditionally followed by pancakes.

Köttsoppa *churt-soppa*
A soup of boiled pieces of beef, vegetables, and dumplings. A hefty meal on a cold day.

Spenatsoppa *spehnat-soppa*
A rich, nourishing soup made from fresh spinach, potatoes, milk, and cream.

Egg dishes Äggrätter

äggröra	*egg-rurra*	scrambled eggs
stekta ägg	*stehkta egg*	baked eggs

Omelet *omelet*
In Sweden, omelets are often filled with pieces of ham, (wild) mushrooms, or spinach.

Pannkaka/Fläskpannkaka *pankaaka/flesk-pankaaka*
Pancakes are very popular in Sweden and are eaten with raspberry or blueberry jam. **Fläskpannkaka** is a thick pancake filled with bacon and baked in the oven.

Fish and seafood Fisk och skaldjur

Swedes enjoy a variety of fish and seafood, and you will
find a good selection in most restaurants and supermarkets.
If you visit Sweden in August, you will no doubt enjoy a
kräftkalas (crayfish party). There is not much meat on a crayfish,
but when helped down with a few glasses of **akvavit** (aquavit ➤ 50) and
some salad and cheese, it makes for an unforgettable evening.

forell	*foorel*	trout
hummer	*heummer*	lobster
kolja	*kolya*	haddock
lax	*lax*	salmon
makrill	*makril*	mackerel
musslor	*meussloor*	mussels
ostron	*oostron*	oysters
räkor	*rairkoor*	shrimp [prawns]
röding	*rurding*	char
rödspätta	*rurd-spetta*	plaice
sjötunga	*sjur-teunga*	sole
skarpsill	*skarp-sil*	herring [whitebait]
tonfisk	*toonfisk*	tuna
torsk	*torshk*	cod

Strömming *strurming*
Sprats (small Baltic herring) filleted and sandwiched in pairs with dill and
butter in the middle. Fried and eaten hot with mashed potatoes or just cold.

Böckling *burkling*
Buckling (or bloaters) are smoked Baltic herring – mild and delicious.

Rimmad lax med stuvad potatis
reemahd lahks mehd stewahd potahtihs
Lightly salted salmon with creamed potatoes and dill.

Halstrad forell med färskpotatis
hahlstrahd forel mehd fairskpotahtihs
Grilled trout with new potatoes.

Stuvad abborre *stewahd abborreh*
Perch poached with onion, parsley, and lemon. Served with potatoes.

Smörgåsbord

If you have never heard of typical Swedish food, you may at least have heard of the famous **smörgåsbord**. You can find this on weekends in most large restaurants and hotels throughout the year. It is a buffet meal on a grand scale, laid out on a large, beautifully decorated table. The table is laden with hot and cold dishes, and there is no need to order an appetizer!

You start at one end of the table, usually the one with the cold seafood dishes, marinated herrings, **Janssons frestelse**, and salads. Then you work your way through the cold meats, **köttbullar**, sausages, omelets, and vegetables, and end up at the cheeseboard and desserts. Then you start all over again. The price is set, and you can eat as much as you like.

At Christmastime, the **smörgåsbord** becomes a **julbord**, served in homes and restaurants alike. You will find that the Swedes tend to drink **akvavit** (aquavit) or beer with this, although an accompanying glass of wine is becoming more common for those who find **akvavit** too strong.

Meat and poultry Kött och fågel

anka	*anka*	duck
bacon	*baykon*	bacon
biffkött	*bif-churt*	beef
biffstek	*bif-stehk*	steak
fasan	*fasaan*	pheasant
fläskkött	*flesk-churt*	pork
hare	*hareh*	rabbit
kalkon	*kalkoon*	turkey
kalvkött	*kalv-churt*	veal
korv	*korv*	sausages
köttbullar	*churt-beullar*	meatballs
kyckling	*chewkling*	chicken
lamm	*lumb*	lamb
skinka	*shinkaa*	ham

Älgstek (Renstek) med svampsås
ail-stehk (rehnstehk) mehd svampsos
Roast moose (reindeer) with mushroom sauce; served with baked potatoes.

Kåldolmar med gräddsås och lingon
koldolmahr mehd graidsos ok leengon
Minced meat and rice stuffed in cabbage leaves; served with a cream-based gravy and wild cranberries.

Sjömansbiff *shurmahnsbif*
Casserole of fried beef, onions, and potatoes, braised in beer.

Vegetables Grönsaker

blomkål	_bloom-kawl_	cauliflower
champinjoner	_shampin-yooner_	mushrooms
grönsallad	_grurn-salad_	lettuce
gurka	_geurka_	cucumber
haricots verts	_arikaw vair_	green beans
(röd) kål	_(rurd) kawl_	(red) cabbage
kålrot	_kawlroot_	rutabaga [swede]
lök	_lurk_	onions
morötter	_moorurter_	carrots
paprika	_paaprika_	peppers (red, green)
potatis	_pootaatis_	potatoes
ris	_rees_	rice
rovor	_roovor_	turnips
schalottenlök	_shalotten-lurk_	shallots [spring onions]
tomater	_toomaater_	tomatoes
vitlök	_veet-lurk_	garlic
äggplanta	_egg-planta_	eggplant [aubergine]
ärtor	_airtoor_	peas
ättiksgurka	_ettiks-geurka_	pickled gherkins

Salad Sallader

blandsallad	_blandsalad_	mixed salad
grönsallad	_grurn-salad_	green salad
potatissallad	_pootaatis-salad_	potato salad
skaldjurssallad	_skaal-yeurs-salad_	seafood salad
tomater och lök	_toomaater ock lurk_	tomato and onion salad

Sillsallad _sil-salad_
Beet and herring salad. It also includes apples, gherkins, potatoes, onions, and cream. A delicious Christmas salad.

Västkustsallad _vestkeust-salad_
A shrimp [prawn] and mussel salad served with mushrooms, tomatoes, lettuce, cucumber, asparagus, and dill.

Cheese Ost

Most Swedish cheeses are hard and come in a variety of flavors and strengths. Swedes love cheese, and they often start the day with an open faced cheese sandwich and a cup of coffee or tea.

Herrgårdsost *hairrgawrds-oost*
A semi-hard cheese with large holes and a nutty flavor.

Svecia *svehsia*
One of the most popular semi-hard cheeses. Varies in strength from region to region.

Grevé *greveh*
A semi-hard cheese with a taste between Dutch Gouda and Swiss Emmentaler.

Mesost *mehs-oost*
A soft, sweet, yellowish whey cheese.

Ädelost *airdel-oost*
A blue cheese with a sharp taste, similar to French Roquefort.

Kryddost *krewdd-oost*
A sharp, strong cheese with caraway seeds.

Västerbotten *vester-botten*
A sharp, tangy, hard and very strong cheese from the north of Sweden.

Dessert Efterrätter

äppelpaj/äppelkaka	*eppel-pie/eppel-kaaka*	apple pie/apple tart
fruktsallad	*freukt-salad*	fruit salad
glass	*glas*	ice cream
jordgubbar med grädde	*yoord-geubbar mehd greddeh*	strawberries and cream

Friterad camembert med hjortronsylt
fritehrad camembert mehd yoortron-sewlt
Deep-fried camembert with cloudberry jam. Cloudberries are only found in cold climates. They have a tangy flavor that goes well with the cheese.

Ostkaka *oost-kaaka*
This curd cake is a traditional dessert from southern Sweden. It is sometimes made with almonds and is served with jam.

Våfflor *voffloor*
Waffles served with jam and whipped cream. Waffles are often eaten as a snack and are favorites with most children.

Marängsviss *mareng-svis*
Meringues served with whipped cream and chocolate sauce.

Fruit Frukt

apelsiner	apel_seener_	oranges
bananer	ban_aaner_	bananas
blåbär	blaw-bair	blueberries
citron	see_troon_	lemon
grapefrukt	grape-freukt	grapefruit
hallon	hallon	raspberries
jordgubbar	_yoord_-geubbar	strawberries
körsbär	churs-bair	cherries
persikor	_pairshikoor_	peaches
plommon	ploommon	plums
smultron	smeultron	wild strawberries
(vatten)melon	(vatten)me_loon_	(water)melon
vindruvor	veen-dreuvor	grapes
äpplen	epplen	apples

Alcoholic drinks Alkoholhaltiga drycker

Apart from wine, alcoholic drinks in Sweden are probably the most expensive in Europe, due to the high taxes. As a result, most Swedes don't drink alcohol on a daily basis. Alcohol (with the exception of class I and II beers, see below) is only sold in state-run shops (**systembolaget**), which you will find in every town, although not in remote areas or villages. **Systembolaget** and restaurants carry all types of drink. But when you go to a restaurant, make sure you know the price of a drink before you order.

Aperitifs Aperitif

Pre-dinner drinks. More or less the same as anywhere, with sherry, Martini, and whisky topping the list, followed closely by gin and tonic and vodka.

Beer Öl

Beer is probably the most popular drink in Sweden, and there are many good Swedish breweries. Beer with an alcohol content above 3% (**starköl** – class III) can only be bought in **systembolaget**, whereas classes I (**lättöl**) and II (below 3% alcohol content) can be bought in ordinary stores. You will find many well-known international beers, but the most common are Carlsberg, Heineken, and Swedish brews such as Pripps.

Do you have (any) …?	**Har ni …?** *haar nee*	
bottled beer/canned beer	**öl på flaska/burköl**	
	url paw flaska/beurk-url	
draft [draught]/low-alcohol	**fatöl**/**lättöl** *faat-eurl/let-url*	

Wine Viner

Wine prices are very competitive in the state-run stores as well as in restaurants, since the government imports wines in bulk. You can find good, reasonably priced table wine as well as Champagne.

The selection is vast with a variety of wines from France, Italy, Spain, Germany, Australia, and California available.

Can you recommend a … wine?	**Kan ni föreslå ett … vin?** *kun nee furreh-slaw et … veen*
red/white/blush [rosé]	**rött/vitt/rosé** *rurt/vit/roseh*
dry/sweet/sparkling	**torrt/sött/mousserande** *tort/surt/moosehrande*
I'd like the house wine, please.	**Jag skulle vilja ha husets vin, tack.** *yaag skeulleh vilya haa heusets veen tuck*

Aquavit Aqvavit

Aqvavit – a grain- or potato-based spirit – is something of a national drink, served in very small, ice-cold glasses. It is very strong and goes excellently with marinated herring dishes, crayfish, and, of course, **smörgåsbord**. It is often served with a beer chaser.

Renat (Brännvin) *rehnat (bren-veen)*
Colorless type of **aqvavit**, without flavor.

Skåne *skawneh*
Another type of **aqvavit**, flavored with aniseed and caraway seeds, yellowish.

Herrgårdsakvavit *hairrgawrds-akvaveet*
Aqvavit, flavored with caraway seeds and whisky.

Spirits and liqueurs Sprit och likör

Glögg *glurg*
Similar to a mulled wine, **glögg** also contains sugar, port, lemon rind, and various spices – and is very much a part of Christmas celebrations. It can be bought ready-made in a bottle or made at home. Don't forget the almonds and raisins.

Punsch *peunsh*
This is not an aperitif but an after-dinner, sweet liqueur, made from arrack [arak], sugar, and pure alcohol. It is often served warm with the traditional pea soup, (**ärtsoppa**).

brandy/gin/whisky	**cognac/gin/whisky** *konyak/jin/whisky*
rum/vodka/port	**rom/vodka/portvin** *rom/vodka/port-veen*
liqueur	**likör** *likurr*

straight/neat	**ren/"som den är"**
	rehn/som den air
on the rocks [with ice]	**med is** *mehd ees*
with water/tonic water	**med vatten/med tonic**
	mehd vatten/mehd tonik
I'd like a single/double …	**Jag skulle vilja ha en liten/**
	dubbel(stor) … *yaag skeulleh vilya haa*
	en leeten/deubbel (stoor)

Non-alcoholic drinks Alkoholfria drycker

For afternoon tea or coffee you can do no better than the typical Swedish **konditori** (patisserie/coffee shop). You can help yourself to as many cups as you like while indulging in a slice of **prinsesstårta** (sponge cake with cream and custard, covered with green marzipan), **mazarin** (almond tart, topped with icing), or a **wienerbröd** (Danish pastry). Try the **saffransbulle** (saffron bun) and **pepparkaka** (ginger cookies) at Christmas. Most **konditori** are self-service, but some of the more elegant ones and those in hotels have waitress service.You can also have a soft drink (**läsk**) or fruit juice. Tea is commonly drunk with lemon, no milk.

Kaffe *kaffeh*

Coffee is definitely the national drink, and it is always freshly brewed. It is commonly drunk black, but ask for **mjölk** (milk) or **grädde** (cream) if you like it that way. You can also find all manner of coffee drinks, such as espresso and cappuccino.

I'd like …	**Jag skulle vilja ha …**
	yaag skeulleh vilya haa …
tea/with milk/with lemon	**thé/med mjölk/med citron**
	teh/mehd myulk/mehd ceetroon
(hot) chocolate	**(varm) choklad** *(varm) shooklaad*
cola/lemonade	**coca-cola/sockerdricka**
	kawka-kawla/socker-dricka
fruit juice	**fruktjuice** *freukt-yoos*
orange/pineapple/tomato	**apelsin/ananas/tomat**
	apelseen/ananas/toomaat
milk shake	**milkshake** *milk-shake*
mineral water	**mineralvatten** *mineraal-vatten*
carbonated/non-carbonated [still]	**med kolsyra/utan kolsyra**
	mehd kawl-sewra/eutan kawl-sewra

Menu Reader

This Menu Reader is an alphabetical glossary of terms that you may find in a menu. Certain traditional dishes are cross-referenced to the relevant page in the *Course by course* section, where they are described in more detail.

bakad	*baakad*	baked
blodig	*bloodig*	rare/underdone
brynt	*brewnt*	sautéed
bräserad	*brehsehrahd*	braised
friterad	*freetenrahd*	deep-fried
fylld	*fewld*	stuffed
förlorat	*furlooraht*	poached *(eggs)*
genomstekt	*yehnomstehkt*	well-done
grillad	*grillahd*	grilled
i bitar	*ee beetahr*	diced
i gryta	*ee grewtah*	stewed
inlagd	*inlagd*	marinated
kluven	*klueven*	diced
kokt	*kookt*	boiled
kryddad/kryddstark	*krewdahd/ krewd-stahrk*	spicy
marinerad	*mahreenehrahd*	marinated
medium	*mehdeeyewm*	medium
panerad	*pahnenrahd*	breaded
pocherad	*poshehrahd*	poached
riktigt blodig	*reekteegt bloodig*	very rare
rökt	*rurkt*	smoked
stekt	*stehkt*	fried/sautéed
stuvad	*stewad*	stewed
ugnsbrynt	*ewngns-brewnt*	oven-browned
ugnstekt	*ewngnstehkt*	roasted
ångkokt	*ongkookt*	steamed

A

abborre perch

alkoholisk dryck alcoholic drink

alkoholfria drycker
non-alcoholic drinks

ananas pineapple

anka duck; duckling

ansjovis anchovies; marinated
anchovies

apelsin orange

apelsinjos/apelsinjuice
orange juice

aprikoser apricots

avokado avocado

älgstek (renstek) med svampsås
roast moose (reindeer) with
mushroom sauce ➤ 46

B

bakad baked

bakverk pastries

bakelse piece of cake

banan banana

barnmatsedel
children's menu

basilika basil

bål punch

ben leg/on the bone

biff steak

bigarråer sweet morello
cherries

bit slice

björnbär
blackberries

björnstek roast bear

blandade assorted

blandade grönsaker
mixed vegetables

blandade kryddor mixed herbs

blandade nötter assorted nuts

blandsallad mixed salad

blomkål cauliflower

blåa vindruvor black grapes

blåbär blueberries

blåbärssylt blueberry jam

blåmusslor mussels

bog shoulder *(cut of meat)*

bondbönor broad beans

bordsvin table wine

bouquet garni mixed herbs

braxen bream; sea bream

broiler spring chicken

brylépudding crème caramel

brysselkål Brussel sprouts

brytbönor kidney beans

brännvin aquavit (grain- or
potato-based spirit) ➤ 50

bröd bread

brödsmulor bread crumbs

bröst breast

buljong consommé

bulle bun

böckling smoked herring

bönor beans [pulses]
bönskott bean sprouts

C champinjoner mushrooms

chilipeppar chili pepper
chips potato chips [crisps]
chocklad chocolate
citron lemon
citronjuice lemon juice
cognac brandy

D dadlar dates

dagens meny menu of the day
dagens rätt dish/speciality of the day
dessertvin dessert wine
dillsås dill sauce
dragon tarragon

E efterrätt dessert

enbär juniper berries
endiv endive
en dubbel double *(a double shot)*
en halv flaska half bottle
enkel plain
entrecote sirloin steak

F falukorv lightly spiced sausage for frying

fasan pheasant
fatöl draft [draught] beer
fet fatty, rich *(sauce)*
fikon figs
filé filet mignon
filmjölk drinking yogurt
fisk fish
fläsk pork
fläskben pork on the bone/leg of pork
fläskfilé fillet of pork
fläskkarré loin of pork
fläskkorv spicy, boiled pork sausage
fläsklägg knuckle of pork
fläskpannkaka thick pancake filled with bacon ➤ 44
forell trout
franskbröd white bread *(French recipe)*
friterad deep-fried
friterad camembert med hjortronsylt deep-fried Camembert with cloudberry jam ➤ 48
friterade fritters
frukost breakfast
frukostflingor cereal
frukt fruit

fruktjuice fruit juice

från grillen grilled

fullkornsmjöl whole wheat flour

fylld (med) stuffed (with)

fyllda oliver stuffed olives

fylligt full-bodied *(wine)*

fågel poultry

får mutton

fårost ewe's milk cheese

fänkål fennel

färsk (frukt) fresh (fruit)

färska fikon fresh figs

färska räkor unshelled shrimp
[prawns] ➤ 43

färskpotatis new potatoes

förlorat ägg poached egg

förrätter first course

G **garnering**
garnish/trimming

gelé jelly

get kid *(goat)*

getost goat's milk cheese

gin och tonic gin and tonic

glass ice cream

glutenfritt gluten free

glögg mulled wine with port and
spices, served hot ➤ 50

grapefrukt grapefruit

gratinerad au gratin

gratäng gratin

gravlax marinated
salmon

grevé semi-hard cheese

grillad barbecued/grilled

grillad kyckling grilled chicken

grillspett skewered

gryta pot roast, stew
or casserole

gurka cucumber

gås goose

gädda sea perch

grädde cream

gräddfil sour cream

gräslök chives

grön paprika green peppers

gröna bönor green beans

grönsaker vegetables *(general)*

grönsakssoppa vegetable soup

grönsallad green salad

gröna vindruvor white grapes

gröt porridge

H **hallon** raspberries

halstrad fisk grilled fish

halstrad forell med färskpotatis
grilled trout with new
potatoes ➤ 45

hamburgare hamburger

haricots verts string beans

hasselbackspotatis oven-baked potatoes, coated in bread crumbs

hasselnötter hazelnuts

havre corn

havsabborre sea bass

havskräfta large shrimp [Dublin prawns] *(sea crayfish)*

hemlagad homemade

herrgårdsakvavit aquavit flavored with caraway seeds and whisky ➤ 49

herrgårdsost semi-hard cheese with a nutty flavor

het hot *(temperature)*

hjort deer

hjortron cloudberries

hjortron sylt cloudberry jam

honung honey

hovmästarsås dill sauce *(for marinated salmon)*

hummer lobster

husets specialitet specialties of the house

huvudrätter main course

hårdkokt hard-boiled *(egg)*

hårt bröd crispbread

hälleflundra halibut

i bitar sliced

i gryta stewed

i olja in oil

ingefära ginger

inlagd i ättika (vinäger) marinated in vinegar

inlagd sill marinated *(pickled)* herring

is ice

isterband sausage of pork, barley, and beef, for frying

J jordgubbar strawberries

jordnötter peanuts

jos/juice juice

julbord buffet of hot and cold Swedish specialties served at Christmas time

järpe hazel hen

K kaffe coffee

kaka cake

kalkon turkey

kall soppa cold soup

kallskuret cold dish

kalops beef stew

kalvbräss sweetbreads

kalvkött veal

kalvsylta pickled pig's feet [brawn]

kammussla scallops

kanderad frukt candied fruit

kanel cinnamon

kantareller chanterelle mushrooms

kapris caper

karaff carafe

karameller candy [sweets]

karré tenderloin *(smoked)*

katrinplommon prunes

kex cookies [biscuits]

kikärtor chickpeas

kiwifrukt kiwi fruit

klimp dumpling

kokosnöt coconut

kokt stewed

kokta katrinplommon stewed prunes

kokt potatis boiled potatoes

kokt skinka boiled ham

kokt ägg boiled egg

kolgrillad charcoal-grilled

kolja haddock

kolsyrad/t carbonated [fizzy] *(drinks)*

kompott stewed fruit

konserverad frukt canned fruit

korv sausage

korvar sausages

kotlett cutlet

kotletter chops

köttsoppa substantial beef and vegetable soup with dumplings ➤ 44

krabba crab

krasse watercress

kronärtskockor artichokes

kroppkakor potato dumplings, filled with bacon and onions

krusbär gooseberry

kryddad seasoned

kryddad pepparsås hot pepper sauce

kryddost sharp, strong cheese with caraway seeds

kryddor seasoning/spices

kryddstarkt spicy

kräfta crayfish

kummel hake

kummin caraway

kvark fresh curd cheese

kyckling chicken

kycklingbröst breast of chicken

kycklinglever chicken liver

kycklingsoppa chicken broth

kylda drycker cold drinks

kylt chilled *(wine, etc.)*

kål cabbage

kåldolmar cabbage leaves stuffed with minced meat and rice ➤ 46

kålrot turnip

källkrasse watercress

körsbär cherries

körvel chervil
kött meat *(general)*
köttbullar meatballs
köttfärs minced beef
kött och grönsakssoppa meat and vegetable broth
köttsås bolognese sauce

L **lagerblad** bay leaf
lageröl lager
lamm lamb
lammgryta lamb stew
landgång long open-faced sandwich
lax salmon
lever liver
leverpastej pâté
lingonsylt lingonberry jam
linser lentils
liten förrätt appetizers
lägg shank *(top of leg)*
läsk soft drink
löjrom bleak roe with chopped, raw onions, and sour cream and eaten on toast ➤ 43 .
lök onions
löskokt soft boiled *(eggs)*
lövbiff fried thinly sliced beef, with onions

M **mackrill** mackerel
majonnäs mayonnaise
majs sweet corn
mald minced
mandarin tangerine
mandel almond/sugared almond
mandeltårta almond tart
marmelad marmalade
marsipan marzipan
marulk monkfish
maräng meringue
marängsviss meringues served with cream and chocolate sauce ➤ 48
matjesill marinated herring
matsedel menu
medaljong small fillets of cut meat
med benet kvar on the bone
med citron with lemon
med florsocker icing
med grädde with cream [white] *(coffee)*
med is on the rocks/iced *(drinks)*
med kolsyra carbonated [fizzy] *(drinks)*
med mjölk with milk/white *(coffee)*
med socker with sugar
med vitlök in garlic
mellanmål snacks
meny set menu

mesost soft, sweet, whey cheese

middag dinner *(evening mealtime)*

mineralvatten mineral water

mjukost soft cheese

mjuk pepparkaka ginger cake

mjöl flour

mjölk milk

mogen ripe

morkulla woodcock

morötter carrots

mot extra kostnad extra charge

mousserande sparkling

mousserande vin sparkling wine

mullbär mulberry

multe mullet

munk donut

muskot nutmeg

musslor clams

mustigt full-bodied *(wine)*

mycket kryddad highly seasoned

mycket torrt very dry
(wine, etc.)

mynta mint *(herb)*

mäktig rich *(sauce)*

mördegstårta tart *(sweet or savory)*

mört roach *(type of fish)*

N nejlikor cloves

nejonögon lamprey

nektarin
nectarine

njure kidney

nudlar noodles

nyponsoppa rose-hip
compote served with whipped
cream and almond flakes

O odlade champinjoner
cultivated mushrooms

ojäst bröd unleavened bread

oliver olives

omelett omelet

ost hard cheese

ostkaka curd cake served with jam
➤ 47

ostkex crackers

ostron oysters

oxkött beef/ox

oxrullader
braised rolls of beef

oxsvans oxtail

P paj pie

palsternacka parsnips

panerad breaded *(cutlet, etc.)*

pannbiff hamburger *(when listed as
main meal)*

pannkakor pancakes

pasta/pastarätter pasta

pastej pâté

peppar pepper *(condiment)*

pepparkakor ginger cookies ➤ 51

pepparrotssås horseradish sauce

persika peach

persilja parsley

piggvar turbot

pittabröd pita bread

plommon plums

plättar baby pancakes served with jam and whipped cream

pocherad poached

pomegranat äpple pomegranates

pommes frites French fries

portion portion

portvin port

potatis potato

potatismos mashed potato

prinsesstårta sponge cake with vanilla custard, whipped cream, and jam, covered in light green marzipan

prinskorv small pork sausage, similar to frankfurters

pumpa pumpkin

punsch sweet liqueur, made from arrack [arak], sugar, and pure alcohol ➤ 49

purjolök leeks

pytt i panna chunks of fried meat, onion, potatoes, often served with a fried egg

på beställning made on request

pärlande sparkling

pärlhöns guinea fowl

päron pear

R **rabarber** rhubarb

ragu beef stew

rapphöna partridge

ren neat *(straight)*

ren reindeer

renat flavorless, clear spirit (aquavit) ➤ 49

renskav minced leg of reindeer

renstek roast reindeer

revbensspjäll spareribs

rimmad cured

rimmad lax lightly salted salmon ➤ 45

ris rice

riven grated

rocka ray, skate

rom rum

rosé blush *(wine)*

rosmarin rosemary

rostat bröd toast *(bread)*

rostbiff roast beef

rova turnip

rumpstek rump steak

russin raisins

rå raw

rådjur venison

rådjursstek roast of venison

rågbröd rye bread

rädisa radish

räkor shrimp [prawns]

rätt dish

röda vinbär red currants

rödbeta beet

rödkål red cabbage

röd paprika sweet red peppers

rökt smoked

rökt ål smoked eel

rökt fisk smoked fish

rökt lax smoked salmon

rökt renstek smoked reindeer

rökt skinka smoked ham

rönnbärsgelé rowanberry jelly

rörd soppa cream soup

rött red *(wine)*

S **sadel** *(saddle)*

saffran saffron

saffransbulle saffron buns *(served at Christmas)* ➤ 51

saft squash *(fruit cordial)*

salamikorv salami

sallad salad

salladshuvud lettuce

saltad salted

saltade jordnötter salted peanuts

saltgurka salted, pickled gherkins

salvia sage

sardiner sardines

schalottenlök shallots

schnitzel escallope

selleri celery root/celery

senap mustard

sherry sherry

sill herring

sillsallad beet and herring salad ➤ 47

sirap syrup

sjömansbiff casserole of fried beef, onions, and potatoes, braised in beer ➤ 46

sjötunga sole

skaldjur seafood

skaldjurssallad seafood salad

skinka ham

skogssvamp all field fungi

sky gravy

skåne type of aquavit flavored with aniseed and caraway ➤ 49

smultron wild strawberries

småbröd rolls

småkakor cookies

smårätter snacks

småsill whitebait

smör butter

smördeg pastry

smörgås sandwich/Swedish open-faced sandwich

smörgåsbord buffet of hot and cold Swedish specialties

sniglar snails

socker sugar

sockerdricka lemonade

sockerkaka sponge cake

sockerärtor sugar snap peas [mangetout]

sodavatten soda water

soppa soup

S.O.S. (smör, ost och sill) small plate of marinated herring, bread and butter, and cheese ➤ 43

sparris asparagus

specialitet för landsdelen local specialty

spenat spinach

spenatsoppa spinach soup ➤ 44

sprit spirits

spädgris sucking pig

squash squash *(vegetable)*

stark sharp/strong *(flavor)*

starkt kryddad hot *(spicy)*

stek roast

stekt fried/sautéed

stekt fisk fried fish

stekt kyckling fried chicken

stekt potatis sautéed potatoes

stekt ägg fried egg

strömming sprats *(small Baltic herrings)*

strömmingsflundror Baltic herrings, filleted and sandwiched in pairs, fried, with dill and butter filling ➤ 45

stuvad abborre perch poached with onion, parsley, and lemon ➤ 45

sufflé soufflé

sultana sultana/raisin

sur sour *(taste)*

svamp mushroom *(generic term for all types of fungi)*

svart black *(coffee)*

svarta vinbär

black currants

svecia semi-hard cheese

svensk punsch Swedish punch *(sweet liqueur)*

sylt jam

sås sauce/gravy

söt sweet

sötningsmedel sweetener

sötpotatis sweet potato

sötsur sås sweet-and-sour sauce

T T-benstek T-bone steak

thé tea

tillägg supplement

timjan thyme

tomater tomatoes

tomatsås tomato sauce

tonfisk tuna

tonic tonic water

torkade dadlar dried dates

torkade fikon dried figs

torr dry

torsk cod

toast skagen toast with chopped shrimp in mayonnaise, topped with bleak roe ➤ 43

tunga tongue

tunnbröd Swedish flat bread (*similar to pita bread*)

tunn sås light (*sauce, etc.*)

två personer for two

tårta sponge-based fruit or cream cake

U ugnsbakad fisk baked fish

ungsstekt kyckling roast chicken

ungsstekt potatis roast potatoes

utan kaffein decaffeinated

V vaktel quail

valfria tillbehör choice of side dishes

valnötter walnuts

vanilj vanilla

vaniljsås custard

varm chocklad hot chocolate

varm korv hot dog

varmrätter main course

varmt hot

vatten water

vattenmelon watermelon

vaxbönor butter beans

vegetarisk meny vegetarian menu

vermouth vermouth

vetemjöl plain flour

vilda champinjoner field/button mushrooms

vildand wild duck

vilt game

vin wine

vinaigrettesås vinaigrette [French dressing]

vinbär currants

vindruvor grapes

vinlistan wine list

vispgrädde whipped cream

vit sås white sauce

vitkål white cabbage

vitkålssallad coleslaw

vitling whiting
vitlök garlic
vitlöksmajonnäs garlic mayonnaise
vitlökssås garlic sauce
vitt bröd white bread
vol au vent vol-au-vent (*pastry filled with meat or fish*)
våfflor (med sylt och grädde) waffles (*with jam and whipped cream*)
vårlök spring onions
västerbotten strong, tangy, hard cheese
västkustsallad seafood in mixed green salad, asparagus, and dill ➤ 47

ägg eggs
äggplanta eggplant [aubergine]
äggula egg yolk
äggröra scrambled eggs
äggula egg yolk
äggvita egg white
älg elk
älgfilé fillet of elk
älgstek roast of elk
äppelpaj apple pie/tart
äppelringar apple fritters
äpple apple
ärtor peas
ärtsoppa yellow pea soup ➤ 44
ättiksgurka sweet, pickled gherkins

WX YZ **wienerbröd** Danish pastry
wienerschnitzel breaded veal cutlet
yoghurt yogurt
zucchino zucchini [courgettes]

Ö **öl** beer

Å **ål** eel
ångkokt steamed
ångkokt fisk steamed fish

Ä **ädelost** blue cheese

Travel

ESSENTIAL

1/2/3 ticket(s) to …	**en/två/tre biljett(er) till …** *en/tvaw/treh bilyetter til*
To …, please.	**Till …, tack.** *til … tuck*
one-way [single]	**enkel biljett** *enkel bilyet*
round-trip [return]	**returbiljett** *reteur-bilyet*
How much …?	**Hur mycket …?** *heur mewcket*

Safety Säkerhet

Would you accompany me to the bus stop?	**Vill ni följa med mig till busshållplatsen?** *vil nee furlya mehd may til beuss-holplatsen*
I don't want to … on my own.	**Jag vill inte … ensam.** *yaag vil inteh … ensam*
stay here	**stanna kvar** *stanna kvaar*
walk home	**promenera hem** *proomenehra hem*
I don't feel safe here.	**Jag känner mig inte trygg här.** *yaag chenner may inteh trewgg hair*

POLICE ➤ 159; EMERGENCY ➤ 224

Arrival Ankomst

Visitors from the United States, Canada, Australia, and the United Kingdom only need a valid passport. British citizens can also enter on a visitor's passport, as well as a British excursion document, but the latter is only valid for a 60-hour stay.

Duty free into Sweden:	Cigarettes	Cigars	Tobacco	Spirits	Wine
EU citizens	200	50	250 g.	1 l.	1 l.
Non-EU citizens	400	100	500 g.	1 l.	1 l.
U.K.	200 or	50 or	250 g.	1 l. and	2 l.
U.S.	200	100	2 kg.	1 l. or	1 l.
Canada	200	50	400 g.	1 l. or	1 l.
Australia	250 or	50 or	250 g.	1 l. or	1 l.

Kan jag få se ert pass, tack?	May I see your passport, please?
Vad är syftet med ert besök?	What's the purpose of your visit?
Vem reser ni med?	Who are you here with?

Passport control Passkontroll

We have a joint passport.
Vi har gemensamt pass.
vee haar yemehnsamt pus

The children are on this passport.
Barnen är på detta pass.
baarnen air paw detta pus

I'm here on vacation [holiday]/business.
Jag är här på semester/på affärsresa.
yaag air hair paw semester/paw affairs-rehsa

I'm just passing through.
Jag är bara på genomresa.
yaag air baara paw yehnom-rehsa

I'm going to …
Jag ska resa till … *yaag skaa rehsa til*

I'm on my own.
Jag är ensam. *yaag air ensam*

I'm with my family.
Jag är här med min familj.
yaag air hair mehd min famil'

I'm with a group.
Jag är i en turistgrupp.
yaag air ee en teurist-greupp

WHO ARE YOU WITH? ➤ 120

Customs Tull

I have only the normal allowances.	**Jag har bara den tillåtna ransonen.** *yaag haar baara den tilawtna ransoonen*
It's a gift.	**Det är en gåva.** *det air en gawva*
It's for my personal use.	**Det är för mitt personliga bruk.** *det air fur mit pair-shoonliga breuk*

Har ni något att förtulla?	Do you have anything to declare?
Ni måste betala tull för det här.	You must pay duty on this.
Var köpte ni det här?	Where did you buy this?
Var snäll och öppna den här väskan.	Please open this bag.
Har ni något mer bagage?	Do you have any more luggage?

I would like to declare …	**Jag skulle vilja förtulla …** *yaag skeulleh vilya furteulla*
I don't understand.	**Jag förstår inte.** *yaag furstawr inteh*
Does anyone here speak English?	**Finns det någon här som talar engelska?** *fins det nawgon hair som taalar engelska*

PASSKONTROLL	passport control
GRÄNS	border crossing
TULL	customs
INGET ATT FÖRTULLA	nothing to declare
VAROR ATT FÖRTULLA	goods to declare
TAXFRIA VAROR	duty-free goods

Duty-free shopping Taxfri shopping

What currency is this in?	**Vilken valuta är det här i?** *vilken valeuta air det hair ee*
Can I pay in …	**Kan jag betala med …** *kun yaag betaala mehd*
dollars	**dollar** *dollar*
kronor	**kronor** *kroonor*
pounds (sterling)	**(engelska) pund** *(engelska) peund*

Plane Flyg

International flights operate mainly out of Stockholm, but there are internal flights – operated by SAS, Transwede, Malmö Aviation, and a few smaller operators – that go to most Swedish cities. Some carriers offer package deals.

Tickets and reservations Biljetter och bokningar

When is the … flight to New York?	**När går … flyget till New York?** *nair gawr … flewget til New York*
first/last	**första/sista** *fursta/sista*
When is the next flight to New York?	**När går nästa flyg till New York?** *nair gawr nesta flewg til New York*
I'd like two … tickets to New York.	**Jag skulle vilja ha två … biljetter till New York.** *yaag skeulleh vilya haa tvaw … bilyetter til New York*
one-way [single]	**enkel** *enkel*
round-trip [return]	**retur** *reteur*
first class	**första klass** *fursta klas*
business class	**affärsklass** *affairs-klas*
economy class	**turistklass** *teurist-klas*
How much is a flight to …?	**Vad kostar flyget till …?** *vaad kostar flewget til*
Are there any supplements/reductions?	**Är det några tillägg/rabatter?** *air det nawgra tillegg/rabatter*
I'd like to … my reservation for flight number …	**Jag skulle vilja … min bokning till flyg nummer …** *yaag skeulleh vilya … min bookning til flewg neummer*
cancel/change/confirm	**avbeställa/ändra/bekräfta** *aavbestella/endra/bekrefta*

Inquiries about the flight Förfrågningar om flyg

How long is the flight?	**Hur länge tar flygresan?** *heur lengeh taar flewg-rehsan*
What time does the plane leave?	**Hur dags flyger planet?** *heur dax flewger plaanet*
What time will we arrive?	**När anländer vi?** *nair kommer vee fram*
What time do I have to check in?	**Hur dags måste jag checka in?** *heur dax mosteh yaag checka in*

Checking in Checka in

Where is the check-in desk for flight ...?

Var är incheckningen för flyget ...? *vaar air incheckningen fur flewget*

I have ...

Jag har ... *yaag haar*

three suitcases to check in

tre väskor att checka in *treh veskoor at checka in*

two carry-ons [pieces of hand luggage]

två handbagage *tvaw hand-bahgaash*

How much luggage is allowed free?

Hur mycket gratis bagage får man ha? *heur mewcket graatis bagaash fawr man haa*

Er(t) biljett/pass, tack.	Your ticket/passport, please.
Vill ni sitta vid fönstret eller vid mittgången?	Would you like a window or an aisle seat?
Rökare eller icke rökare?	Smoking or non-smoking?
Var snäll och gå till avgångshallen.	Please go through to the departure lounge.
Hur många resväskor har ni?	How many pieces of baggage do you have?
Ni har övervikt.	You have excess baggage.
Ni måste betala ett tillägg på ... kronor.	You'll have to pay a supplement of ... kronor.
Det där är för tungt/för stort handbagage.	That's too heavy/large for hand baggage.
Packade ni väskorna själv?	Did you pack these bags yourself?
Innehåller de några vassa eller elektriska/elektroniska artiklar?	Do they contain any sharp or electronic items?

ANKOMST	arrivals
AVGÅNG	departures
SÄKERHETSKONTROLL	security check
LÄMNA INGA VÄSKOR UTAN UPPSIKT	do not leave bags unattended

BAGGAGE ➤ 71

69

Information Information/Upplysningar

Is flight … delayed?	**Är det någon försening på flyg …?** *air det nawgon fursehning paw flewg*
How late will it be?	**Hur försenat är det?** *heur fursehnat air det*
Has the flight from … landed?	**Har flyget från … landat?** *haar flewget frawn … landat*
Which gate does flight … leave from?	**Vid vilken gate går flyg nummer …?** *veed vilken gayt gawr flewg neummer*

Boarding Gå ombord

Your boarding pass [card], please.	**Ert boardingkort, tack.** *ehrt boarding-koort tuck*
Could I have a drink/ something to eat, please?	**Kan jag få något att dricka/något att äta, tack?** *kun yaag faw nawgot at dricka/ nawgot at airta tuck*
Please wake me for the meal.	**Kan ni väcka mig innan maten.** *kun nee vecka may innan maaten*
What time will we arrive?	**När anländer vi?** *nair unlender vee*
An airsickness bag, please.	**Kan jag få en flygsjukpåse, tack.** *kun yaag faw en flewg-sheuk-pawseh tuck*

Arrival Ankomst

Where is/are (the) …?	**Var finns …?** *vaar fins*
buses	**bussarna** *beussarna*
car rental	**biluthyrningen** *beel-euthewrningen*
currency exchange	**växelkontoret** *vexel-kontooret*
exit	**utgången** *eutgongen*
taxis	**taxi** *taxi*
Is there a bus into town?	**Finns det en buss in till stan?** *fins det en beuss in til staan*
How do I get to the … hotel?	**Hur kommer jag till hotell …?** *heur kommer yaag til hootel*

Baggage Bagage

There are luggage carts available at all airports and most train stations. You will also find porters at most airports and train stations. If you use one, the customary tip is SEK 5–7 per piece of luggage.

Porter! Excuse me!	**Bärare! Ursäkta!** *bairareh eurshekta*
Could you take my luggage to …?	**Kan ni ta mitt bagage till …?** *kun nee taa mit bagaash til*
a taxi/bus	**en taxi/en buss** *en taxi/en beuss*
Where is/are (the) …?	**Var finns …?** *vaar fins*
luggage carts [trolleys]	**bagagekärror** *bagaash chairroor*
baggage check [left-luggage office]	**effektförvaringen** *effekt-furvaaringen*
baggage reclaim	**bagagehallen** *bagaash-hallen*
Where is the luggage from flight …?	**Var är bagaget från flyg …?** *vaar air bagaashet frawn flewg*

Loss, damage, and theft Förlust, skada och stöld

I've lost my baggage.	**Jag har förlorat mitt bagage.** *yaag haar furloorat mit bagaash*
My baggage has been stolen.	**Mitt bagage har blivit stulet.** *mit bagaash haar bleevit steulet*
My suitcase was damaged.	**Min resväska blev skadad.** *min rehs-veska blehv skaadad*
Our baggage has not arrived.	**Vårt bagage har inte anlänt.** *vawrt bagaash haar inteh unlent*

Hur ser ert bagage ut?	What does your baggage look like?
Har ni bagagekvittot?	Do you have the claim check [reclaim tag]?
Ert bagage …	Your luggage …
har möjligen skickats till …	may have been sent to …
kommer möjligen senare idag	may arrive later today
Var snäll och kom tillbaka imorgon.	Please come back tomorrow.
Ring detta nummer för att kontrollera om ert bagage har anlänt.	Call this number to check if your baggage has arrived.

POLICE ➤ 159; COLOR ➤ 143

Train Tåg

The Swedish State Railway (**SJ**) operates an extensive network that covers the whole country. The system is reliable and comfortable. Trains leave Stockholm for other big towns every hour or two.

The new X2000 train, reaching speeds up to 200 kmph, operates to Göteborg, Malmö, and Karlstad. Long-distance trains have restaurant cars and/or buffets, and there are also sleepers and couchettes for both first and second class.

Two children under 15 travel free when accompanied by an adult and there are a number of discounts for families, students, and senior citizens. Inquire about other discount programs, such as the **reslustkort** (wanderlust card), valid for a year, at only SEK150–200. This card gives you various reductions, for example, half-price second-class travel on certain trains. On some trains, marked "R" or "IC," you must reserve a seat (price SEK20), which can be done right up to the time of departure.

For extraordinary scenery, try the northern **Inlandsbanan** (Inland Railway) service, which runs from Mora in Dalarna to Gällivare beyond the Arctic circle. The **Vildmarksexpressen** (Wilderness Express) has old 1930s coaches and a gourmet restaurant, and runs on the same line between Östersund and Gällivare, with stops and excursions. For further details, contact Inlandståget AB, Kyrkogatan 56, S-831-34 Östersund, ☎ (0)63-12-76-92.

Full-fare tickets can be bought outside Sweden free of sales tax [VAT], which is charged on tickets bought in Sweden. Ask a travel agent.

Eurocity *eurositee*
International express train with first and second class.

Intercity *intehrsitee*
Long-distance train with first and second class. These have sleepers, couchettes, and restaurants or buffet cars.

Lokaltåg *lookaltawg*
Small local train.

Pendeltåg *pendeltawg*
Train serving the suburbs.

To the station Till stationen

How do I get to the train station?	**Hur kommer jag till järnvägsstationen?** *heur kommer yaag til yairnvairgs-stashoonen*
Do trains to Göteborg leave from … station?	**Avgår tåg till Göteborg från … stationen?** *gawr det tawg til yurtehbor' frawn … stashoonen*
How far is it?	**Hur långt är det?** *heur longt air det*
Can I leave my car there?	**Kan jag lämna min bil där?** *kun yaag lemna min beel dair*

At the station Vid stationen

Where is/are the …?	**Var finns …?** *vaar fins*
baggage check [left-luggage office]	**effektförvaringen** *effekt-furvaaringen*
currency exchange	**valutaväxeln** *valeuta-vexeln*
information desk	**informationen** *informashoonen*
lost and found [lost property office]	**hittegodsexpeditionen** *hitteh-goods-expedishoonen*
platforms	**plattformen** *platformen*
snack bar	**barserveringen** *baarservehringen*
ticket office	**biljettkontoret** *bilyet-kontooret*
waiting room	**väntrummet** *vent-reummet*

INGÅNG	entrance
UTGÅNG	exit
TILL PLATTFORMEN	to the platforms
INFORMATION	information
BILJETTKONTOR	reservations
ANKOMST	arrivals
AVGÅNG	departures

DIRECTIONS ➤ 94

73

Tickets Biljetter

Swedish State Railway offers a number of discount programs for parents traveling with children, as well as travel cards allowing discounted fares on certain trains. For more information ➤ 72.

I'd like a … ticket to Malmö.	**Jag skulle vilja ha en … biljett till Malmö.** *yaag skeulleh vilya haa en … bilyet til malmeur*
one-way [single]	**enkel** *enkel*
round-trip [return]	**retur** *reteur*
first/second class	**första/andra klass** *fursta/andra klas*
concessionary	**rabatt** *rabatt*
I'd like to reserve a(n) … seat.	**Jag skulle vilja reservera en plats …** *yaag skeulleh vilya reservehra en plats*
aisle seat	**vid mittgången** *veed mitgongen*
window seat	**vid fönstret** *veed feunstret*
Is there a sleeping car [sleeper]?	**Finns det sovvagn?** *fins det sawv-vungn*
I'd like a(n) … berth.	**Jag skulle vilja ha en … bädd.** *yaag skeulleh vilya haa en … bed*
upper/lower	**över/under** *urver/eunder*

Price Pris

How much is that?	**Hur mycket kostar det?** *heur mewcket kostar det*
Is there a reduction for …?	**Blir det rabatt för …?** *bleer det rabatt fur*
children/families	**barn/familjer** *baarn/famil-yer*
senior citizens	**pensionärer** *pangshoonairer*
students	**studerande** *steudehrande*

NUMBERS ➤ 216; DAYS OF THE WEEK ➤ 218

Queries Förfrågningar

Do I have to change trains?	**Behöver jag byta tåg?** *behurver yaag bewta tawg*
Is it a direct train?	**Är det ett direkttåg?** *air det et direkt-tawg*
You have to change at …	**Ni måste byta i …** *nee mosteh bewta ee*
How long is this ticket valid?	**Hur länge gäller den här biljetten?** *heur lengeh yeller den hair bilyetten*
Can I take my bicycle on the train?	**Kan jag ta med mig cykeln på tåget?** *kun yaag taa mehd may sewkeln paw tawget*
Can I return on the same ticket?	**Kan jag åka tillbaka på samma biljett?** *kun yaag awka tilbaaka paw samma bilyet*
In which car [coach] is my seat?	**I vilken vagn är min plats?** *ee vilken vangn air min plats*
Is there a dining car on the train?	**Finns det restaurangvagn på tåget?** *fins det resteurang-vangn paw tawget*

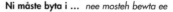

– Jag skulle vilja ha en biljett till Halmstad.
(I'd like a ticket to Halmstad, please.)
– Enkel eller retur? (One-way or round-trip?)
– En returbiljett, tack. (Round-trip, please.)
– Det blir femhundratio (510) kronor, tack.
(That's 510 kronor, please.)
– Behöver jag byta tåg?
(Do I have to change trains?)
– Ja, ni behöver byta tåg i Jönköping.
(Yes, you have to change at Jönköping.)
– Tack. (Thank you.)

Train times Tågtider

Could I have a timetable, please?	**Kan jag få en tidtabell, tack?** *kun yaag faw en teed-tabell tuck*
When is the … train to Sundsvall?	**När går … tåget till Sundsvall?** *nair gawr … tawget til seundsvall*
first/next/last	**första/nästa/sista** *fursta/nesta/sista*

How frequent are trains to …?	**Hur ofta går tågen till …?** _heur ofta gawr tawgen til_
once/twice a day	**en gång/två gånger om dagen** _en gong/tvaw gonger om daagen_
five times a day	**fem gånger om dagen** _fem gonger om daagen_
every hour	**varje timme** _varyeh timmeh_
What time do they leave?	**Hur dags avgår tågen?** _heur dax gawr tawgen_
on the hour	**varje heltimme** _varyeh hehl-timmeh_
20 minutes past the hour	**tjugo minuter efter varje heltimme** _chewgoo mineuter efter varyeh hehl-timmeh_
What time does the train stop at …?	**Hur dags stannar tåget i …?** _heur dax stannar tawget ee_
What time does the train arrive at …?	**Hur dags anländer tåget i …?** _heur dax unlender tawget ee_
How long is the trip [journey]?	**Hur länge tar resan?** _heur lengeh taar rehsan_
Is the train on time?	**Går tåget i tid?** _gawr tawget ee teed_

Departures Avgång

Which platform does the train to … leave from?	**Från vilken plattform avgår tåget till …?** _frawn vilken platform aavgawr tawget til_
Where is platform 4?	**Var är plattform fyra?** _vaar air platform fewra_
over there	**där borta** _dair borta_
on the left/right	**till vänster/höger** _til venster/hurger_
Where do I change for …?	**Var måste jag byta till …?** _var mosteh yaag bewta til_
How long will I have to wait for a connection?	**Hur länge behöver jag vänta på anslutning?** _heur lengeh behurver yaag venta paw ansleutning_

TIME ➤ 220; DIRECTIONS ➤ 94

Boarding Påstigning

Is this the right platform for …?
Är det här rätta plattformen till …? *air det hair retta platformen til*

Is this the train to …?
Är det här tåget till …? *air det hair tawget til*

Is this seat taken?
Är den här platsen upptagen? *air den hair platsen eupptaagen*

That's my seat.
Det här är min plats. *det hair air min plats*

Here's my reservation.
Jag har reserverad plats. *yaag haar reservehrad plats*

Are there any seats/ berths available?
Finns det några lediga platser/bäddar? *fins det nawgra lehdiga platser/beddar*

Do you mind if …?
Har ni något emot att …? *haar nee nawgot emoot at*

I sit here
jag sitter här *yaag sitter hair*

I open the window
jag öppnar fönstret *yaag urpnar furnstret*

On the journey På resan

How long are we stopping here for?
Hur länge stannar vi här? *heur lengeh stannar vee hair*

When do we get to …?
När anländer vi i …? *nair unlender vee ee*

Have we passed …?
Har vi passerat …? *haar vee passehrat*

Where is the dining/ sleeping car?
Var är restaurangvagnen/sovvagnen? *vaar air resteurang-vangnen/sawv-vangnen*

Where is my berth?
Var är min bädd? *vaar air min bed*

I've lost my ticket.
Jag har tappat min biljett. *yaag haar tappat min bilyet*

ALARM	alarm
AUTOMATISKA DÖRRAR	automatic doors
NÖDBROMS	emergency break

TIME ➤ 220

Long-distance bus [Coach]
Långfärdsbuss

Long-distance buses (**långfärdsbussar**) are efficient, relatively cheap, and run daily between all major towns and resorts.

Where is the bus [coach] station?	**Var är bussterminalen?** *vaar air beuss-terminaalen*
When's the next bus [coach] to …?	**När går nästa buss till …?** *nair gawr nesta beuss til*
Where does it leave from?	**Var avgår den från?** *vaar aavgawr den frawn*
Where are the bus [coach] bays?	**Var är hållplatsen?** *vaar air holplatsen*
Does the bus [coach] stop at …?	**Stannar bussen i …?** *stannar beussen ee*
How long does the trip [journey] take?	**Hur länge tar resan?** *heur lengeh taar rehsan*
Are there … on board?	**Finns det … ombord?** *fins det … omboord*
refreshments/toilets	**mat och dryck/toaletter** *maat ock drewck/tooaletter*

Bus/Streetcar [Tram] Bus/Spårvagn

Buses in Sweden are excellent and well maintained. Buses run frequently and are well integrated with other means of transportation. They usually run from 5:00 a.m. to midnight or later on weekends.

Stockholm used to have a streetcar network and some lines are now being re-introduced. Göteborg has long had an ecologically friendly streetcar network.

Where is the bus stop?	**Var är busshållplatsen?** *vaar air beuss-holplatsen*
Where can I get a bus/ streetcar [tram] to …?	**Var går bussen/spårvagnen till …?** *vaar gawr beussen/spawr-vangnen til*
What time is the bus to Djurgården?	**Hur dags går bussen till Djurgården?** *heur dax gawr beussen til yeur-gawrden*

Ni måste gå till hållplatsen där borta.	You need that stop over there.
Ni måste ta buss nummer …	You need bus number …
Ni måste byta buss vid …	You must change buses at …

BUSSHÅLLPLATS	bus stop
RÖKNING FÖRBJUDEN	no smoking
UTGÅNG/NÖDUTGÅNG	exit/emergency exit

DIRECTIONS ➤ 94; TIME ➤ 220

Buying tickets Köpa biljetter

Tickets, valid for one hour once stamped, can be bought from the bus driver. You can also buy discount 20-unit cards from **pressbyrån** (newsstands found at subway stations). Children and senior citizens pay half price.

Where can I buy tickets?	**Var kan jag köpa biljetter?** *vaar kun yaag churpa bilyetter*
A … ticket to Gamla Stan, please.	**En … biljett till Gamla Stan, tack.** *en bilyet til gamla staan tuck*
one-way [single]/round-trip [return]	**enkel/retur** *enkel/reteur*
A booklet of tickets, please.	**Ett rabatthäfte, tack.** *ett rabatt-hefteh tuck*
How much is the fare to …?	**Hur mycket kostar biljetten till …?** *heur mewcket bilyetten til*

Traveling Resa

Is this the right bus/streetcar [tram] to …?	**Är det här rätta bussen/spårvagnen till …?** *air det hair retta beussen/spawr-vangnen til*
Could you tell me when to get off?	**Kan ni tala om för mig när jag ska stiga av?** *kun nee taala om fur may nair yaag skaa steega aav*
Do I have to change buses?	**Behöver jag byta buss?** *behurver yaag bewta beuss*
How many stops are there to …?	**Hur många hållplatser är det till …?** *heur monga holplatser air det til*

BILJETTKONTOR	ticket office
BILJETTAUTOMAT	ticket vending machine

– Ursäkta mig. Är det här rätta bussen till Stadshuset?
(Excuse me. Is this the right bus to the town hall?)

– Ja, det är nummer åtta. (Yes, number 8.)

– En biljett till Stadshuset, tack.
(One ticket to the town hall, please.)

– Det blir nitton (19) kronor. (That's 19 kronor.)

– Kan ni tala om för mig när jag ska stiga av?
(Could you tell me when to get off?)

– Det är fyra hållplatser härifrån.
(It's four stops from here.)

NUMBERS ➤ 216; DIRECTIONS ➤ 94

Subway [Metro] Tunnelbana

The subway in Stockholm (**tunnelbana**) is efficient and easy to use. It runs from 5:00 a.m. to midnight. Tickets, valid for one hour from the time they are stamped, can be bought from the ticket booths. You can also buy a discount card from a newsstand (**pressbyrån**). Children and senior citizens travel at half price. Tourist tickets are also available. You can use subway tickets for bus trips as well.

General inquiries Allmänna förfrågningar

Where's the nearest subway [metro] station?	**Var är närmaste tunnelbanestation?** *vaar air <u>nair</u>masteh teunnel-baane-sta<u>shoon</u>*
Where can I buy a ticket?	**Var kan jag köpa en biljett?** *vaar kun yaag churpa en bil<u>yet</u>*
Could I have a map of the subway [metro], please?	**Kan jag få en tunnelbanekarta, tack?** *kun yaag faw en teunnel-baane-kaarta tuck*

Traveling Resa

Which line should I take for …?	**Vilken linje ska jag ta till …?** *<u>vilk</u>en linyeh skaa yaag taa til*
Is this the right train for …?	**Är det här rätta tåget till …?** *air det hair retta <u>tawg</u>et til*
Which stop is it for …?	**Vilken är den närmaste hållplatsen till …?** *<u>vilk</u>en air den <u>nair</u>masteh holplatsen til*
How many stops is it to …?	**Hur många hållplatser är det till …?** *heur monga holplatser air det til*
Is the next stop …?	**Är nästa hållplats …?** *air nesta holplats*
Where are we?	**Var är vi?** *vaar air vee*
Where do I change for …?	**Var måste jag byta till …?** *vaar mosteh yaag bewta til*
What time is the last train to …?	**Hur dags går sista tåget till …?** *heur dax gawr sista <u>tawg</u>et til*

⊘ **ANDRA LINJER/BYTE**	to other lines/transfer ⊖

NUMBERS ➤ 216; BUYING TICKETS ➤ 74, 79

Ferry Färjor

Regular boat and ferry services, carrying trains, cars, and passengers, link Sweden to neighboring countries as well as to the U.K. Ferry services from Stockholm to the vacation destinations of Åland and Gotland in the Baltic Sea are very popular, as are the ferries to Finland. Not to be missed are the ferry/steamer trips from Stockholm to the small islands around it, Skärgården (the archipelago).

When is the … car ferry to Gotland?	**Hur dags går … bilfärjan till Gotland?** *heur dax gawr beel-fairyan til gotland*
first/next/last	**första/nästa/sista** *fursta/nesta/sista*
hovercraft/ship	**svävare/båt** *svaivareh/bawt*
A round-trip [return] ticket for …	**En returbiljett till …** *en returr-bilyet til*
one car and one trailer [caravan]	**en bil och en husvagn** *en beel ock en heus-vangn*
two adults and three children	**två vuxna och tre barn** *tvaw veuxna ock treh baarn*
I want to reserve a … cabin.	**Jag vill boka en … hytt.** *yaag vil booka en … hewtt*
single/double	**enkel/dubbel** *enkel/deubbel*

LIVBÄLTE/FLYTVÄST	life preserver [lifebelt]
LIVBÅT	lifeboat
SAMLINGSPLATS	muster station
INGEN INGÅNG	no access

Boat trips Båtresor

Is there a …?	**Finns det någon …?** *fins det nawgon*
boat trip/river cruise	**båttur/flodkryssning** *bawt-teur/flood-krewsning*
What time does it leave?	**Hur dags går den?** *heur dax gawr den*
What time does it return?	**Hur dags kommer den tillbaka?** *heur dax kommer den tilbaaka*
Where can we buy tickets?	**Var kan vi köpa biljetter?** *vaar kun vee churpa bilyetter*

TIME ➤ 220; BUYING TICKETS ➤ 74, 79

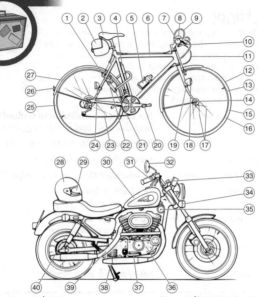

1	brake pad **broms**	21	lock **lås**
2	bicycle bag **cykelväska**	22	generator [dynamo] **dynamo**
3	saddle **sadel**	23	chain **kedja**
4	pump **pump**	24	rear light **bakljus**
5	water bottle **vattenflaska**	25	rim **fälg**
6	frame **ram**	26	reflectors **reflex**
7	handlebars **handtag**	27	fender [mudguard] **stänkskärm**
8	bell **ringklocka**	28	helmet **hjälm**
9	brake cable **bromskabel**	29	visor **skärm**
10	gear shift [lever] **växlar**	30	fuel tank **bensintank**
11	gear control cable **växelkabeln**	31	clutch lever **kopplingspedal**
12	inner tube **innerslang**	32	mirror **spegel**
13	front/back wheel **framhjul/bakhjul**	33	ignition switch **tändning**
14	axle **axel**	34	turn signal [indicator] **visare**
15	tire [tyre] **däck**	35	horn **signalhorn**
16	wheel **hjul**	36	engine **motor**
17	spokes **ekrar**	37	gear shift [lever] **växelspaken**
18	bulb **lampa**	38	kick stand [main stand] **kickstart**
19	headlamp **framljus**	39	exhaust pipe **avgasrör**
20	pedal **pedal**	40	chain guard **kedjeskärm**

REPAIRS ➤ 89

Bicycle/Motorbike
Cykel/Motorcykel

Sweden's uncrowded roads make bicycling very popular, and
you can rent a bike almost anywhere, including Stockholm. It
costs around SEK120 per day, and package deals can also be
arranged. Note that helmets are required for drivers and passengers on
motorcycles/mopeds. Inquire at the local tourist office.

I'd like to rent a …	**Jag skulle vilja hyra en …** *yaag skeulleh vilya hewra en*
3-/10-speed bicycle	**cykel med 3/10 växlar** *sewkel mehd treh/teeoo vexlar*
moped	**moped** *moopehd*
motorbike	**motorcykel** *mootor-sewkel*
How much does it cost per day/week?	**Hur mycket kostar det per dag/per vecka?** *heur mewcket kostar det pairr daag/ pairr vecka*
Do you require a deposit?	**Behöver ni handpenning?** *behurver nee hand-penning*
The brakes don't work.	**Bromsarna fungerar inte.** *bromsarna feungehrar inteh*
There are no lights.	**Det finns inget ljus.** *det fins inget yeus*
The front/rear tire [tyre] has a flat [puncture].	**Det är punktering på fram-/bakhjulet.** *det air punktehring paw fram-yeulet/ baak-yeulet*

Hitchhiking Lifta

Where are you heading?	**Vart är du på väg?** *vart skaa du taa vairgen*
I'm heading for …	**Jag är på väg till …** *yaag air paw vairg til*
Is that on the way to …?	**Är det på vägen till …?** *air det paw vairgen til*
Could you drop me off …?	**Kan du släppa av mig …?** *kun deu sleppa aav may*
here/at …	**här/vid …** *hair/veed*
at the … exit	**vid … utfart** *veed … eutfaart*
downtown	**i centrum** *ee sentreum*
Thanks for giving me a lift.	**Tack för liften.** *tuck fur liften*

DIRECTIONS ➤ 94; NUMBERS ➤ 216

Taxi/Cab Taxi

You can find a taxi at stands marked **Taxi**. You can also flag them down in the street or you can order one by phone. The sign **Ledig** lit up indicates that the taxi is available. Taxis have meters, and overcharging is not a problem.

Where can I get a taxi?	**Var kan jag få tag på taxi?** *vaar kun yaag faw taag paw taxi*
Do you have the number for a taxi?	**Har ni numret till taxi?** *haar nee neumret til taxi*
I'd like a taxi ...	**Jag skulle vilja ha en taxi ...** *yaag skeulleh vilya haa en taxi*
now	**nu** *neu*
in an hour	**om en timme** *om en timmeh*
for tomorrow at 9:00	**imorgon klockan nio (09.00)** *ee morron klockan neeoo*
The pick-up address is ...	**Adressen är ...** *adressen air*
I'm going to ...	**Jag ska åka till ...** *yaag skaa awka til*

◎ **LEDIG**	for hire ◎

Please take me to (the) ...	**Var snäll och kör mig till ...** *vaar snel ock chur may til*
airport	**flygplatsen** *flewg-platsen*
train station	**järnvägsstationen** *yairnvairgs-stashoonen*
this address	**denna adress** *denna adress*
How much will it cost?	**Hur mycket kommer det att kosta?** *heur mewcket kommer det at kosta*
How much is that?	**Hur mycket är det?** *heur mewcket air det*
Keep the change.	**Behåll växeln.** *behol vairxeln*

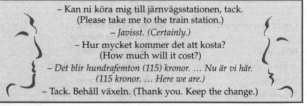

– Kan ni köra mig till järnvägsstationen, tack.
(Please take me to the train station.)
– *Javisst. (Certainly.)*
– Hur mycket kommer det att kosta?
(How much will it cost?)
– *Det blir hundrafemton (115) kronor. ... Nu är vi här.
(115 kronor. ... Here we are.)*
– Tack. Behåll växeln. (Thank you. Keep the change.)

Car/Automobile Bil

Although there are not many highways in Sweden, driving in the countryside is a real pleasure. The roads are wide, uncrowded, and well maintained – and the scenery is breathtaking. There are also many idyllic spots and rest areas where you can picnic and even go for a swim.

If you are taking a car into Sweden you will need:

- a valid driver's license, international driving permit, or EU license
- car registration documents
- a Green Card (insurance)
- a national identity (country of origin) sticker
- a red reflector warning triangle

The minimum driving age is 18, and 21 for rental cars. Seat belts are required for everybody in the car, and children under seven should be secured in the back seat in a child's seat. All vehicles, including motorcycles, must have running lights [dipped headlights] on at all times.

Drinking and driving is a very serious offense, and the police are free to stop motorists to breathalize them whenever they want.

Conversion chart

km	1	10	20	30	40	50	60	70	80	90	100	110	120	130
miles	0.62	6	12	19	25	31	37	44	50	56	62	68	74	81

Speed Limits

	Built-up area kmph (mph)	Main road kmph (mph)	Highway [motorway] kmph (mph)
Cars	50 (31)	90 (56)	110 (68)
Cars towing a trailer [caravan]	50 (31)	70 (44)	70 (44)

Fuel

Gas [Petrol]	Leaded	Unleaded	Diesel
bensin	**med bly**	**blyfri**	**diesel**
benseen	*mehd blew*	*blewfree*	*deesel*

Car rental Biluthyrning

You can find all the major international car rental companies, as well as local agencies, in large towns and at airports. To rent a car, you need to have a valid driver's license, held for at least three years, and a passport.

Where can I rent a car?	**Var kan jag hyra en bil?** *vaar kun yaag hewra en beel*
I'd like to rent a(n) …	**Jag skulle vilja hyra en …** *yaag skeulleh vilya hewra en*
2-/4-door car	**bil med två/fyra dörrar** *beel mehd tvaw/fewra durrar*
automatic	**bil med automatväxel** *beel mehd aatoomaat-vexel*
car with 4-wheel drive	**bil med fyrhjulsdrift** *beel mehd fewr-yeulsdrift*
car with air conditioning	**bil med luftkonditionering** *beel mehd leuft-kondishoonering*
I'd like it for a day/week.	**Jag behöver den för en dag/en vecka.** *yaag behurver den fur en daag/en vecka*
How much does it cost per day/week?	**Hur mycket kostar det per dag/vecka?** *heur mewcket kostar det pairr daag/vecka*
Is insurance included?	**Är försäkring inkluderad?** *air fursairkring inkleudehrad*
Are there special weekend rates?	**Har ni särskilda helgrabatter?** *haar nee sairshilda hel'-rabatter*
Can I return the car at …?	**Kan jag lämna tillbaka bilen vid …?** *kun yaag lemna tilbaaka beelen veed*
What sort of fuel does it take?	**Vilken bensin tar den?** *vilken benseen taar den*
Where is the high [full]/low [dipped] beam?	**Var är helljuset/halvljuset?** *vaar air hehl-yeuset/halv-yeuset*
Could I have full insurance?	**Kan jag få en helförsäkring?** *kun yaag faw en hehl-fursairkring*

Gas [Petrol] station Bensinstation

Where's the next gas [petrol] station, please?	**Ursäkta, var är närmaste bensinstation?** *eurshekta vaar air nairmasteh benseen-stashoon*
Is it self-service?	**Är det själv-service?** *air det shelv-service*
Fill it up, please.	**Fyll tanken, tack.** *fewll tanken tuck*
... liters, please.	**... liter, tack.** *leeter tuck*
premium [super]/regular	**premium/vanlig** *prehmieum/vaanlig*
lead-free/diesel	**blyfri/diesel** *blewfree/deesel*
I'm at pump number ...	**Jag är vid tank nummer ...** *yaag air vid tank neummer*
Where is the air pump/ water?	**Var finns luft/vatten?** *vaar fins leuft/vatten*

LITERPRIS	price per liter

Parking Parkering

Street parking is metered in towns and can be costly. A blue circular sign with a red "x" tells you where parking is prohibited. Some areas also have alternate-side-of-street parking.

Is there a parking lot [car park] nearby?	**Finns det en parkeringsplats i närheten?** *fins det en parkehrings-plats ee nairhehten*
What's the charge per hour/day?	**Vad kostar det per timme/dag?** *vaad kostar det pairr timmeh/daag*
Do you have some change for the parking meter?	**Har ni växel till parkeringsmätaren?** *haar nee vexel til parkehrings-mairtaren*
My car has been booted [clamped]. Who do I call?	**Min bil har försetts med hjullås. Vem kan jag kontakta?** *min beel haar fursets mehd yeul-laws. vem kun yaag kontakta*

NUMBERS ➤ 216; DIRECTIONS ➤ 94

Breakdown Motorstopp

For accidents or breakdowns, contact the police or **Larmtjänst** (24-hour road service) by calling (Stockholm) 241000 or cheap rate 020 910040.

Most big gas stations have mechanics on duty. In case of serious injuries, call the emergency services, ☎ 112.

Where is the nearest garage?	**Var finns närmaste bilverkstad?** *vaar fins nairmasteh beel-vairkstud*
My car broke down.	**Min bil har gått sönder.** *min beel haar got surnder*
Can you send a mechanic/ tow [breakdown] truck?	**Kan ni skicka en mekaniker/en bärgningsbil?** *kun nee shicka en mekaaniker/en ber'nings-beel*
I'm a member of …	**Jag är medlem i …** *yaag air mehdlem ee*
My license plate [registration] number is …	**Mitt registreringsnummer är …** *mit rejistrehrings-neummer air*
The car is …	**Bilen är …** *beelen air*
on the highway [motorway]	**på motorvägen** *paw mootor-vairgen*
2 km from …	**2 km från …** *tvaw kilomehter frawn*
How long will you be?	**När kan ni komma?** *nair kun nee komma*

What is wrong? Vad är felet?

My car won't start.	**Min bil startar inte.** *min beel staartar inteh*
The battery is dead.	**Batteriet är slut.** *batteree-et air sleut*
I've run out of gas [petrol].	**Bensinen är slut.** *benseenen air slewt*
I have a flat [puncture].	**Jag har fått punktering.** *yaag haar fot peunktehring*
There's something wrong with …	**Det är något fel med …** *det air nawgot fehl mehd*
I've locked the keys in the car.	**Jag har låst in nycklarna i bilen.** *yaag haar lawst in newcklarna ee beelen*

TELEPHONING ➤ 127; CAR PARTS ➤ 90–91

Repairs Reparationer

Do you do repairs?

Lagar ni bilar?
laagar nee beelar

Can you repair it?

Kan ni laga det här?
kun nee laaga det hair

Please make only
essential repairs.

Var snäll och laga bara det som behövs.
vaar snel ock laaga baara det som behurvs

Can I wait for it?

Kan jag vänta? _kun yaag venta_

Can you repair it today?

Kan ni laga det idag?
kun nee laaga det ee daag

When will it be ready?

När blir det färdigt?
nair bleer det fairdigt

How much will it cost?

Hur mycket kostar det?
heur mewcket kostar det

That's outrageous!

Det är alldeles för dyrt!
det air alldeles fur dewrt

Can I have a receipt
for my insurance?

**Kan jag få ett kvitto för mitt
försäkringsbolag?** _kun yaag faw et
kvittoo fur mit fursairkrings-boolaag_

... fungerar inte.	The ... isn't working.
Jag har inte delarna som behövs.	I don't have the necessary parts.
Jag måste beställa delarna.	I will have to order the parts.
Jag kan bara laga det provisoriskt.	I can only repair it temporarily.
Er bil kan inte lagas – den är för skadad.	Your car is beyond repair.
Vi kan inte laga den.	It can't be repaired.
Den blir färdig ...	It will be ready ...
senare idag	later today
imorgon	tomorrow
om ... dagar	in ... days

DAYS OF THE WEEK ➤ 218; NUMBERS ➤ 216

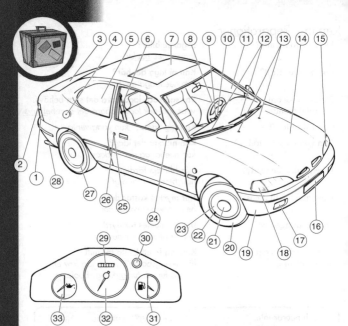

1	taillights [back lights] **bakljus**
2	brakelights **bromsljus**
3	trunk [boot] **bagageutrymme**
4	gas tank door [petrol cap] **lock på bensintank**
5	window **fönster**
6	seat belt **säkerhetsbälte**
7	sunroof **soltak**
8	steering wheel **ratten**
9	ignition **tändning**
10	ignition key **tändningsnyckel**
11	windshield [windscreen] **vindruta**
12	windshield [windscreen] wipers **vindrutetorkare**
13	windshield [windscreen] washer **vindrutespolare**
14	hood [bonnet] **motorhuv**
15	headlights **framljus**
16	license [number] plate **nummerplåt**
17	fog lamp **dimljus**
18	turn signals [indicators] **visare**
19	bumper **kofångare**
20	tires [tyres] **däck**
21	wheel cover [hubcap] **navkapsel**
22	valve **ventil**
23	wheels **hjul**
24	outside [wing] mirror **sidospegel**
25	automatic locks [central locking] **centrallås**
26	lock **lås**
27	wheel rim **fälg**
28	exhaust pipe **avgasrör**
29	odometer [milometer] **vägmätare**
30	warning light **varningsljus**

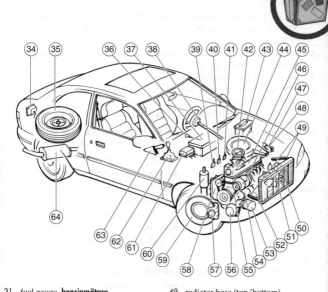

31 fuel gauge **bensinmätare**	49 radiator hose (top/bottom)
32 speedometer **hastighetsmätare**	**kylarslang (uppe/nere)**
33 oil gauge **oljmätare**	50 radiator **kylare**
34 backup [reversing] lights **backljus**	51 fan **fläkt**
35 spare wheel **reservhjul**	52 engine **motor**
36 choke **choke**	53 oil filter **oljefilter**
37 heater **värme**	54 starter motor **startmotor**
38 steering column **rattstång**	55 fan belt **fläktrem**
39 accelerator **gaspedal**	56 horn **signalhorn**
40 pedal **pedal**	57 brake pads **bromsbelägg**
41 clutch **koppling**	58 transmission [gearbox] **växellåda**
42 carburetor **förgasare**	59 brakes **bromsar**
43 battery **batteri**	60 shock absorbers **stötdämpare**
44 air filter **luftfilter**	61 fuses **säkringar**
45 camshaft **kamaxel**	62 gear shift [lever] **växelspak**
46 alternator **generator**	63 handbrake **handbroms**
47 distributor **fördelare**	64 muffler [silencer] **ljuddämpare**
48 points **brytarspetsar**	

REPAIRS ➤ 89

Accidents Olyckor

In the event of an accident:

1. Put your warning triangle 100 meters behind your car;

2. Report the accident to the police (required by law if anyone is injured);

3. Give your name, address, and insurance information to the other party and make a note of any witnesses;

4. Contact your insurance company;

5. Don't make a written statement without advice from a lawyer or motor-club official;

6. Get the police to make a report of the accident.

There's been an accident.	**Det har hänt en olycka** *det haar hent en <u>oo</u>lewcka*
It's …	**Den är …** *den air*
on the highway [motorway]	**på motorvägen** *paw mootor-<u>vair</u>gen*
near …	**nära …** *naira*
Where's the nearest telephone?	**Var är närmaste telefon?** *vaar air <u>nair</u>masteh tele<u>faw</u>n*
Call …	**Ring efter …** *ring efter*
an ambulance	**en ambulans** *en ambeu<u>lans</u>*
a doctor	**en doktor** *en doktor*
the fire department [brigade]	**brandkåren** <u>*brand*</u>*kawren*
the police	**polisen** *poo<u>lee</u>sen*
Can you help me, please?	**Kan ni hjälpa mig?** *kun nee yelpa may*

Injuries Personskador

There are people injured.	**Någon har blivit skadad.** *nawgon haar bleevit skaadad*
No one is hurt.	**Ingen är skadad.** *ingen air skaadad*
He's seriously injured.	**Han är allvarligt skadad.** *han air <u>alvaar</u>ligt skaadad*
She's unconscious.	**Hon är medvetslös.** *hoonn air <u>mehd</u>-vehtslurs*
He can't breathe.	**Han kan inte andas.** *han kun inteh andas*
He can't move.	**Han kan inte röra sig.** *han kun inteh rurra say*
Don't move him.	**Flytta honom inte.** *rurr honom inteh*

Legal matters Rättsliga frågor

What's your insurance company?	**Vilket är ert försäkringsbolag?** _vilket air ehrt fursairkrings-boolaag_
What's your name and address?	**Vad är ert namn och adress?** _vaad air ehrt namn ock adress_
The car ran into me.	**Bilen körde på mig.** _beelen churdeh paw may_
The car was going too fast.	**Bilen körde för fort.** _beelen churdeh fur foort_
The car was driving too close.	**Bilen körde för nära.** _beelen churdeh fur naira_
I had the right of way.	**Jag hade förkörsrätt.** _yaag hadeh furchurs-ret_
I was (only) driving ... kmph.	**Jag körde bara i ... km i timmen.** _yaag churdeh baara ee ... kilomehter ee timmen_
I'd like an interpreter.	**Jag behöver en tolk.** _yaag behurver en tolk_
I didn't see the sign.	**Jag såg inte skylten.** _yaag sawg inteh shewlten_
This person saw it happen.	**Denna person såg vad som hände.** _denna pairshoon sawg vaad som hendeh_
The license plate [registration] number was ...	**Registreringsnumret var ...** _rejistrehrings-neumret vaar_

Kan jag får se ert ... , tack?	Can I see your ..., please?
körkort	driver's license
försäkringsbrev	insurance card
bilregistreringspapper	vehicle registration document
Hur dags hände det?	What time did it happen?
Var hände det?	Where did it happen?
Var någon annan inblandad?	Was anyone else involved?
Finns det några vittnen?	Are there any witnesses?
Ni körde för fort.	You were speeding.
Era ljus fungerar inte.	Your lights aren't working.
Ni måste betala böter nu.	You'll have to pay a fine (on the spot).
Ni måste komma till polisstationen och rapportera.	You have to make a statement at the station.

TIME ➤ 220

93

Asking directions
Fråga efter vägen

Excuse me, please.	**Ursäkta mig.** *eurshekta may*
How do I get to …?	**Hur kommer jag till …?** *heur kun yaag komma til*
Where is …?	**Var är …?** *vaar air*
Can you show me where I am on the map?	**Kan ni visa på kartan var jag är?** *kun nee veesa paw kaartan vaar yaag air*
I've lost my way.	**Jag har gått vilse.** *yaag haar got vilseh*
Can you repeat that, please?	**Kan ni upprepa det, tack?** *kun nee eupp-rehpa det tuck*
More slowly, please.	**Lite långsammare, tack.** *leeteh longsammare tuck*
Thanks for your help.	**Tack för hjälpen.** *tuck fur yelpen*

Traveling by car Bilresa

Is this the right road for …?	**Är det här rätta vägen till …?** *air det hair retta vairgen til*
Is it far?	**Är det långt?** *air det longt*
How far is it to … from here?	**Hur långt är det till … härifrån?** *heur longt air det till … haireefrawn*
Where does this road lead?	**Vart går den här vägen?** *vart gawr den hair vairgen*
How do I get onto the highway [motorway]?	**Hur kommer jag till motorvägen?** *heur kommer yaag til mootor-vairgen*
What's the next town called?	**Vad heter nästa stad?** *vaad hehter nesta staad*
How long does it take by car?	**Hur länge tar det med bil?** *heur lengeh taar det mehd beel*

– Ursäkta mig. Hur kommer jag till järnvägsstationen?
(Excuse me, please. How do I get to the train station?)

– *Ta tredje gatan till höger och sen är det rakt fram.*
(Take the third right, and it's straight ahead.)

– Tredje gatan till höger. Är det långt härifrån?
(Third on the right. Is it far?)

– *Det tar tio minuter till fots. (It's ten minutes on foot.)*

– Tack för hjälpen. (Thanks for your help.)

– *För all del. (You're welcome.)*

COMMUNICATION DIFFICULTIES ➤ 11

Location Hitta vägen

Det är ...	It's ...
rakt fram	straight ahead
till vänster	on the left
till höger	on the right
i slutet på gatan	at the end of the street
i hörnan	on the corner
runt hörnan	around the corner
i riktning mot ...	in the direction of ...
mitt emot .../bakom ...	opposite .../behind ...
bredvid .../efter ...	next to .../after ...
Gå ner på ...	Go down the ...
sidogatan/huvudgatan	side street/main street
Korsa över ...	Cross the ...
torget/bron	square/bridge
Ta tredje gatan till höger	Take the third right.
Ta till vänster ...	Turn left ...
efter första trafikljusen	after the first traffic light
vid den andra korsningen	at the second intersection [crossroad]

By car Med bil

Det ligger ... härifrån.	It's ... of here.
norr/söder	north/south
öster/väster	east/west
Ta vägen till ...	Take the road for ...
Ni är på fel väg.	You're on the wrong road.
Ni måste åka tillbaka till ...	You'll have to go back to ...
Följ skyltarna mot ...	Follow the signs for ...

How far? Hur långt?

Det är ...	It's ...
nära/långt	close/a long way
fem minuter till fots	5 minutes on foot
tio minuter med bil	10 minutes by car
omkring hundra meter ner	about 100 meters down the road
omkring tio kilometer härifrån	about 10 kilometers away

TIME ➤ 220; NUMBERS ➤ 216

Road signs Vägmärken

KÖR LÅNGSAMT	drive slowly
TRAFIKOMLÄGGNING	detour [diversion]
OMKÖRNING FÖRBJUDEN	no passing [overtaking]
ENKELRIKTAD GATA	one-way street
VÄGEN STÄNGD	road closed
SKOLA	school zone [path]
STOPP	stop
ANVÄND HELLJUS	use headlights

Town plans Stadsplanering

bank	bank
bio	movie theater [cinema]
bussfil/busslinje	bus route
busshållplats	bus stop
flygplats	airport
gågata	pedestrian zone [precinct]
huvudgata/affärsgata	main [high] street/shopping street
informationskontor/turistbyrå	information/tourist office
järnvägsstation	train station
kyrka	church
lekplats/idrottsplats	playing field [sports ground]
Ni är här.	You are here.
park	park
parkeringsplats	parking lot [car park]
polisstation	police station
post	post office
sjukhus	hospital
skola	school
stadion	stadium
taxi	taxi stand [rank]
teater	theater
tunnelbana	subway [metro] station
varuhus	department store
övergångsställe	pedestrian crossing

Sightseeing

Tourist information office Turistbyrå

Tourist information offices (**Turistbyrå**), marked with the international tourist sign (a white "i" on a green background) can be found in the center of most towns. They offer advice on places to stay, tours, and special events. In Stockholm, go to the Sweden House.

Where's the tourist office?	**Var ligger turistbyrån?** *vaar ligger teurist-bewrawn*
What are the main points of interest?	**Vad finns det för sevärdheter?** *vaad fins det fur sehvaird-hehter*
We're here for …	**Vi kommer att vara här …** *vee kommer at vaara hair …*
a few hours	**några timmar** *nawgra timmar*
a day	**en dag** *en daag*
a week	**en vecka** *en vecka*
Can you recommend …?	**Kan ni föreslå …?** *kun nee furreh-slaw*
a sightseeing tour	**en sightseeingtur** *en sightseeing-teur*
an excursion	**en rundtur** *en reundteur*
a boat trip	**en båttur** *en bawt-teur*
Do you have any information on …?	**Har ni någon information om …?** *haar nee nawgon informashoon om …*
Are there any trips to …?	**Finns det några turer till …?** *fins det nawgra teurer till*

Excursions Rundturer

How much does the tour cost?	**Hur mycket kostar turen?** *heur mewcket kostar teuren*
Is lunch included?	**Är lunch inkluderad?** *air leunsh inkleudehrad*
Where do we leave from?	**Var far vi ifrån?** *vaar faar vee ee frawn*
What time does the tour start?	**Hur dags startar turen?** *heur dax staartar teuren*
What time do we get back?	**När kommer vi tillbaka?** *nair kommer vee tilbaaka*
Do we have free time in …?	**Har vi någon ledig tid i …?** *haar vee nawgon lehdig teed ee*
Is there an English-speaking guide?	**Finns det någon engelsk-talande guide?** *fins det nawgon engelsk-taalande guide*

On tour På rundtur

Are we going to see …?	**Kommer vi att se …?** *kommer vee at seh*
We'd like to have a look at the …	**Vi skulle vilja se …** *vee skeulleh vilya seh*
Can we stop here …?	**Kan vi stanna här …?** *kun vee stanna hair*
to take photographs	**för att ta foton** *fur at taa footon*
to buy souvenirs	**för att köpa souvenirer** *fur at churpa sooveneerer*
to use the bathrooms [toilets]	**för att gå på toaletten** *fur at gaw paw tooaletten*
Would you take a photo of us, please?	**Kan ni vara snäll och ta ett foto av oss?** *kun nee vaara snel ock taa et footoo aav os*
How long do we have here/in …?	**Hur länge stannar vi här/i …?** *heur lengeh stannar vee hair/ee*
Wait! … isn't back yet.	**Vänta! … har inte kommit tillbaka ännu.** *venta. … haar inteh kommit tilbaaka enneu*

Sights Sevärdheter

Town maps are displayed in city centers, at bus and subway [underground] stations, and on highways before you arrive in a town. They are also available at tourist offices.

Where is the ...?	**Var är/ligger ...?** *vaar air/ligger*
art gallery	**konstgalleriet** *konst-galeree-et*
botanical garden	**botaniska trädgården** *bootaaniska traird-gawrden*
castle	**slottet** *slottet*
cathedral	**katedralen** *kateh-draalen*
cemetery	**kyrkogården** *chewrkoo-gawrden*
church	**kyrkan** *chewrkan*
downtown area	**centrum** *sentreum*
fountain	**fontänen** *fontairnen*
historic site	**historiska platsen** *histoorisk plats*
market	**torget** *tor-yet*
(war) memorial	**(krigs)monumentet** *(krix)moneumentet*
monastery	**klostret** *klostret*
museum	**muséet** *meusehet*
old town	**gamla stan** *gamla staan*
opera house	**operan** *ooperan*
palace	**slottet** *slottet*
park	**parken** *parken*
parliament building	**riksdagshuset** *rixdax-heuset*
ruins	**ruinerna** *reueenerna*
shopping area	**affärscentrum** *affairs-sentreum*
statue	**statyn** *statewn*
theater	**teatern** *teatern*
tower	**tornet** *toornet*
town hall	**stadshuset** *stads-heuset*
viewpoint	**utsiktpunkten** *eutsikts-peunkten*
Can you show me on the map?	**Kan ni visa mig på kartan?** *kun nee veesa may paw kaartan*

DIRECTIONS ➤ 94

Admission Inträde

Museums are usually open from 10 or 11 a.m. until 4 or 5 p.m. every day of the week, except on certain holidays (Christmas, New Year). The **Stockholmskortet** (Stockholm card), valid for 1–3 days, available from tourist offices, gives free entry to about 70 museums, castles, and other sights, and is also good for public transportation.

Is the … open to the public?	**Är … öppet för allmänheten?** air … eurpet fur allmen-hehten
Can we look around?	**Kan vi titta runt?** kun vee titta reunt
What are the opening hours?	**När är det öppet?** nair air det eurpet
When does it close?	**När stänger det?** nair stenger det
Is … open on Sundays?	**Är … öppet på söndagar?** air … urpet paw surndaagar
When's the next guided tour?	**När blir nästa guidade tur?** nair bleer nesta guidade teur
Do you have a guide book (in English)?	**Har ni någon guidebok (på engelska)?** haar nee nawgon guide-book paw engelska
Can I take photos?	**Är det tillåtet att fotografera?** air det tillawtet at footoo-grafehra
Is there access for the disabled?	**Finns det ingång för rörelsehindrade?** fins det ingong fur rurrelseh-hindrade
Is there an audioguide in English?	**Finns det en audio-guide på engelska?** fins det en audio-guide paw engelska

Paying/Tickets Betala/Biljetter

… tickets, please.	**… biljetter, tack.** … bilyetter tuck
How much is the entrance fee?	**Hur mycket kostar inträdet?** heur mewcket kostar intrairdet
Are there any reductions for …?	**Är det någon rabatt för …?** air det nawgon rabatt fur
children/groups	**barn/grupper** baarn/greupper
senior citizens	**pensionärer** pangshoonairer
students	**studerande** steudehrande
the disabled	**rörelsehindrade** rurrelseh-hindrade
One adult and two children, please.	**En vuxen och två barn, tack.** en veuxen ock tvaw baarn tuck
I've lost my ticket.	**Jag har tappat min biljett.** yaag haar tappat min bilyet

TIME ➤ 220

> – Fem biljetter, tack. Är det någon rabatt?
> (Five tickets, please. Are there any reductions?)
>> – Ja. För barn och pensionärer kostar
>> det tjugofem (25) kronor.
>> (Yes. Children and senior citizens are 25 kronor.)
> – Två vuxna och tre barn, tack.
> (Two adults and three children, please.)
>> – Det blir hundrasextiofem (165) kronor.
>> (That's 165 kronor.)

BESÖKSTIDER	hours [visiting hours]
BLIXTFOTOGRAFERING FÖRBJUDEN	no flash photography
FOTOGRAFERING FÖRBJUDEN	no photography
FRITT INTRÄDE	free admission
INGET TILLTRÄDE/INGEN INGÅNG	no entry
NÄSTA GUIDETUR …	next tour at …
ÖPPET	open
PRESENTSHOP	gift shop
STÄNGT	closed
SISTA TILLTRÄDE 17.00	latest entry at 5 p.m.

Impressions Intryck

It's …	**Det är …** *det air*
amazing/beautiful	**fantastiskt/vackert** *fan<u>tas</u>tiskt/<u>vack</u>ert*
bizarre/strange	**underligt/konstigt** *e<u>un</u>derligt/<u>kon</u>stigt*
incredible	**otroligt** *oo<u>troo</u>ligt*
interesting/boring	**intressant/trist** *intres<u>sant</u>/trist*
magnificent	**storslaget** *<u>stoor</u>slaaget*
romantic	**romantiskt** *ro<u>man</u>tiskt*
stunning	**jättesnygg** *<u>yetteh</u>-snewgg*
superb	**fantastiskt** *fan<u>tas</u>tiskt*
terrible/ugly	**hemskt/fult** *hemskt/feult*
It's a good value.	**Det är god valuta för pengarna.**
	det air good val<u>eu</u>ta fur <u>peng</u>arna
It's a rip-off.	**Det var odrägligt dyrt.**
	det vaar <u>ood</u>rairgligt dewrt
I like it.	**Jag tycker om den.** *yaag <u>tew</u>cker om den*
I don't like it.	**Jag tycker inte om den.**
	yaag <u>tew</u>cker inteh om den

101

absid apse
alkov alcove
altare altar(piece)
arbeten works
av ... by ... (*person*)
avslutat ... completed in ...
århundrade century
ädelsten gemstone
bad baths
bibliotek library
bild picture
bjälke beam
byggd i ... built in ...
byggnad building
började ... started in ...
detalj detail
dog år ... died in ...
drottning queen
duk canvas
dörr door
dörröppning doorway
emalj enamel
fiskben herringbone
flygel wing (*building*)
foajé foyer
frescomålning fresco
fullgjort ... completed in ...
funt font
född i ... born in ...
fönster window
fönster med målat glas stained-glass window
föreläsning lecture
förstörd av ... destroyed by ...
gavel gable
gjord av ... designed by ...

gjutning molding [moulding]
gobeläng tapestry
grav grave/tomb
gravsten headstone
gravvalv crypt
gravyr engraving
grotesk vattenkastare gargoyle
grundad ... founded in ...
guld gold(en)
gyllene gilded
gård courtyard
halft timrad half-timbered
hantverk crafts
havsmålning seascape
höjd height
hörnsten cornerstone
i ... stil in the style of ...
juveler jewelry
järnsmide ironwork
kejsarinna empress
klocka clock
kol charcoal
konst fine arts
konstnär painter
kopparstick etching
kor choir (*stall*)
krona crown
kung king
kungliga våningen apartments (*royal*)
kyrkogård churchyard
landskap landscape/ landscape painting
lera clay
levt ... lived ...
litet torn turret

lövverk foliage	**skyltskåp** display case
marmor marble	**skänkt av ...** donated by ...
mittskep nave	**snideri** carving
modell model	**spira** spire
mur wall	**sten** stone
mur med tinnar battlement	**stilleben** still life
mynt coin	**stöttepelare** buttress
målad av ... painted by ...	**tablå** tableau
målning painting/picture	**tak** ceiling
mästare master	**teckning** drawing
mästerstycke masterpiece	**tegel** brick
möbler furniture	**terracotta** terra-cotta
oljemålning oils	**tillfälligt utställningsföremål** temporary exhibit
ombyggd ... rebuilt in ...	**till låns** on loan
orgel organ (*musical instrument*)	**torn** tower
överhängande overhanging	**trappa** staircase
panel panel	**trappor** stairs
paneler paneling	**trä** wood
paradvåning stateroom	**trädgård** formal garden
pelare pillar	**uppförd ...** erected in ...
pulpet pulpit	**upptäckt ...** discovered in ...
på uppdrag av commissioned by ...	**utforma** design
regeringstid reign	**utformad av ...** designed by ...
representationsvåning stateroom	**utformning** design
restaurerad ... restored in ...	**utställning** exhibition
rustkammare armory	**utställningsföremål** exhibit
scen stage	**vallgrav** moat
... skola school of ...	**valv** vault
silver silver	**vapen** weapon
silversaker silverware	**vattenfärg** watercolor
skala 1:100 scale 1:100	**vaxmodell** waxwork
sketch sketch	**vindbrygga** drawbridge
skugga shadow	**väggmålning** frieze/mural
skulptur sculpture	**yttertak** roof
skyltning display	

Who?/What?/When?
Vem?/Vad?/När?

What's that building? **Vad är det där för byggnad?**
vaad air det dair fur bewgnad

When was it built? **När byggdes den?** *nair bewgdes den*

Who was the artist/architect? **Vem var konstnären/arkitekten?**
vem vaar konstnairen/arkitekten

What style is that? **Vilken stil är det?** *vilken steel air det*

What period is that? **Vilken period är det?** *vilken pairiood air det*

A.D. 98
The Sviones, warriors with fleets of ships, are mentioned in Tacitus' *Germania*.

800–1100
Swedish Vikings raid and invade Britain, Ireland, northern France, North America, and Russia, getting as far as Constantinople. The Vikings were also artists and poets who made positive contributions to the regions they occupied. They traded with many Christian countries, and records of their exploits can be seen on thousands of **runstenar** (rune stones) all over Sweden.

1000
Olof Skötkonung is baptized into the Byzantine church as the first Christian king. However, paganism was still practiced into the twelfth century.

1200–1500
Many churches are built, some in wood, especially in the countryside, with wood sculptures, stained-glass windows, and murals. St. Birgitta founds a monastic order and church, and her book, *Revelations*, is considered a masterpiece of medieval literature. The German Hanseatic League dominates trade.

1477
Uppsala University, the oldest university in Sweden, is founded.

1527
Gustav Vasa, the first king of the Swedish nation-state, implements the Reformation and takes control of the Church's land and wealth. He then uses the wealth to build fortresses and palaces at Uppsala, Vadstena, and Gripsholm.

1541
The first Swedish Bible appears.

1500–1700

Many new towns are built – Stockholm becomes the capital of Sweden.

1700–1800

The era of freedom and enlightenment. The botanist Carl von Linné (aka Carolus Linnaeus, who established the system of botanical nomenclature), publishes his system for classifying plants. Anders Celsius invents the thermometer.

King Gustav III promotes a native Swedish culture. The Stockholm Opera and Dramatic Theatre are built to counteract French influence. Gustav III founds the Swedish Academies of Literature, Music, Art, and History.

1800–1900

The making of modern Sweden. Mining, logging, and the manufacture of wood pulp give rise to a late industrial revolution. Alfred Nobel invents dynamite; Gustav Pasch invents the safety match. Establishment of railroads, universal education, trade unions, and women's movements. Agricultural crisis leads to mass emigration to North America.

1900–

At the beginning of the century, 80 percent of the population are still involved in farming or rural industries. The First World War brings wealth with demand for Swedish products and Swedish industry. The welfare state is created, with innovations in social reform, urban planning, and education. A pace-setter in design and applied arts – Swedish glassware, textiles and furniture exported around the world. Sweden joins the European Union in 1995. In 1998, Stockholm is selected as the cultural capital of Europe.

Places of worship Gudstjänstlokaler

The Swedish church is Lutheran, but there are other denominations which have their own churches. Most churches and cathedrals are open to the public.

Catholic/Protestant church	**katolsk/protestantisk kyrka** *kahtoolsk/protehstahnteesk chewrkah*
mosque	**moské** *moskai*
synagogue	**synagoga** *sinahgooga*
temple	**tempel** *tempehl*
What time is …?	**Hur dags är …?** *heur dax air*
mass/the service	**gudstjänsten** *geuds-chainsten*

In the countryside På landet

I'd like a map of …	**Jag skulle vilja ha en karta över …** *yaag skeulleh vilya haa en kaarta urver*
this region	**denna region** *denna regioon*
walking routes	**vandringsleder** *vandrings-lehder*
cycle routes	**cykelleder** *sewkel-lehder*
How far is it to …?	**Hur långt är det till …?** *heur longt air det til*
Is there a right of way?	**Har man förkörsrätt?** *haar man furchurs-ret*
Is there a trail/scenic route to …?	**Finns det någon led/vacker väg till …?** *fins det nawgon lehd/vacker vairg til*
Can you show me on the map?	**Kan ni visa mig på kartan?** *kun nee veesa may paw kaartan*
I'm lost.	**Jag har kommit vilse.** *yaag haar kommit vilseh*

Organized walks Organiserade vandringar

When does the guided walk start?	**När startar den guidade vandringen?** *nair staartar den guidade vandringen*
When will we return?	**När kommer vi tillbaka?** *nair kommer vee tilbaaka*
Is it a … walk?	**Är det en … led?** *air deht en … lehd*
gentle/medium/tough (hard)	**lätt/mellansvår/jobbig** *let/mellan-svawr/yobbig*
I'm exhausted.	**Jag är uttröttad.** *yaag air eut-trurtad*
How long are we resting here?	**Hur länge stannar vi här?** *heur lengeh stannar vee hair*
What kind of … is that?	**Vad för slags … är det?** *vaad fur slax … air det*
animal/bird	**djur/fågel** *yeur/fawgel*
flower/tree	**blomma/träd** *bloomma/traird*

Geographical features
Geografiska landmärken

beach	**strand** strand
bridge	**bro** broo
canal	**kanal** kanaal
cave	**grotta** grotta
cliff	**klippa** klippa
farm	**bondgård** boond-gawrd
footpath	**fotstig** foot-steeg
forest	**skog** skoog
hill	**kulle** keulle
lake	**sjö** shur
mountain	**berg** ber'
mountain pass	**bergspass** ber's-pus
mountain range	**bergskedja** ber's-chehdya
nature reserve	**naturreservat** nateur-reservaat
panorama	**panorama** panoraama
park	**park** park
peak	**topp** top
picnic area/rest area	**picknickområde/rastplats** piknik-omrawdeh/rastplats
pond	**damm** dumb
rapids	**forsar** foshar
river	**flod** flood
sea	**hav** haav
stream	**å** aw
valley	**dal** daal
viewpoint	**utsiktspunkt** eutsikts-peunkt
village	**by** bew
waterfall	**vattenfall** vattenfall
wood	**skog** skoog

Leisure

Events Evenemang

Sweden is a bedrock of tradition, and you will find events and festivals throughout the year. Look for *Stockholm this Week,* and guides to events from local tourist offices. Not to be missed are the midsummer celebrations in June, folk music festivals, and the Stockholm Water Festival in August.

Do you have a program of events?	**Har ni ett evenemangsprogramm?** *haar nee et evenemangs-proogram*
Can you recommend a ...?	**Kan ni rekommendera någon ...?** *kun nee rekomendehra nawgon*
ballet/concert	**ballett/konsert** *balett/konsair*
movie [film]	**film** *film*
opera/play	**opera/teaterpjäs** *oopera/teater-pyairs*

Availability Tillgång

When does it start?	**När börjar den?** *nair burryar den*
When does it end?	**När slutar den?** *nair sleutar den*
Are there any seats for tonight?	**Finns det några platser ikväll?** *fins det nawgra platser ee kvel*
Where can I get tickets?	**Var kan jag köpa biljetter?** *vaar kun yaag churpa bilyetter*
There are ... of us.	**Vi är ... stycken.** *vee air ... stewcken*
I'd like to reserve ...	**Jag skulle vilja beställa ...** *yaag skeulleh vilya bestella*
three tickets for Sunday evening	**tre biljetter till söndag kväll** *treh bilyetter til surndag kvel*
one ticket for the matinée	**en biljett till matinén** *en bilyet til matinehn*

Tickets Biljetter

How much are the seats?

Hur mycket kostar biljetterna?
heur mewcket kostar bilyetterna

Do you have anything cheaper?

Har ni någonting billigare?
haar nee nawgonting billigareh

I'd like two tickets for tonight's concert.

Jag skulle vilje ha två biljetter till konserten ikväll. *yaag skeulleh vilya haa tvaw bilyetter til konsairen ee kvel*

Can I pay by credit card?

Kan jag betala med kreditkort?
kun yaag betaala mehd kredeet-koort

I'll pay by …

Jag vill betala med … *yaag vil betaala mehd*

Vilket kreditkort har ni?	What credit card do you have?
Vad är numret på er kreditkort?	What's your credit card number?
När löper det ut?	What's the expiration [expiry] date?
Kan ni skriva under här, tack.	Sign here, please.
Ni kan hämta biljetterna …	Please pick up the tickets …
före klockan …	by … p.m.
vid förhandsbeställningar	at the reservation desk

May I have a program, please?

Kan jag få ett programm, tack?
kun yaag faw ett proogram, tuck

Where's the coatcheck [cloakroom]?

Var är garderoben?
vaar air gardeh-rawben

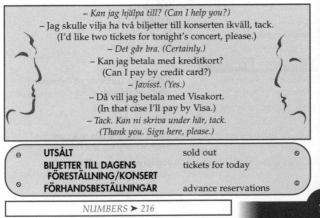

– *Kan jag hjälpa till? (Can I help you?)*
– Jag skulle vilja ha två biljetter till konserten ikväll, tack.
 (I'd like two tickets for tonight's concert, please.)
– *Det går bra. (Certainly.)*
– Kan jag betala med kreditkort?
 (Can I pay by credit card?)
– *Javisst. (Yes.)*
– Då vill jag betala med Visakort.
 (In that case I'll pay by Visa.)
– *Tack. Kan ni skriva under här, tack.*
 (Thank you. Sign here, please.)

UTSÅLT	sold out
BILJETTER TILL DAGENS FÖRESTÄLLNING/KONSERT	tickets for today
FÖRHANDSBESTÄLLNINGAR	advance reservations

NUMBERS ➤ 216

Movies [Cinema] Bio(graf)

All films are shown in the original language with Swedish subtitles. Look in newspapers and tourist publications to find out what is playing.

Is there a movie theater [multiplex cinema] near here?	**Finns det en mångbiograf i närheten?** *fins det en <u>mong</u>-beeoograaf ee <u>nair</u>hehten*
What's playing at the movies [on at the cinema] tonight?	**Vad visas på bio ikväll?** *vaad veesas paw <u>beeoo</u> ee kvel*
Is the film in English?	**Är filmen engelsk?** *air filmen <u>eng</u>elsk*
What time does the film start?	**När börjar filmen?** *nair burryar filmen*
How long is the film?	**Hur länge varar filmen?** *heur laingen vaaraar filmen*
A ..., please.	**En ..., tack.** *en ..., tuck*
box [carton] of popcorn	**påse popcorn** *pawseh popcorn*
chocolate ice cream [choc-ice]	**chockladglass** *shoo<u>klaad</u>-glas*
hot dog	**varm korv** *varm korv*
soft drink	**läskedryck** *<u>les</u>keh-drewck*
small/regular/large	**liten/vanlig/stor** *<u>lee</u>ten/<u>vaan</u>lig/stoor*

Theater På teater

What's playing at the Dramaten Theater?	**Vilken pjäs spelar de på Dramaten?** *<u>vil</u>ken pyairs spehlar deh paw dra<u>maa</u>ten*
Who's the playwright?	**Vem är författaren?** *vem air fur<u>fat</u>taren*
Do you think I'd enjoy it?	**Tror ni att jag skulle tycka om den?** *troor nee at yaag skeulleh tewcka <u>om</u> den*
I don't know much Swedish.	**Jag förstår inte mycket svenska.** *yaag fur<u>stawr</u> inteh mewcket svenska*

Opera/Ballet/Dance
Opera/Balett/Dans

Sweden has many opera, theater, and ballet companies,
which compare with the best in the world. The three largest
cities have large performing arts venues but you can also find
good performances elsewhere, some even staged outdoors in the summer
months.

Where's the theater?	**Var ligger teatern?** *vaar ligger teatern*
Who's the composer/soloist?	**Vem är kompositören/solisten?** *vem air kompositurren/solisten*
Is formal dress required?	**Behöver man klä sig formellt?** *behurver man klair say formellt*
Who's dancing?	**Vem är det som dansar?** *vem air det som dansar*
I'm interested in contemporary dance.	**Jag är intresserad av nutida dans.** *yaag air intressehrad aav neuteeda dans*

Music/Concerts Musik/Konserter

Where's the concert hall?	**Var ligger konserthallen?** *vaar ligger konsair-hallen*
Which orchestra/band is playing?	**Vilken orkester/vilket band spelar där?** *vilken orkester/vilket band spehlar dair*
What are they playing?	**Vad spelar de?** *vaad spehlar de*
Who's the conductor/soloist?	**Vem är dirigent/solist?** *vem air dirigent/solist*
Who's the support band?	**Vilket band backar?** *vilket band backar*
I really like …	**Jag tycker mycket om …** *yaag tewcker mewcket om*
folk music/country music	**folkmusik/country and western** *folk-meuseek/country and western*
jazz	**jazz** *yas*
music of the sixties	**musik från sextiotalet** *meuseek frawn sextioo-taalet*
pop/rock music	**pop/rockmusik** *pop/rock-meuseek*
soul music	**blues och soulmusik** *blues ock soul-meuseek*
Have you ever heard of her/him/them?	**Har ni hört talas om henne/honom/dem?** *haar nee hurt taalas om henneh/honom/dem*
Are they popular?	**Är de populära?** *air deh popeulaira*

Nightlife Kvällsliv

What's there to do in the evenings?	**Vad kan man göra på kvällarna?** *vaad kun man yurra paw kvellarna*
Can you recommend/ suggest a …?	**Kan ni rekommendera/föreslå en/ett …?** *kun nee rekomendehra/furreh-slaw en/et*
Is there a …?	**Finns det …?** *fins det*
bar/restaurant	**en bar/restaurang** *en baar/resteurang*
cabaret	**en kabaré** *en kabareh/*
casino	**ett kasino** *ett kaseeno*
discotheque	**ett diskotek** *ett diskotehk*
gay club	**en gayklubb** *en gay-kleubb*
nightclub	**en nattklubb** *en nut-kleubb*
What type of music do they play?	**Vilken slags musik spelar de?** *vilken slax meuseek spehlar deh*
How do I get there?	**Hur kan jag komma dit?** *heur kun yaag komma deet*
Is there an admission charge?	**Kostar det inträde?** *kostar det intrairdeh*

Admission Inträde

What time does the show start?	**När börjar föreställningen?** *nair burryar furreh-stellningen/showen*
Is there a cover charge?	**Är det kuvertavgift?** *air det keuvair-aavyift*
Is a reservation necessary?	**Behöver man reservera?** *behurver man reservehra*
Do we need to be members?	**Behöver man vara medlem?** *behurver man vaara mehdlem*
Can you have dinner there?	**Kan vi äta där?** *kun vee airta dair*
How long will we have to stand in line [queue]?	**Hur länge behöver vi vänta?** *heur lengeh behurver vee venta*
I'd like a good table.	**Jag skulle vilja ha ett bra bord.** *yaag skeulleh vilya haa et braa boord*

INKLUDERAR EN DRINK	includes one complimentary drink
ENDAST FÖR MEDLEMMAR	members only

Children Barn

Can you recommend something for the children?	**Kan ni föreslå något för barnen?** *kun nee furreh-slaw nawgot fur baarnen*
Are there changing facilities here for babies?	**Finns det skötrum för barn här?** *fins det shurt-reumm fur baarn hair*
Where are the bathrooms [toilets]?	**Var finns toaletten?** *vaar finns tooaletten*
amusement arcade	**spelautomater** *spehl-aatoomaater*
fairground	**nöjesfält** *nur-yesfelt*
kiddie [paddling] pool	**barnbassäng** *baarnbaseng*
playground	**lekplats** *lehk-plats*
play group	**lekgrupp** *lehk-greupp*
zoo	**djurpark** *yeur-park*

Babysitting Barnvakt

Can you recommend a reliable babysitter?	**Kan ni rekommendera en pålitlig barnvakt?** *kun nee rekomendehra en pawleetlig baarnvakt*
Is there constant supervision?	**Blir de under uppsikt hela tiden?** *bleer de eunder euppsikt hehla teeden*
Is the staff properly trained?	**Är personalen utbildad?** *air pairshoonaalen eutbildad*
When can I bring them?	**När kan jag ta hit dem?** *nair kun yaag taa heet dem*
I'll pick them up at …	**Jag hämtar dem vid …** *yaag hemtar dem veed*
We'll be back by …	**Vi kommer tillbaka vid …** *vee kommer tilbaaka veed*
She's 3, and he's 18 months.	**Hon är tre år och han är arton månader.** *hoonn air treh awr ock han air aarton mawnader*

Sports Sport

Swedes are outdoor people, and there are excellent sports facilities everywhere, ranging from golf, fishing (salmon fishing in particular), tennis, soccer, and all kinds of water sports to skiing and ice hockey.

Spectator Åskådarsport

Is there a soccer [football] game [match] this Saturday?	**Är det någon fotbollsmatch på lördag?** *air det nawgon footbolls-match paw lurdag*
Which teams are playing?	**Vilka lag spelar?** *vilka laag spehlar*
Can you get me a ticket?	**Kan ni skaffa mig en biljett?** *kun nee skaffa may en bilyet*
What's the admission charge?	**Vad kostar inträdesbiljetten?** *vaad kostar intrairdes-bilyetten*
Where's the racetrack [racecourse]?	**Var ligger kapplöpningsbanan?** *vaar ligger hestkap-lurpnings-baanan*
Where can I place a bet?	**Var kan jag spela totto?** *vaar kun yaag spehla toottoo*
What are the odds on …?	**Vad är vinstchansen på …?** *vaad air vinst-chansen paw*
athletics	**idrott** *eedrot*
basketball	**basket** *basket*
baseball	**baseboll** *baseboll*
canoeing	**kanoting** *kanooting*
cycling	**cykel** *sewkel*
golf	**golf** *golf*
horseracing	**hästkapplöpning** *hestkap-lurpning*
field hockey/ice hockey	**landhockey/ishockey** *landhockey/ees-hockey*
rock climbing	**klippbestigning** *klip-besteegning*
rowing	**rodd** *roodd*
rugby	**rugby** *reuggbew*
soccer [football]	**fotboll** *footboll*
swimming	**simning** *simning*
tennis/table tennis	**tennis/bordtennis** *tennis/boordtennis*
volleyball	**volleyboll** *volleyboll*

Participating Spela sport

Is there a … nearby?	**Finns det en/ett … i närheten?** *fins det en/et … ee nairhehten*
golf course	**golfbana** *golfbaana*
sports club	**sportklubb** *sport-kleubb*
Are there any tennis courts?	**Finns det några tennisbanor?** *finns det nawgra tennis-baanoor*
What's the charge per …?	**Vad kostar det per …?** *vaad kostar det pairr*
day/hour	**dag/timme** *daag/timmeh*
game/round	**spel/runda** *spehl/reunda*
Do I need to be a member?	**Behöver jag vara medlem?** *behurver yaag vaara mehdlem*
Where can I rent …?	**Var kan jag hyra …?** *vaar kun yaag hewra*
boots	**stövlar** *sturvlar*
clubs	**klubbor** *kleubboor*
equipment	**utrustning** *eut-reustning*
a racket	**en racket** *en racket*
Can I get lessons?	**Kan jag ta lektioner?** *kun yaag taa lekshooner*
Do you have a fitness room?	**Har ni ett gym?** *haar nee et gym*
Can I join in?	**Får jag vara med?** *fawr yaag vaara mehd*

Tyvärr, det är fullbokat.	I'm sorry. We're booked.
Det blir handpenning på …	There is a deposit of …
Vilken storlek tar ni?	What size are you?
Ni behöver ett passfoto.	You need a passport-size photo.

OMKLÄDNINGSRUM	changing rooms
FISKE FÖRBJUDET	no fishing
ENDAST FISKEKORT	permit holders only

At the beach På stranden

Sandy beaches are found in the south and on the southwest coast. Around Stockholm you can swim and dive from the small islands in the archipelago – and you can even swim in the water around Stockholm itself. Rivers and inland lakes are also good for swimming and boating, and there is minimal pollution.

Is the beach pebbly/sandy?	**Är stranden stenig/sandig?** *air stranden stehnig/sandig*
Is there a … here?	**Finns det … här?** *fins det … hair*
children's pool	**en barnbassäng** *en baarn-baseng*
swimming pool	**en simbassäng** *en sim-baseng*
indoor/open-air	**inomhus/utomhus** *inomheus/eutomheus*
Is it safe to swim/dive here?	**Kan man simma/dyka här utan risk?** *kun man simma/dewka hair eutan risk*
Is it safe for children?	**Är det barnsäkert?** *air det baarn-sairkert*
Is there a lifeguard?	**Finns det livräddare?** *fins det leev-reddare*
I want to rent a/some …	**Jag skulle vilja hyra …** *yaag skeulleh vilya hewra*
deck chair	**en solstol** *en sool-stool*
jet-ski	**en jet-ski** *en jet-ski*
motorboat	**en motorbåt** *en mootor-bawt*
diving equipment	**dykarutrustning** *dewkar-eut-rustning*
umbrella [sunshade]	**en solparasol** *en sool-parasoll*
surfboard	**en surfbräda** *en seurf-brairda*
water skis	**vattenskidor** *vatten-sheedoor*
for … hours.	**på … timmar** *paw … timmar*

Skiing Skidåkning

Swedes grow up with skiing: cross-country in the south and downhill in the north. There are many excellent ski resorts in the north, offering superb skiing and first-class facilities. Many hotels offer three- to seven-day package deals, including transportation and accommodation. A number of travel companies organize package vacations to the larger resorts, such as Åre, Storlien, and Sälen. In June, try Riksgränsen for a taste of skiing in the midnight sun.

Long-distance buses (**långfärdsbussar**) are efficient, relatively cheap, and run daily to all major towns and resorts. In winter, they are particularly popular with ski enthusiasts, with companies offering all-inclusive three- to seven-night vacation packages. For more information, visit the **Cityterminalen** (Central Bus Station), just above the train station in Stockholm, or any travel agent.

Is there much snow?	**Finns det mycket snö?** *fins det mewket snur*
What's the snow like?	**Hur är snön?** *heur air snurn*
heavy/icy	**djup/med skare** *yeup/mehd skaare*
powdery/wet	**nysnö/blötsnö** *newsnur/blurt-snur*
I'd like to rent some …	**Jag skulle vilja hyra …** *yaag skeulleh vilya hewra*
poles/skis	**stavar/skidor** *staavar/sheedoor*
skates	**skridskor** *skriskoor*
ski boots	**skidpjäxor** *sheed-pyaixoor*
These are too …	**De här är för …** *deh hair air fur*
big/small	**stora/små** *stoora/smaw*
They're uncomfortable.	**De är obekväma.** *deh air oobekvairma*
A lift pass for a day/five days, please.	**Ett liftpass för en dag/för fem dagar, tack.** *et liftpus fur en daag/fur fem daagar, tuck*
I'd like to join the ski school.	**Jag skulle vilja gå i skidskolan.** *yaag skeulleh vilya gaw ee sheed-skoolan*
I'm a beginner.	**Jag är nybörjare.** *yaag air new-burryareh*
I'm experienced.	**Jag har erfarenhet.** *yaag haar airrfaarenheht*

ÄGGLIFT	cable car/gondola
STOLLIFT	chair lift
DRAGLIFT	drag lift

Making friends
Göra bekantskap
Introductions Presentation

Greetings vary according to how well you know someone. The following is a guide. It is polite to shake hands when you meet and say good-bye. When being introduced to a group, men will shake hands first with the women and then with the men.

There are two terms for "you": **du** (informal/referring to one person) and **ni** (informal/referring to more than one person) are used when talking to relatives, friends, colleagues, children, between young people, and in work situations. **Ni** (formal/referring to one or more people) is used in other situations, although you will hear more and more people nowadays address each other with the informal **du.**

As in many countries, titles are more commonly used by the older generation, and you will hear the words for Mr. (**herr**), Mrs. (**fru**) and Miss (**fröken**, abbreviated to **frk**) being used as well as other professional titles, e.g., doctor (**doktor**), engineer (**ingenjör**), etc.

Hello, we haven't met.	**Hej, vi har inte träffats förut.** *hay, vee haar inteh treffats furreut*
My name is …	**Mitt namn är …** *mit namn air*
May I introduce …?	**Får jag presentera …?** *fawr yaag present<u>eh</u>ra*
Pleased to meet you.	**Trevligt att träffas.** *trehvligt at treffas*
What's your name?	**Vad heter ni/du?** *vaad hehter nee/deu*
How are you?	**Hur står det till?** *heur stawr det til*
Fine, thanks. And you?	**Bra, tack. Och ni/du?** *braa, tuck. ock nee/deu*

– Hej. Hur står det till? (Hello. How are you?)
– *Bra, tack. Och du? (Fine, thanks. And you?)*
– Bara bra, tack. (Fine, thanks.)

Where are you from?
Var kommer du ifrån?

Where are you from?	**Var kommer du ifrån?** *vaar kommer deu eefrawn*
Where were you born?	**Var är du född?** *vaar air deu furdd*
I'm from ...	**Jag kommer från ...** *yaag kommer frawn*
Australia	**Australien** *aaeustraalee-en*
Britain	**Storbritannien** *stoorbritannee-en*
Canada	**Kanada** *kanada*
England	**England** *england*
Ireland	**Irland** *eerland*
Scotland	**Skottland** *scotland*
the U.S.	**USA** *eu es aa*
Wales	**Wales** *vayles*
Where do you live?	**Var bor du?** *vaar boor deu*
What part of Sweden are you from?	**Vilken del av Sverige kommer du ifrån?** *vilken dehl aav svairryeh kommer deu eefrawn*
Norway	**Norge** *norryeh*
Denmark	**Danmark** *danmark*
Finland	**Finland** *finland*
We come here every year.	**Vi åker hit varje år.** *vee awker heet varyeh awr*
It's my/our first visit.	**Det är första gången jag/vi är här.** *det air fursta gongen yaag/vee air hair*
Have you ever been to ...?	**Har du varit i ...?** *haar deu vaarit ee*
the U.K./U.S.	**Storbritannien/USA** *stoorbritannee-en/eu es aa*
Do you like it here?	**Trivs du här?** *trivs deu hair*
What do you think of the ...?	**Vad tycker du om ...?** *vaad tewcker deu om*
I love the ... here.	**Jag tycker om ... här.** *yaag tewcker om ... hair*
I don't really like the ... here.	**Jag tycker inte om ... här.** *yaag tewcker inteh om ... hair*
food/people	**maten/människorna** *maaten/mennishoorna*

119

Who are you with?
Vem är du här med?

Who are you with?	**Vem är du här med?**
	vem air deu hair mehd
I'm on my own.	**Jag är ensam här.**
	yaag air ensam hair
I'm with a friend.	**Jag är här med en vän.**
	yaag air hair mehd en ven
I'm with ...	**Jag är här med ...** *yaag air hair mehd*
my husband/wife	**min man/fru** *min man/freu*
my family	**min familj** *min famil'*
my children/parents	**mina barn/föräldrar**
	meena baarn/furreldrar
my boyfriend/girlfriend	**min pojkvän/flickvän**
	min poyk-ven/flick-ven
my father/son	**min far/son** *min faar/sawn*
my mother/daughter	**min mor/dotter** *min moor/dotter*
my brother/sister	**min bror/syster** *min broor/sewster*
my uncle (*paternal/maternal*)	**min farbror/morbror**
	min farbroor/moorbroor
my aunt (*paternal/maternal*)	**min faster/moster**
	min faster/mooster
What's your son's/ wife's name?	**Vad heter din son/fru?**
	vaad hehter din sawn/freu
Are you married?	**Är du gift?** *air deu yift*
I'm ...	**Jag är ...** *yaag air*
married/single	**gift/ogift** *yift/ooyift*
divorced/separated	**skild/separerad** *shild/separehrad*
engaged	**förlovad** *furlawvad*
We live together.	**Vi bor tillsammans.** *vee boor tilsammans*
Do you have any children?	**Har ni några barn?**
	haar nee nawgra baarn
We have two boys and a girl.	**Vi har två pojkar och en flicka.**
	vee haar tvaw poykar ock en flicka
How old are they?	**Hur gamla är de?** *heur gamla air deh*
They're ten and twelve.	**De är tio och tolv år.**
	deh air teeoo ock tolv awr

What do you do?
Vad sysslar du med?

What do you do?	**Vad sysslar du med?** *vaad sewslar deu mehd*
What are you studying?	**Vad studerar du?** *vaad steudehrar deu*
I'm studying ...	**Jag studerar ...** *yaag steudehrar*
I'm in ...	**Jag är inom ...** *yaag air inom*
business	**affärsvärlden** *affairs-vairden*
engineering	**teknologi** *teknolawgee*
sales	**försäljning** *fursel'ning*
Who do you work for ...?	**Vilken firma jobbar du på?** *vilken feerma yobbar deu paw*
I work for ...	**Jag jobbar på ...** *yaag yobbar paw*
I'm (a/an) ...	**Jag är ...** *yaag air*
accountant	**revisor** *reveesor*
housewife	**hemmafru** *hemmafreu*
student	**studerande** *steudehrande*
retired	**pensionär** *pangshoonair*
self-employed	**egen företagare** *yaag air ehgen furreh-taagare*
between jobs	**mittemellan jobb** *mit ehmellan yob*
What are your interests/ hobbies?	**Har du några hobbies eller intressen?** *haar deu nawgra hobbies eller intressen*
I like ...	**Jag tycker om ...** *yaag tewcker om*
music	**musik** *meuseek*
reading	**att läsa** *at lairsa*
sports	**sport** *sport*
I play ...	**Jag spelar ...** *yaag spehlar*
Would you like to play ...?	**Vill du spela ...?** *vil deu spehla*
cards	**kort** *koort*
chess	**schack** *shack*

What weather! Vilket väder!

What a lovely day!	**Vilken härlig dag!** _vilken hairlig daag_
What terrible weather!	**Vilket hemskt väder!** _vilket hemskt vairder_
It's hot/cold today!	**Det är hett/kallt idag!** _det air het/kalt ee daag_
Is it usually this warm?	**Brukar det vara så här varmt?** _breukar det vaara saw hair varmt_
Do you think it's going to ... tomorrow?	**Tror ni att det kommer att ... imorgon?** _troor nee at det kommer at ... ee morron_
be a nice day	**bli en vacker dag** _blee en vacker daag_
rain	**regna** _rengna_
snow	**snöa** _snura_
What's the weather forecast for tomorrow?	**Vad är väderleksutsikterna för imorgon?** _vaad air vairder-lehks-eutsikterna fur ee morron_
It's ...	**Det är ...** _det air_
cloudy	**molnigt** _mawlnigt_
foggy	**dimmigt** _dimmigt_
icy	**fruset** _freuset_
stormy	**stormigt** _stormigt_
windy	**blåsigt** _blawsigt_
It's raining.	**Det regnar.** _det rengnar_
It's snowing.	**Det snöar.** _det snurar_
It's sunny.	**Det är soligt.** _det air sooligt_
Has the weather been like this for long?	**Har vädret varit så här länge?** _haar vairdet vaarit saw hair lengeh_
What's the pollen count?	**Hur är pollenhalten?** _heur air pollen-halten_
high/medium/low	**hög/mitt emellan/låg** _heurg/mit emellan/lawg_
Will it be good weather for skiing?	**Blir det bra väder för skidåkning?** _bleer det braa vairder fur sheed-awkning_

⊘ **VÄDERLEKSRAPPORT**	weather forecast ⊘

122

Enjoying your trip? Trivs du med resan?

Är du på semester?	Are you on vacation?
Hur reste du hit?	How did you get here?
Var bor du?	Where are you staying?
Hur länge har du varit här?	How long have you been here?
Hur länge ska du stanna?	How long are you staying?
Vad har du gjort hittills?	What have you done so far?
Vart ska du åka sedan?	Where are you going next?
Trivs du med semestern?	Are you enjoying your vacation?

I'm here on …	**Jag är här …** *yaag air hair*
business	**på affärsresa** *paw affairs-rehsa*
vacation [holiday]	**på semester** *paw semester*
We came by …	**Vi kom med …** *vee kom mehd*
train/bus/plane	**tåg/buss/flygplan** *tawg/beuss/flewg-plaan*
car/ferry	**bil/färja** *beel/fairya*
I have a rental [hire] car.	**Jag har en hyrbil.** *yaag haar en hewr-beel*
We're staying in/at …	**Vi bor på …** *vee boor paw*
a campsite	**en campingplats** *en kamping-plats*
a guesthouse	**ett pensionat** *et pangshoonaat*
a hotel	**ett hotell** *et hootel*
a youth hostel	**ett vandrarhem** *paw et vandrar-hem*
with friends	**hos vänner** *hoos venner*
Can you suggest …?	**Kan du föreslå …?** *kun deu furreh-slaw*
things to do	**vad man kan göra** *vaad man kun yurra*
places to eat	**var man kan äta** *vaar man kun airta*
places to visit	**sevärdheter** *sehvaird-hehter*
We're having a great time.	**Vi trivs utomordentligt.** *vee trivs eutom-ordentligt*
We're having a terrible time.	**Vi trivs inte alls.** *vee trivs inteh als*

Invitations Inbjudan

Would you like to have dinner with us on …?	**Vill du äta middag med oss på …?** *vil deu airta <u>midd</u>ag mehd os paw*
Are you free for lunch?	**Får jag bjuda på lunch?** *fawr yaag byeuda paw leunsh*
Can you come for a drink this evening?	**Kan du komma på en drink i kväll?** *kun deu komma paw en drink ee kvel*
We are having a party. Can you come?	**Vi ska ha fest. Kan du komma?** *vee skaa haa fest. kun deu komma*
May we join you?	**Får vi göra er sällskap?** *fawr vee yeara ehr selskaap*
Would you like to join us?	**Vill du följa med oss?** *vil deu furlya mehd os*

Going out Gå ut

What are your plans for …?	**Vad har du för planer för …?** *vaad haar deu fur plaaner fur*
today/tonight	**idag/ikväll** *ee daag/ee kvel*
tomorrow	**imorgon** *ee morron*
Are you free this evening?	**Är du ledig ikväll?** *air deu lehdig ee kvel*
Would you like to …?	**Har du lust att …?** *haar deu leust at*
go dancing	**gå och dansa** *gaw ock dansa*
go for a drink	**gå på en drink** *gaw paw en drink*
go out for a meal	**gå ut och äta** *gaw eut ock airta*
go for a walk	**gå på en promenad** *gaw paw en proome<u>naad</u>*
go shopping	**gå och shoppa** *gaw ock shoppa*
I'd like to go to …	**Jag skulle vilja gå till …** *yaag skeulleh vilya gaw til*
I'd like to see …	**Jag skulle vilja se …** *yaag skeulleh vilya seh*
Do you enjoy …?	**Tycker du om …?** *tewcker deu om*

Accepting/Declining
Acceptera/Avböja

In Sweden, people tend to pay for themselves in restaurants, except when there has been a specific invitation. If you are invited to somebody's home for dinner, always take a small gift. And do not forget to phone or write within the next few days to **tacka för senast** – that is to say, "thank you for last time."

Thank you. I'd love to.	**Tack, det vill jag gärna.** *tuck, det vil yaag yairna*
Thank you, but I'm busy.	**Tack, men jag är upptagen.** *tuck, men yaag air eupp-taagen*
May I bring a friend?	**Får jag ta med en vän?** *fawr yaag taa mehd en ven*
Where shall we meet?	**Var ska vi träffas?** *vaar skaa vee treffas*
I'll meet you …	**Jag möter dig …** *yaag murter day*
in front of your hotel	**framför ditt hotell** *framfur dit hootel*
I'll call for you at 8.	**Jag hämtar dig klockan åtta.** *yaag hemtar day klockan otta*
Could we make it a bit later/earlier?	**Kan vi träffas lite senare/tidigare?** *kun vee treffas leeteh sehnareh/teedigareh*
How about another day?	**Ska vi träffas en annan dag?** *skaa vee treffas en anan daag*
That will be fine.	**Det blir bra.** *det bleer braa*

Dining out/in Äta ute/inne

Let me buy you a drink.	**Får jag bjuda på en drink.** *fawr yaag byeuda paw en drink*
Do you like …?	**Tycker du om …?** *tewcker deu om*
What are you going to have?	**Vad vill du ha?** *vaad vil deu haa*
That was a lovely meal.	**Det var en underbar middag.** *det vaar en eunderbaar middag*

TIME ➤ 220

Encounters Sammanträffanden

Do you mind if …?	**Har du något emot att …?** *haar deu nawgot emoot at*
I sit here/I smoke	**jag sitter här/jag röker** *yaag sitter hair/yaag rurker*
Can I get you a drink?	**Får jag bjuda på en drink?** *fawr yaag byeuda paw en drink*
I'd love to have some company.	**Jag skulle vilja ha lite sällskap.** *yaag skeulleh vilya haa leeteh selskaap*
What's so funny?	**Vad skrattar du åt?** *vaad skrattar deu awt*
Is my Swedish that bad?	**Är min svenska så dålig?** *air min svenska saw dawlig*
Shall we go somewhere quieter?	**Ska vi gå på ett lugnare ställe?** *skaa vee gaw paw et lungnareh stelleh*
Leave me alone, please!	**Kan du lämna mig ifred, tack!** *kun deu lemna may ee frehd, tuck*
You look great!	**Vad du ser vacker ut!** *vaad deu sehr vacker eut*
Would you like to come home with me?	**Vill du komma hem med mig?** *vil deu komma hem mehd may*
I'm not ready for that.	**Jag är inte beredd på det.** *yaag air inteh bered paw det*
I'm afraid we have to leave now.	**Vi måste tyvärr gå nu.** *vee mosteh tewvairr gaw neu*
Thanks for the evening.	**Tack för ikväll.** *tuck fur ee kvel*
It was great.	**Det var trevligt.** *det vaar trehvligt*
Can I see you again tomorrow?	**Kan vi träffas imorgon?** *kun vee treffas ee morron*
See you soon.	**Hoppas vi ses snart.** *hoppas vee sehs snaart*
Can I have your address?	**Kan jag få din adress?** *Kun yaag faw din adress*

Telephoning Telefon

Public telephone booths take either phone cards or coins. Phone cards (**telefonkort**) are available at post offices, newsstands (**pressbyrån**), and some stores and department stores. To phone home from Sweden, dial 00 followed by: 61, Australia; 1, Canada; 353, Ireland; 64, New Zealand; 27, South Africa; 44, United Kingdom; 1, United States.

Can I have your telephone number?	**Kan jag få ditt telefonnummer?** *kun yaag faw dit telefawn-neummer*
Here's my number.	**Här är mitt nummer.** *hair air mit neummer*
Please call me.	**Var snäll och ring mig.** *vaar snel ock ring may*
I'll give you a call.	**Jag ringer dig.** *yaag ringer day*
Where's the nearest telephone booth?	**Var finns närmaste telefonkiosk?** *vaar fins nairmasteh telefawn-chosk*
May I use your phone?	**Får jag låna din telefon?** *fawr yaag lawna din telefawn*
It's an emergency.	**Det gäller en nödsituation.** *det yeller en nurd-sitteu-aashoon*
I'd like to call someone in England.	**Jag behöver ringa någon i England.** *yaag behurver ringa nawgon ee england*
What's the area [dialling] code for …?	**Vad är riktnumret till …?** *vaad air rikt-neumret til*
I'd like a phone card, please.	**Kan jag få ett telefonkort?** *kun yaag faw et telefawn-koort*
What's the number for Information [Directory Enquiries]?	**Vilket nummer är det till Nummerbyrån?** *vilket neummer air det til neummer-bewrawn*
I'd like the number for …	**Jag skulle vilja ha numret till …** *yaag skeulleh vilya haa neumret til*
I'd like to call collect [reverse the charges].	**Jag skulle vilja beställa ett Ba-samtal.** *yaag skeulleh vilya bestella et beh-aa-samtaal*

Speaking Tala på telefon

Hello. This is …	**Hej. Det är …** *hay. det air*
I'd like to speak to …	**Jag skulle vilja tala med …** *yaag skeulleh vilya taala mehd*
Extension …	**Anknytning …** *anknewtning*
Speak louder, please.	**Var snäll och tala högre.** *vaar snel ock taala hurgreh*
Speak more slowly, please.	**Var snäll och tala långsammare.** *vaar snel ock taala long-sammareh*
Could you repeat that, please.	**Kan ni upprepa det, tack.** *kun nee eupp-rehpa det tuck*
I'm afraid he's/she's not in.	**Tyvärr, han/hon är inte här.** *tewvairr, han/hoonn air inteh hair*
You have the wrong number.	**Ni har fått fel nummer.** *nee haar fot fehl neummer*
Just a moment, please.	**Ett ögonblick, tack.** *et urgonblick tuck*
Hold on, please.	**Vänta ett ögonblick, tack.** *venta et urgonblick tuck*
When will he/she be back?	**När är han/hon tillbaka?** *nair air han/hoonn tilbaaka*
Will you tell him/her that I called?	**Kan ni säga honom/henne att jag ringde?** *kun nee saya honom/heneh at yaag ringde*
My name is …	**Mitt namn är …** *mit namn air*
Would you ask him/her to call me?	**Kan ni be honom/henne ringa mig?** *kun nee beh honom/heneh ringa may*
I must go now.	**Jag måste sluta nu.** *yaag mosteh sleuta neu*
Thank you for calling.	**Tack för att du ringde.** *tuck fur at deu ringde*
I'll be in touch.	**Jag hör av mig snart.** *yaag hur aav may snaart*
Bye.	**Hej då.** *hay daw*

128

Stores & Services

Although Sweden still has many small, specialty shops, they are slowly giving way to shopping centers (**Köpcentrum**), especially in larger towns. Many chain and department stores, such as **Åhléns**, **Kappahl**, and **Hennes & Mauritz**, have branches all over the country, all selling good quality goods. In the well-established Stockholm department store **NK**, you can find almost anything. Many towns have colorful markets, and the traditional Christmas market in Stockholm is reminiscent of times gone by.

ESSENTIAL

I'd like …	**Jag skulle vilja ha …**
	yaag skeulleh vilya haa
Do you have …?	**Har ni …?** haar nee
How much is that?	**Hur mycket kostar det?**
	heur mewcket kostar det
Thank you.	**Tack.** tuck

ÖPPET	open
STÄNGT	closed
REA(LISATION)	sale

129

Stores and services
Affärer och service

Where is …?	**Var finns …?** *vaar fins*
Where's the nearest …?	**Var finns närmaste …?** *vaar fins nairmasteh*
Is there a good …?	**Finns det en bra …?** *fins det en braa*
Where's the main shopping mall [centre]?	**Var ligger affärscentrum?** *vaar ligger affairs-sentreum*
Is it far from here?	**Är det långt härifrån?** *air det longt haireefrawn*
How do I get there?	**Hur kommer jag dit?** *heur kommer yaag deet*

Stores Affärer

bakery	**bageri** *baageree*
bank	**bank** *bunk*
bookstore	**bokhandel** *book-handel*
butcher	**slaktare** *slaktareh*
camera store	**fotoaffär** *footoo-affair*
tobacconist	**tobaksaffär** *toobax-affair*
clothing store [clothes shop]	**klädaffär** *klaird-affair*
convenience store	**närbutik** *nair-beuteek*
delicatessen	**delikatessaffär/charkuteri** *delikatess-affair/sharkeuteree*
department store	**varuhus** *vaareu-heus*
drugstore	**apotek** *apootehk*
fish store [fishmonger]	**fiskaffär** *fisk-affair*
florist	**blomsteraffär** *blomster-affair*
gift store	**presentaffär** *present-affair*
greengrocer	**grönsaksaffär** *grurnsaaks-affair*
health food store	**hälsokostaffär** *helsoo-kost-affair*
jeweler	**juvelerare** *yeuveleh-rareh*

liquor store [off-licence]	**systembolag** sew*stem*-boolaag
newsstand [newsagent]	**tidningskiosk** teednings-chosk
pastry/coffee shop	**konditori** kon*dee*-toree
pharmacy [chemist]	**apotek** apoo*tehk*
produce store	**livsmedelsaffär** livs-*mehdels*-af*fair*
music store	**musikaffär** meuseek-af*fair*
shoe store	**skoaffär** skoo-af*fair*
souvenir store	**souvenirbutik** sooveneer-beuteek
sporting goods store	**sportaffär** sport-af*fair*
supermarket	**snabbköp** snub-churp
toy store	**leksaksaffär** lehksaaks-af*fair*

Services Olika tjänster

clinic	**klinik** kli*neek*
dentist	**tandläkare** *tand*-lairkare
doctor	**läkare** *lairkare*
dry cleaner	**kemtvätt** chehm-tvet
hairdresser/barber	**damfrisör/herrfrisör** hairr-fri*surr*/daam-fri*surr*
hospital	**sjukhus** sheuk-heus
laundromat	**snabbtvätt** snub-tvet
optician	**optiker** *optiker*
police station	**polisstation** poo*lees*-stashoon
post office	**post** post
travel agency	**resebyrå** rehse-*bewraw*

Opening hours Öppettider

Stores are usually open weekdays from 9 or 10 a.m. to 6 p.m., Saturdays until 1 or 4 p.m. Some of the bigger department stores are open on Sunday afternoons, as are some supermarkets. Corner stores (**närbutik**) and small shops in the subway stations are open late in the evenings.

When does the … open/close?	**När öppnar/stänger …?** *nair eurpnar/stenger*
Are you open in the evening?	**Har ni öppet på kvällarna?** *haar nee urpet paw kvellarna*
Where's the …?	**Var ligger …?** *vaar ligger*
cashier [cash desk]	**kassan** *kassan*
escalator	**rulltrappan** *reull-trappan*
elevator [lift]	**hissen** *hissen*
store directory [guide]	**informationen** *informashoonen*
first [ground (U.K.)] floor	**bottenvåningen** *botten-vawningen*
second [first (U.K.)] floor	**första våningen** *fursta vawningen*
Where's the … department?	**Var ligger … avdelningen?** *vaar ligger … aavdehlningen*

ÖPPETTIDER	business hours
INGÅNG	entrance
RULLTRAPPA	escalator
UTGÅNG	exit
NÖDUTGÅNG/UT-NÖD	emergency exit
HISS	elevator [lift]
BRANDUTGÅNG	fire exit
DAMTOALETT/HERRTOALETT	restroom (women/men)
TRAPPOR	stairs

Service Betjäning

Can you help me?	**Kan ni hjälpa mig?** *kun nee yelpa may*
I'm looking for …	**Jag letar efter …** *yaag lehtar efter*
I'm just browsing.	**Jag tittar bara.** *yaag tittar baara*
It's my turn.	**Det är min tur.** *det air min teur*
Do you have any …?	**Har ni några …?** *haar nee nawgra*
I'd like to buy …	**Jag skulle vilja köpa …** *yaag skeulleh vilya churpa*
Could you show me …?	**Kan ni visa mig några …?** *kun nee veesa may nawgra*
How much is this/that?	**Hur mycket kostar det här/det där?** *heur mewcket kostar det hair/det dair*
That's all, thanks.	**Det var allt, tack.** *det vaar alt tuck*

God morgon/God middag.	Good morning/afternoon.
Kan jag hjälpa er?	Can I help you?
Jag ska bara kontrollera det.	I'll just check that for you.
Är det allt?	Is that everything?
Något annat?	Anything else?

– *Kan jag hjälpa er? (Can I help you?)*
– Nej tack, jag tittar bara.
(No, thanks. I'm just browsing.)
– *Varsågod. (Fine.)*
– Ursäkta mig. (Excuse me.)
– *Ja, kan jag hjälpa er? (Yes? Can I help you?)*
– Hur mycket kostar det? (How much is that?)
– *Hm, jag ska bara kontrollera det. … Det kostar*
hundrafyrtiofem (145) kronor.
(Um, I'll just check that for you. … That's 145 kronor.)

REA	clearance [sale]
SJÄLVBETJÄNING	self-service

Preferences Jag föredrar

I want something …	**Jag skulle vilja ha något …** *yaag skeulleh vilya haa nawgot*
It must be …	**Den/det måste vara …** *den/det mosteh vaara*
big/small	**stor(t)/liten(t)** *stoor(t)/leeten(t)*
cheap/expensive	**billig(t)/dyr(t)** *billig(t)/dewr(t)*
dark/light (color)	**mörk(t)/ljus(t)** *murk(t)/yeus(t)*
light/heavy	**lätt/tung(t)** *let/teung(t)*
oval/round/square	**oval/rund/fyrkantig** *oovaal/reund/fewrkantig*
genuine/imitation	**äkta/imitation** *ekta/immitashoon*
I don't want anything too expensive.	**Jag vill inte ha någonting för dyrt.** *yaag vil inteh haa nawgonting fur dewrt*
In the region of … kronor.	**Någonting omkring … kronor.** *nawgonting omkring … kroonor*
Do you have anything …?	**Har ni något …?** *haar nee nawgot*
larger/smaller	**större/mindre** *sturreh/mindreh*
better quality	**av bättre kvalitet** *aav bettreh kvaliteht*
cheaper	**billigare** *billigareh*

Vilken … vill ni ha?	What … would you like?
färg/form	color/shape
kvalitet/kvantitet	quality/quantity
Hur många vill ni ha?	How many would you like?
Vilken sort vill ni ha?	What kind would you like?
Vilket pris hade ni tänkt er ?	What price range are you thinking of?

Can you show me …?	**Kan ni visa mig …?** *kun nee veesa may*
this one/these	**den här/dom här** *den hair/dom hair*
that one/those	**den där/dom där** *den dair/dom dair*
the one in the window/ display case	**den i fönstret/vitrinet** *den ee furnstret/vitreenet*
some others	**några andra** *nawgra andra*

COLOR ➤ 143

Conditions of purchase Köpvillkor

Is there a guarantee?	**Finns det garanti?**
	fins det garantee
Are there any instructions with it?	**Finns det en bruksanvisning?**
	fins det en breuks-anveesning

Out of stock Slut på lagret

Jag är ledsen, vi har inga.	I'm sorry. We don't have any.
Det är slut på lagret.	We're out of stock.
Kan jag visa er något annat/ en annan typ?	Can I show you something else/ a different kind?
Ska vi beställa det åt er?	Shall we order it for you?

Can you order it for me?	**Kan ni beställa det åt mig?**
	kun nee bestella det awt may
How long will it take?	**Hur länge tar det?** *heur lengeh taar det*
Is there another store that sells ...?	**Finns det någon annan affär som säljer ...?** *fins det nawgon anan affair som selyer*

Decisions Beslut

That's not quite what I want.	**Det är inte riktigt vad jag vill ha.**
	det air inteh riktigt vaad yaag vil haa
No, I don't like it.	**Nej, jag tycker inte om det.**
	nay yaag tewcker inteh om det
That's too expensive.	**Det är för dyrt.** *det air fur dewrt*
I'd like to think about it.	**Jag behöver tänka på det.**
	yaag behurver tenka paw det
I'll take it.	**Jag tar den.** *yaag taar den*

– God morgon, jag skulle vilja ha en sweatshirt.
(Good morning. I'm looking for a sweatshirt.)

– *Javisst, vilken färg vill ni ha?*
(Certainly. What color would you like?)

– Orange, tack. Och den måste vara stor.
(Orange, please. And I want something big.)

– *Här är en. Den kostar tvåhundratjugofem (225) kronor.*
(Here you are. That's 225 kronor.)

– Hm, det är inte riktigt vad jag vill ha. Tack.
(Hmm, that's not quite what I want. Thank you.)

Paying Betalning

Sales tax [VAT] (**MOMS**) is imposed on almost all goods and services and is included in the stated price. If you live outside the EU, you can reclaim the tax when you return home.

Where do I pay?	**Var kan jag betala?** *vaar kun yaag betaala*
How much is that?	**Hur mycket kostar det?** *heur mewcket kostar det*
Could you write it down?	**Kan ni skriva det?** *kun nee skreeva det*
Do you accept traveler's checks [cheques]?	**Tar ni resecheckar?** *taar nee rehse-checkar*
I'll pay by …	**Jag vill betala …** *yaag vil betaala*
cash	**kontant** *kontant*
credit card	**med kreditkort** *mehd kredeet-koort*
I don't have any smaller change.	**Jag har inte mindre växel.** *yaag haar inteh mindreh vexel*
Sorry, I don't have enough money.	**Jag har inte tillräckligt med pengar.** *yaag haar inteh tilreckligt mehd pengar*
Could I have a receipt, please?	**Kan jag få ett kvitto, tack?** *kun yaag faw et kvittoo tuck*
I think you've given me the wrong change.	**Jag tror ni har gett mig fel växel.** *yaag troor nee haar yet may fehl vexel*

Hur vill ni betala?	How are you paying?
Kortet har inte blivit accepterat.	This transaction has not been approved/accepted.
Det här kortet gäller inte.	This card is not valid.
Kan jag få se ytterligare ligitimation.	May I have additional identification?
Har ni mindre växel?	Do you have any smaller change?

BETALA HÄR	please pay here

136

Complaints Klagomål

This doesn't work.	**Den här fungerar inte.**
	den hair fungehrar inteh
Can you exchange this, please?	**Kan ni byta den, tack?**
	kun nee bewta den tuck
I'd like a refund.	**Kan jag få pengarna tillbaka.**
	kun yaag faw pengarna tilbaaka
Here's the receipt.	**Här är kvittot.** *hair air kvittoot*
I don't have the receipt.	**Jag har inte kvittot.**
	yaag haar inteh kvittot
I'd like to see the manager.	**Jag vill tala med chefen.**
	yaag vil taala mehd shehfen

Repairs/Cleaning
Reparationer/Tvätt och rengöring

This is broken. Can you repair it?	**Det här är trasigt. Kan ni laga det?**
	det hair air traasigt. kun nee laaga det
Do you have … for this?	**Har ni … till det här?**
	har nee … til det hair
a battery	**ett batteri** *et batteree*
replacement parts	**reservdelar** *reserv-dehlar*
There's something wrong with …	**Det är något fel på …**
	det air nawgot fehl paw
Can you … this?	**Kan ni … den här?**
	kun nee … den hair
clean	**göra ren/tvätta** *yurra rehn/tvetta*
press	**stryka** *strewka*
patch	**laga** *laaga*
Could you alter this?	**Kan ni göra en ändring på det här?**
	kun nee yurra en endring paw det hair
When will it be ready?	**När blir det klart?** *nair bleer det klart*
This isn't mine.	**Det här är inte min.** *det hair air inteh min*
There's … missing.	**… saknas.** *… saaknas*

TIME ➤ 220; DATES ➤ 218

Bank/Currency exchange
Bank/Växelkontor

Cash can be obtained from ATMs (cash machines) – **Bankomat** – with MasterCard, Visa, Eurocard, American Express, and other international credit cards. Remember to bring your passport when you change money. Most banks close at 3 p.m., but some are open later one day a week.

Where's the nearest …?	**Var ligger närmaste …?** _vaar ligger nairmasteh …_
bank	**bank** _bunk_
currency exchange office [bureau de change]	**växelkontor** _vexel-kontoor_

VÄXELKONTOR/ UTLÄNDSK VALUTA	currency exchange
ÖPPET/STÄNGT	open/closed
KASSA	cashiers

Changing money Växla pengar

Can I exchange foreign currency here?	**Kan jag växla pengar här?** _kun yaag vexla pengar hair_
I'd like to change some dollars/ pounds into kronor.	**Jag skulle vilja växla dollar/pund till kronor.** _yaag skeulleh vilya vexla dollar/peund till kroonor_
I want to cash some traveler's checks [cheques].	**Jag skulle vilja lösa in några resecheckar.** _yaag skeulleh vilya lursa in nawgra rehse-checkar_
What's the exchange rate?	**Vad är växelkursen?** _vaad air vexel-keursen_
How much commission do you charge?	**Hur mycket är expeditionsavgiften?** _heur mewcket air expedishoons-aavyiften_
Could I have some small change, please?	**Kan jag få lite växel, tack?** _kun yaag faw leeteh vexel tuck_
I've lost my traveler's checks. These are the numbers.	**Jag har tappat mina resecheckar. Här är numren.** _yaag haar tappat meena rehse-checkar. hair air neumren_

Security Säkerhet

Kan jag få se ...?	Could I see ...?
ert pass	your passport
en legitimation	some identification
ert bankkort	your bank card
Vad är er adress?	What's your address?
Var bor ni?	Where are you staying?
Fyll i blanketten, tack.	Fill out this form, please.
Underteckna här, tack.	Please sign here.

ATMs (Cash machines) Bankomater

Can I withdraw money on my credit card here?
Kan jag ta ut pengar på mitt kreditkort här? *kun yaag taa eut pengar paw mit kredeet-koort hair*

Where are the ATMs/ (cash machines)?
Var finns det bankomater? *vaar fins det bankoomaater*

Can I use my ... card in the cash machine?
Kan jag använda mitt ... kort i maskinen? *kun yaag anvenda mit ... koort ee masheenen*

The cash machine has eaten my card.
Maskinen har tagit mitt kort. *masheenen haar tagit mit koort*

BANKOMATER — automated teller (ATM)/ cash machine

The monetary unit is the **krona** (singular) or **kronor** (plural). As other countries, such as Iceland, also have the same name for their currency, the Swedish krona/kronor is abbreviated to SEK.

The krona is divided into **öre.**   100 öre = 1 krona (SEK)

Coins: 50 öre
1 krona, 5 and 10 kronor

Banknotes: 20, 50, 100, 500, and 1,000 kronor

The Euro (€) – the common European currency – was introduced in 1999, when it was worth approximately $1. However, banknotes and coins will not come into circulation until at least 2002.

Pharmacy Apotek

Pharmacies are called **apotek** and are found everywhere. They also sell their own brands of toiletries and cosmetics, but you will have to go to a department store if you want international commercial brands. For all-night or weekend service, check the pharmacy window, newspapers, or tourist offices.

Where's the nearest (all-night) pharmacy?
Var är närmaste (nattöppet) apotek?
vaar air nairmasteh apootehk

What time does the pharmacy open/close?
När öppnar/stänger apoteket?
nair urpnar/stenger apootehket

Can you make up this prescription for me?
Kan ni göra iordning det här receptet åt mig? *kun nee yurra ee ordning det hair receptet awt may*

Shall I wait?
Ska jag vänta?
skaa yaag venta

I'll come back for it.
Jag kommer tillbaka.
yaag kommer tilbaaka

Dosage instructions Instruktion för dosering

How much should I take?
Hur mycket ska jag ta?
heur mewcket skaa yaag taa

How many times a day should I take it?
Hur många gånger om dagen ska jag ta det? *heur monga gonger om daagen skaa yaag taa det*

Is it suitable for children?
Är det lämpligt för barn?
air det lempligt fur baarn

Ta ...	Take ...
... tabletter/... teskedar	... tablets/... teaspoons
före/efter måltiden	before/after meals
med vatten	with water
hel(a)	whole
på morgonen/på kvällen	in the morning/at night
i ... dagar	for ... days

DOCTOR ➤ 161

Asking advice Rådfrågning

I'd like some medicine for …	**Jag behöver medicin mot …** *yaag behurver mediseen moot*
a cold	**förkylning** *furchewlning*
a cough	**hosta** *hoosta*
diarrhea	**diarré** *deeareh*
a hangover	**baksmälla** *baaksmella*
hay fever	**hösnuva** *hur-sneuva*
insect bites	**insektsbett** *insekts-bet*
a sore throat	**halsont** *hals-oont*
sunburn	**solbränna** *sool-brenna*
motion [travel] sickness	**åksjuka** *awk-sheuka*
an upset stomach	**ont i magen** *oont ee maagen*
Can I get it without a prescription?	**Kan jag få det utan recept?** *kun yaag faw det eutan resept*
Can I have some …?	**Kan jag få …?** *kun yaag faw*
antiseptic cream	**antiseptisk salva** *antiseptisk salva*
aspirin	**huvudvärkstabletter (aspirin)** *heuvud-vairks-tabletter (aspireen)*
condoms	**kondomer** *kondawmer*
cotton [cotton wool]	**bomullsvadd** *boomeulls-vadd*
gauze [bandages]	**gasbinda** *gaasbinda*
insect repellent	**insektsmedel** *insekts-mehdel*
painkillers	**smärtstillande medel** *smairt-stillande mehdel*
vitamins	**vitamintabletter** *vitameen-tabletter*

Toiletries Toalettartiklar

I'd like some …	**Jag skulle vilja ha …** *yaag skeulleh vilya haa*
after shave	**rakvatten** *raak-vatten*
after-sun lotion	**efter-solkräm** *efter-soolkrairm*
deodorant	**deodorant** *deh-odorant*
razor blades	**rakblad** *raakblaad*
sanitary napkins [towels]	**bindor** *bindoor*
soap	**tvål** *tvawl*
sun block	**solkräm med extra skydd** *sool-krairm mehd extra shewdd*
sunscreen	**skyddssolkräm** *sheuds-soolkrairm*
factor …	**faktor …** *faktor*
tampons	**tamponger** *tamponger*
tissues	**pappersnäsdukar** *pappers-nairsdeukar*
toilet paper	**toalettpapper** *tooalet-papper*
toothpaste	**tandkräm** *tand-krairm*

Haircare Hårprodukter

comb	**kam** *kam*
conditioner	**hårbalsam** *hawr-balsam*
hair mousse/gel	**hårmousse/gelé** *hawr-mooss/shehleh*
hair spray	**hårspray** *hawr-spray*
shampoo	**schampo** *shampoo*

For the baby För babyn

baby food	**barnmat** *baarn-maat*
baby wipes	**våtservetter för barn** *vawt-servetter fur baarn*
diapers [nappies]	**blöjor** *blur-yoor*
sterilizing solution	**steriliseringsvätska** *sterilisehrings-vairtska*

Clothing Kläder

General Allmänt

I'd like … **Jag skulle vilja ha …**
yaag skeulleh vilya haa

Do you have any …? **Har ni några …?** *haar nee nawgra*

DAMKLÄDER	ladieswear
HERRKLÄDER	menswear
BARNKLÄDER	childrenswear

Color Färger

I'm looking for something in … **Jag söker något i …**
yaag surker nawgot ee

beige **beige** *behsh*

black **svart** *svart*

blue **blått** *blot*

brown **brunt** *breunt*

green **grönt** *grurnt*

gray **grått** *grott*

orange **orange** *ooransh*

pink **rosa** *rawsa*

purple **lila** *leela*

red **rött** *rurt*

white **vitt** *vit*

yellow **gult** *geult*

light … **ljus …** *yeus*

dark … **mörk …** *murk*

I want a darker/lighter shade. **Jag skulle vilja ha en mörkare/ljusare nyans.** *yaag skeulleh vilya haa en murkareh/yeusareh newans*

Do you have the same in …? **Har ni samma i …?**
haar nee samma ee

Clothes and accessories
Kläder och accessoarer

belt (man's/woman's)	**bälte/skärp**	_belteh/shairp_
bikini	**bikini**	_bikeeni_
blouse	**blus**	_bleus_
bra	**behå**	_beh-haw_
briefs	**trosor**	_troosor_
cap	**mössa**	_meursa_
coat (man's/woman's)	**rock/kappa**	_rock/kappa_
dress	**klänning**	_klenning_
handbag	**handväska**	_hand-veska_
hat	**hatt**	_hut_
jacket	**jacka**	_yacka_
jeans	**jeans**	_jeans_
leggings	**tights**	_tights_
pants (U.S.)	**(lång)byxor**	_long-bewxoor_
panty hose [tights]	**strumpbyxor**	_streump-bewxoor_
raincoat (man's/woman's)	**regnrock/regnkappa**	
	rengn-rock/rengn-kappa	
scarf	**halsduk**	_hals-deuk_
shirt (man's)	**skjorta**	_shoorta_
shorts	**shorts**	_shorts_
skirt	**kjol**	_chool_
socks	**sockar**	_sockar_
stockings	**strumpor**	_streumpoor_
suit (man's/woman's)	**kostym/dräkt**	_kostewm/drekt_
sweater	**tröja**	_trur-ya_
sweatshirt	**sweatshirt**	_sweatshirt_
swimming trunks/swimsuit	**badbyxor/baddräkt**	
	baad-bewxoor/baad-drekt	
T-shirt	**T-skjorta**	_teh-shoorta_
tie	**slips**	_slips_
trousers	**byxor**	_bewxoor_
underpants	**kalsonger**	_kalsonger_
with long/short sleeves	**med lång/kort ärm**	_mehd long/kort airm_
with a V-/round neck	**V-ringad/rund i halsen**	
	veh-ringad/reund ee haalsen	

Shoes Skor

boots	**stövlar** *sturvlar*
flip-flops	**badsandaler** *baad-sandaaler*
running [training] shoes	**träningsskor** *trairnings-skoor*
sandals	**sandaler** *sandaaler*
shoes	**skor** *skoor*
slippers	**tofflor** *toffloor*

Walking/Hiking gear Utrustning för fotvandring

knapsack	**ryggsäck** *rewgg-seck*
walking boots	**vandrarkängor** *vandrar-chengoor*
waterproof jacket [anorak]	**vattentät jacka/anorak** *vatten-tairt yacka/anorak*
windbreaker [cagoule]	**vindtät jacka** *vindtairt yacka*

Fabric Tyg

I want something in …	**Jag skulle vilja ha något i …** *aag skeulleh vilyah haa nawgot ee*
cotton	**bomull** *boomeull*
denim	**denim** *denim*
lace	**spets** *spets*
leather	**läder** *lairder*
linen	**linne** *linneh*
wool	**ull** *eull*
Is this …?	**Är detta …?** *air detta*
pure cotton	**ren bomull** *rehn boomeull*
synthetic	**syntetiskt** *sewntehtiskt*
Is it hand/machine washable?	**Kan det tvättas för hand/i maskin?** *kun det tvettas fur hand/ee masheen*

ENDAST KEMTVÄTT	dry clean only
ENDAST HANDTVÄTT	handwash only
STRYK INTE/STRYK EJ	do not iron
EJ KEMTVÄTT/KEMTVÄTTAS EJ	do not dry clean

Does it fit? Passar det?

Can I try this on?	**Kan jag prova den här?** *kun yaag proova den hair*
Where's the fitting room?	**Var är provrummet?** *vaar air <u>proov</u>-reummet*
It fits well. I'll take it.	**Den passar bra. Jag tar den.** *den passar braa. yaag taar den*
It doesn't fit.	**Den passar inte.** *den passar inteh*
It's too ...	**Den är för ...** *den air fur*
short/long	**kort/lång** *kort/long*
tight/loose	**trång/lös** *trong/lurs*
Do you have this in size ...?	**Har ni den här i storlek ...?** *haar nee den hair ee stoorlehk*
What size is this?	**Vilken storlek är det här?** *<u>vilk</u>en stoorlehk air det hair*
Could you measure me, please?	**Kan ni mäta mig, tack?** *kun nee mairta may tuck*
I don't know Swedish sizes.	**Jag känner inte till svenska storlekar.** *yaag <u>chenn</u>er inteh til svenska <u>stoor</u>lehkar*

Size Storlek

	Dresses/Suits							Women's shoes			
American	8	10	12	14	16	18		6	7	8	9
British	10	12	14	16	18	20		$4^{1/2}$	$5^{1/2}$	$6^{1/2}$	$7^{1/2}$
Continental	36	38	40	42	44	46		37	38	40	41

	Shirts				Men's shoes							
American } British	15	16	17	18	5	6	7	8	$8^{1/2}$	9	$9^{1/2}$	10 11
Continental	38	41	43	45	38	39	41	42	43	43	44	44 45

EXTRA STOR/LARGE (XL)	extra large (XL)
STOR (L)	large (L)
MEDIUM (M)	medium (M)
LITEN (S)	small (S)

1 centimeter (cm.) = 0.39 in.	1 inch = 2.54 cm.
1 meter (m.) = 39.37 in.	1 foot = 30.5 cm.
10 meters = 32.81 ft.	1 yard = 0.91 m.

Health and beauty
Hälsa och skönhet

I'd like a ...	**Jag skulle vilja ha ...** *yaag skeulleh vilya haa*
facial	**ansiktsbehandling** *ansikts-behandling*
manicure	**manikyr** *manikewr*
massage	**massage** *masaash*
waxing	**benvaxning** *behn-vaxning*

Hairdresser Hårfrisör

A ladies' hairdresser is a **damfrisör** and a men's hairdresser or barber is a **herrfrisör**. A tip of 10 percent is standard.

I'd like to make an appointment for ...	**Jag skulle vilja boka en tid till ...** *yaag skeulleh vilya booka en teed til*
Can you make it a bit earlier/later?	**Kan jag få komma lite tidigare/senare?** *kun yaag faw komma leeteh teedigareh/ sehnare*
I'd like a ...	**Jag vill ha ...** *yaag vil haa*
cut and blow-dry	**klippning och föning** *kliping ock furning*
shampoo and set	**tvätt och läggning** *tvet ock legning*
trim	**klippning av topparna** *kliping av topparna*
I'd like my hair ...	**Jag vill ha mitt hår ...** *yaag vil haa mit hawr*
highlighted	**med blonda slingor** *mehd blonda slingor*
permed	**permanentat** *permanentat*
Don't cut it too short.	**Klipp det inte för kort.** *klip det inteh fur kort*
A little more off the ...	**Klipp lite mer ...** *klip leeteh mehr*
back/front	**baktill/framtill** *baaktil/framtil*
neck/sides	**i nacken/på sidorna** *ee nacken/paw seedorna*
top	**på toppen** *paw toppen*
That's fine, thanks.	**Det är bra, tack.** *det air braa tuck*

Household articles
Hushållsartiklar

I'd like a(n)/ some …	**Jag skulle vilja ha en(ett)/några …** *yaag skeulleh vilya haa en/et/nawgra*
adapter	**adapter** *adapter*
alumin[i]um foil	**aluminiumfolie** *aleumeenium-foolyeh*
bottle opener	**flasköppnare** *flask-urpnareh*
can [tin] opener	**konservöppnare** *konserv-urpnareh*
clothes pins [pegs]	**klädnypor** *klaird-newpoor*
corkscrew	**korkskruv** *kork-skreuv*
light bulb	**glödlampa** *glurd-lampa*
matches	**tändstickor** *tend-stickor*
paper napkins	**pappersservetter** *pappers-servetter*
plastic wrap [cling film]	**plastfolie** *plast-foolyeh*
plug (electrical)	**stickkontakt** *stick-kontakt*
plug (sink, basin)	**propp** *prop*
scissors	**sax** *sax*
screwdriver	**skruvmejsel** *skreuv-maysel*

Cleaning items Rengöringsmedel

bleach	**klormedel** *klawr-mehdel*
dishcloth	**disktrasa** *disk-traasa*
dishwashing [washing-up] liquid	**diskmedel** *disk-mehdel*
garbage [refuse] bags	**soppåsar** *soop-pawsar*
detergent [washing powder]	**tvättmedel** *tvet-mehdel*

Dishes/Utensils [Crockery/Cutlery] Porslin/Bestick

bowls	**djupa tallrikar** *yeupa tallrikar*
cups	**koppar** *koppar*
forks/knives	**gafflar/knivar** *gafflar/kneevar*
spoons/teaspoons	**skedar/teskedar** *shehdar/teh-shehdar*
glasses	**glas** *glaas*
mugs	**muggar** *meuggar*
plates	**tallrikar** *tallrikar*

Jeweler Juvelerare

Could I see …?	**Kan jag få se …?**
	kun yaag faw seh
this/that	**det här/det där**
	det hair/det dair
It's in the window/	**Det är i skyltfönstret/i vitrinet.**
display cabinet.	*det air ee shewlt-furnstret/ee vitreenet*
alarm clock	**väckarklocka** *veckar-klocka*
battery	**batteri** *batteree*
bracelet	**armband** *armband*
brooch	**brosch** *brawsh*
chain	**kedja** *chehdya*
clock	**klocka** *klocka*
earrings	**örhängen** *urrhengen*
necklace	**halsband** *halsband*
ring	**ring** *ring*
watch	**armbandsklocka** *armbands-klocka*

Materials Olika råmaterial

Is this real silver/gold?	**Är det här äkta silver/guld?**
	air det hair ekta silver/geuld
Is there a certificate for it?	**Har ni certifikat på det?**
	haar nee sertifikaat paw det
Do you have anything in …?	**Har ni någonting i …?**
	har nee nawgonting ee
copper	**koppar** *koppar*
crystal (quartz)	**kristall** *kreestall*
cut glass	**slipat glas** *sleepat glaas*
diamond	**diamant** *deeamant*
enamel	**emalj** *ehmal'*
gold/gold plate	**guld/gulddoublé** *geuld/geuld-deubleh*
pearl	**pärla** *pairla*
pewter	**tenn** *ten*
platinum	**platina** *platina*
silver/silver plate	**silver/nysilver** *silver/newsilver*
stainless steel	**rostfritt stål** *rost-frit stawl*

149

Newsstand [Newsagent]/ Tobacconist Tidningskiosk/ Tidningsaffär

Foreign newspapers can usually be found at train stations or airports, or in bookstores or newsstands in major cities. **Pressbyrån** are the most common newsstands, where you can also buy tobacco, certain food items, candy, and chocolate, as well as subway and bus cards.

Do you sell English-language books/newspapers?	**Säljer ni böcker/tidningar på engelska?** *selyer nee burker/teedningar paw engelska*
I'd like a(n)/some …	**Jag skulle vilja ha en (ett)/några …** *yaag skeulleh vilyah haa en/et/nawgra*
book	**bok** *book*
candy [sweets]	**lite godis** *leeteh goodis*
chewing gum	**tuggummi** *teugg-geummi*
chocolate bar	**chockladkaka** *shooklad-kaaka*
cigarettes (pack of)	**paket cigaretter** *pakeht sigaretter*
cigars	**cigarrer** *sigarrer*
dictionary	**lexikon** *lexicon*
English–Swedish	**engelska-svenska** *engelska-svenska*
envelopes	**kuvert** *keuvair*
guidebook of …	**guidebok över …** *guide-book urver*
lighter	**tändare** *tendareh*
magazine	**veckotidning** *veckoo-teedning*
map	**karta** *kaarta*
map of the town	**stadskarta** *stats-kaarta*
matches	**tändstickor** *tend-stickoor*
newspaper	**tidning** *teedning*
American/English	**amerikansk/engelsk** *amerikaansk/engelsk*
pen	**kulspetspenna** *keulspets-penna*
road map of …	**vägkarta över …** *vairg-kaarta urver*
stamps	**frimärken** *free-mairken*
tobacco	**tobak** *toobuck*
writing paper	**brevpapper** *brehv-papper*

Photography Fotografering

I'm looking for a(n) … camera.	**Jag skulle vilja köpa en … kamera.** yaag skeulleh vilya churpa en … <u>kaa</u>mera
automatic	**automatisk** aatoo<u>maa</u>tisk
compact	**kompakt** kom<u>pakt</u>
disposable	**engångskamera** ehngongs-<u>kaa</u>mera
SLR (single lens reflex)	**med enkellinsreflex** mehd enkel-lins-re<u>flex</u>
I'd like a(n) …	**Jag skulle vilja ha …** yaag skeulleh vilya haa
battery	**ett batteri** et bat<u>tee</u>ree
camera case	**ett kamerafodral** et <u>kaa</u>mera-foo<u>draal</u>
electronic flash	**en elektronisk blixt** en elek<u>trawn</u>isk blixt
filter	**ett filter** et filter
lens	**ett objektiv** et obyek<u>teev</u>
lens cap	**ett linsskydd** et lins-shewdd

Film/Processing Framkallning

I'd like (a) … film.	**Jag skulle vilja ha en … film.** yaag skeulleh vilya haa en … film
black and white	**svart-vit** svart-veet
color	**färg** fair'
24/36 exposures	**tjugofyra/trettiosex exponeringar** cheugoo-<u>few</u>ra/tretteeoo-<u>sex</u> expo<u>neh</u>ringar
I'd like this film developed, please.	**Jag skulle vilja ha den här filmen framkallad.** yaag skeulleh vilya haa den hair filmen <u>fram</u>kallad
Would you enlarge this, please?	**Kan ni förstora det här?** kun nee fur<u>stoo</u>ra det hair
How much do … exposures cost?	**Hur mycket kostar … exponeringar?** heur mewcket kostar … expo<u>neh</u>ringar
When will my photos be ready?	**När blir korten klara?** nair bleer koorten klaara
I'd like to pick up my photos.	**Jag skulle vilja hämta mina kort.** yaag skeulleh vilya hemta meena koort
Here's the receipt.	**Här är kvittot.** hair air kvittoot

Post office Posten

Post offices are easily recognized by the yellow **Post** sign. Mailboxes [postboxes] are bright yellow, except those for local mail, which are blue. The post office only handles mail; for telephoning, sending telegrams, and faxing you have to go to a **tele office**. Business hours are 9 a.m. to 6 p.m. and until 1 p.m. on Saturdays. Don't forget to take a ticket with your number.

General inquiries Allmänna förfrågningar

Where is the post office?	**Var ligger posten?** *vaar ligger posten*
What time does the post office open/close?	**När öppnar/stänger posten?** *nair urpnar/stenger posten*
Does it close for lunch?	**Stänger den för lunch?** *stenger den fur leunsh*
Where's the mailbox [postbox]?	**Var är postlådan?** *vaar air post-lawdan*
Is there any mail for me?	**Finns det någon post till mig?** *fins det nawgon post til may*

Buying stamps Frimärken

I'd like to send these postcards to …	**Jag skulle vilja skicka de här vykorten till …** *yaag skeulleh vilya shicka de hair vew-koorten til*
A stamp for this postcard/letter, please.	**Kan jag få ett frimärke till det här vykortet/brevet, tack.** *kun yaag faw et free-mairke til det hair vew-koortet/brehvet tuck*
A stamp for …, please.	**Ett frimärke för …, tack.** *et free-mairke fur … tuck*
What's the postage for a letter to …?	**Vad är portot för ett brev till …?** *vaad air portot fur et brehv til*

> – Hej, jag skulle vilja skicka de här vykorten till USA.
> (Hello, I'd like to send these postcards to the U.S.)
> – Hur många har ni? (How many?)
> – Nio, tack. (Nine, please.)
> – Det blir sju och femtio gånger nio: sextiosju och femtio, tack.
> (That's 7.50 (kronor) times nine: 67.50 kronor, please.)

Sending packages Skicka paket

I want to send this package [parcel] by …	**Jag vill skicka det här paketet …** *yaag vil shicka det hair pakehtet*
airmail	**som flygpost** *som flewg-post*
special delivery [express]	**express** *express*
registered mail	**rekommenderat** *rekomendehrat*
It contains …	**Det innehåller …** *det inneholler*

Fyll i tulldeklarationen, tack.	Please fill out the customs declaration form.
Vad är värdet?	What's the value?
Vad finns inuti?	What's inside?

Telecommunications Telekommunikationer

I'd like a phone card, please.	**Jag skulle vilja ha ett telefonkort, tack.** *yaag skeulleh vilya haa et telefawn-koort tuck*
10/20/50 units	**10/20/50 enheter** *teeo/cheugoo/femteeoo ehn-hehter*
Do you have a photocopier?	**Har ni en kopiator?** *haar nee en kopiaator*
I'd like to send a message …	**Jag skulle vilja skicka ett meddelande …** *yaag skeulleh vilya shicka ett mehd-dehlande*
by e-mail/fax	**via e-post/fax** *veea e-post/fax*
What's your e-mail address?	**Vad är er e-postadress?** *vaad air ehr e-post-adress*
Can I access the Internet here?	**Kan jag komma in på Internet här?** *kun yaag komma in paw internet hair*
What are the charges per hour?	**Vad kostar det per timme?** *vaad kostar det per timmeh*
How do I log on?	**Hur loggar jag in?** *heur loggar yaag in*

PAKET	packages [parcels]
NÄSTA TÖMNING	next collection
ALLMÄN POST	general delivery [poste restante]
FRIMÄRKEN	stamps
TELEGRAM	telegrams

153

Souvenirs Souvenirer

There is no shortage of souvenirs – from ceramics and
woodcraft items to traditional Lapp handicrafts made from
reindeer antlers and skin. The following are a few suggestions.

candlesticks	**ljusstakar** *yeus-staakar*
Christmas decorations	**juldekorationer** *yeul-dekorashooner*
clogs	**träskor** *traiskoor*
crystal (glass)	**kristallglas** *kreestall-glaas*
Dala horse (red wooden horse)	**dalahäst** *daala-hest*
dolls	**dockor** *dockoor*
glassware	**glas** *glaas*
handicrafts	**hemslöjd** *hem-sluyd*
horn work	**något i horn** *nawgot ee hoorn*
jewelry	**smycken** *smewcken*
Lapp handicrafts	**sameslöjd** *saameh-sluyd*
porcelain	**porslin** *poshleen*
pottery	**keramik** *cherameek*
reindeer antlers	**renhorn** *rehn-hoorn*
smoked salmon	**rökt lax** *rurkt lax*
tablecloth	**duk** *deuk*
textiles	**textilvaror** *texteel-vaaroor*
wood carvings	**träfigurer** *trair-figeurer*
wooden knife	**träkniv** *trair-kneev*
wooden spoon	**träsked** *trair-shehd*

Gifts Presenter

bottle of wine	**en flaska vin** *en flaska veen*
box of chocolates	**en chockladask** *en shooklaad-ask*
calendar	**en kalender** *en kalender*
key ring	**en nyckelring** *en newckel-ring*
postcards	**vykort** *vew-koort*
scarf	**scarf** *skaaf*
souvenir guide	**souvenirguide** *sooveneer-guide*
tea towel	**diskhandduk** *disk-handdeuk*
T-shirt	**T-skjorta** *teh-shoorta*

Music Musik

I'd like a …	**Jag skulle vilja ha …** *yaag skeulleh vilya haa*
cassette	**en kassett** *en kasett*
compact disc	**en CD-skiva** *en seh-deh-sheeva*
record	**en skiva** *en sheeva*
videocassette	**en videofilm** *en video-film*
Who are the popular native singers/bands?	**Vilka svenska sångare/band är populära nu?** *vilka svenska songareh/band air popeu-laira neu*

Toys and games Leksaker och spel

I'd like a toy/game …	**Jag skulle vilja ha en leksak/ett spel …** *yaag skeulleh vilya haa en lehk-saak/et spehl*
for a boy	**till en pojke** *til en poykeh*
for a 5-year-old girl	**till en 5-årig flicka** *til en fem-awrig flicka*
ball	**en boll** *en bol*
chess set	**ett schackspel** *et shack-spehl*
doll	**en docka** *en docka*
electronic game	**ett elektroniskt spel** *et elektrawniskt spehl*
teddy bear	**en nalle** *en nalleh*
pail and shovel [bucket and spade]	**en hink och spade** *en hink ock spaadeh*

Antiques Antikviteter

How old is this?	**Hur gammalt är det här?** *heur gammalt air det hair*
Do you have anything from the … era?	**Har ni något från … perioden/talet?** *haar nee nawgot frawn … pairiooden/taalet*
Can you send it to me?	**Kan ni skicka den till mig?** *kun nee shicka den til may*
Will I have problems with customs?	**Får jag problem i tullen?** *fawr yaag prooblehm ee teullen*
Is there a certificate of authenticity?	**Finns det ett äkthetsbevis?** *fins det et ekthehts-bevees*

WHO?/WHAT?/WHEN? ➤ 104

Supermarket/Minimart
Snabbköp/Närbutik

Supermarkets, such as ICA, Konsum, and Åhléns, can be found in most large towns and cities and offer an excellent selection of foods. Large supermarkets, such as Obs, can be found in the suburbs. Many corner shops (**närbutik**), as well as newsstands (**pressbyrån**), sell a good range of food, too. In Stockholm, the market halls, **Östermalmshallen** and **Hötorgshallen**, sell fresh meat, fish, and poultry, as well as reindeer and moose.

At the supermarket I snabbköpet

Excuse me. Where can I find (a) …?	**Ursäkta mig, var finns …?** *eurshekta may, vaar fins*
Do I pay for this here?	**Ska jag betala här?** *skaa yaag betaala hair*
Where are the carts [trolleys]/baskets?	**Var finns shoppingvagnarna/korgarna?** *vaar fins shopping-vag-narna/kor-yarna*
Is there a … here?	**Finns det …här?** *fins det … hair*
bakery	**ett bageri** *et baageree*
pharmacy	**ett apotek** *et apootehk*
delicatessen	**en delikatessaffär** *en delikatess-affair*

KONSERVER	canned foods
MEJERIPRODUKTER	dairy products
FÄRSK FISK	fresh fish
FÄRSKT KÖTT	fresh meat
FÄRSKVAROR	fresh produce
DJUPFRYSTA VAROR	frozen foods
HUSHÅLLSARTIKLAR	household goods
FÅGEL	poultry
BRÖD OCH KONDITORIVAROR	bread and cakes

Weights and measures

- 1 kilogram or kilo (kg.) = 1000 grams (g.); 100 g. = 3.5 oz.; **1 kg.** = 2.2 lb.; 1 oz. = **28.35 g.**; 1 lb. = **453.60 g.**
- **1 liter (l.)** = 0.88 imp. quart or 1.06 U.S. quart; 1 imp. quart = **1.14 l.**; 1 U.S. quart = **0.951 l.**; 1 imp. gallon = **4.55 l.**; 1 U.S. gallon = 3.8 l.

Food hygiene Livsmedelshygien

ÄT INOM ... DAGAR EFTER ÖPPNANDET	eat within ... days of opening
MÅSTE FÖRVARAS I KYLSKÅP	keep refrigerated
KAN LAGAS I MIKROUGN	microwaveable
LÄMPLIGT FÖR VEGETARIANER	suitable for vegetarians
FÖRBRUKAS INNAN ...	use by ...

At the minimart I närbutiken

I'd like some of that/those.	**Jag skulle vilja ha lite av det här/det där.** *yaag skeulleh vilya haa leeteh aav det hair/det dair*
this one/that one	**den här/den där** *den hair/den dair*
these/those	**de här/de där** *deh hair/deh dair*
to the left/right	**till vänster/till höger** *til venster/til hurger*
over there/here	**där borta/här** *dair borta/hair*
Where is/are the ...?	**Var finns ...?** *vaar fins*
I'd like ...	**Jag skulle vilja ha ...** *yaag skeulleh vilya haa*
a kilo (of)/half a kilo (of)	**ett kilo/ett halvt kilo** *et keelo/et halft keelo*
a liter (of)/half a liter (of)	**en liter/en halv liter** *en leeter/en halv leeter*
... slices of ham	**... skivor skinka** *... skivoorr shinka*
apples	**äpplen** *epplen*
beer	**öl** *url*
bread	**bröd** *brurd*
coffee	**kaffe** *kaffeh*
cheese	**ost** *oost*
cookies [biscuits]	**kex/småkakor** *kex/smaw-kaakor*
eggs	**ägg** *egg*
ham	**skinka** *shinka*
jam	**sylt** *sewlt*
milk	**mjölk** *myulk*
potato chips [crisps]	**chips** *chips*
soft drinks	**läskedrycker** *leskeh-drewcker*
tomatoes	**tomater** *toomaater*
That's all, thanks.	**Det var allt, tack.** *det vaar alt tuck*

Provisions/Picnic På picknick

beer	**öl** *url*
butter	**smör** *smur*
cakes	**kakor** *kaakor*
cheese	**ost** *oost*
cooked meats	**lite kallskuret** *leeteh kal-skeuret*
cookies [biscuits]	**kex/småkakor** <u>smaw</u>-kaakor/kex
grapes	**vindruvor** *veen-dreuvoor*
instant coffee	**snabb-kaffe** *snaab-kaafer*
lemonade	**sockerdricka** *socker-dricka*
margarine	**margarin** *marga<u>reen</u>*
oranges	**apelsiner** *apel<u>seen</u>er*
rolls (bread)	**småfranska** *smaw-franska*
sausage	**korv** *korv*
tea bags	**thépåsar** *teh-pawsar*
wine	**vin** *veen*
yogurt	**yoghurt** *yawgeurt*

Sweden is full of wonderful smelling bakeries (**bageri**) and coffee/pastry
shops (**konditori**). Try afternoon coffee or tea at a **konditori** with homemade
Danish pastries (**wienerbröd**) – or a cinnamon bun (**kanelbulle**). Or try an
open sandwich (**smörgås**) topped with shelled shrimp or egg, and
anchovies on rye bread. Hot dogs (**varm korv**) are a favorite with the
Swedes, and are sold from kiosks on practically every street.

Police Polisen

Crime, theft, accidents, or lost property should be reported to the nearest police station (**Polisstation**), open 24 hours a day. To get the police in an emergency, ☎ 112.

Where's the nearest police station?	**Var ligger närmaste polisstation?** *vaar ligger nairmasteh poolees-stashoon*
Does anyone here speak English?	**Talar någon engelska här?** *taalar nawgon engelska hair*
I want to report a(n) …	**Jag vill anmäla en(ett) …** *yaag vil anmairla en/ett*
accident	**olycka** *oolewcka*
attack	**attack** *attack*
mugging	**överfall** *urverfall*
rape	**våldtäkt** *vold-tekt*
My child is missing.	**Mitt barn har kommit bort.** *mit baarn haar kommit bort*
Here's a photo of him/her.	**Här är ett foto på honom/henne.** *hair air et footoo paw honom/henneh*
Someone's following me.	**Någon följer efter mig.** *nawgon furlyer efter may*
I need an English-speaking lawyer.	**Jag behöver en engelsktalande advokat.** *yaag behurver en engelsk-taalande advookaat*
I need to make a phone call.	**Jag behöver ringa ett samtal.** *yaag behurver ringa et samtaal*
I need to contact the … Consulate.	**Jag behöver kontakta … konsulatet.** *yaag behurver kontakta … konseulaatet*
American/British	**amerikanska/engelska** *amerikaanska/engelska*

Kan ni beskriva honom/henne?	Can you describe him/her?
av manligt kön/av kvinnligt kön	male/female
blond/brunett	blond(e)/brunette
rödhårig/gråhårig	red-headed/gray-haired
långt/kort hår	long/short hair
skallig	balding
hur lång/ungefärlig längd …	approximate height …
ålder (ungefärlig) …	aged (approximately) …
Han/hon var klädd i …	He/She was wearing …

CLOTHES ➤ 144; COLOR ➤ 143

Lost property / Theft
Förlorade egendomar / Stöld

I want to report a theft.	**Jag skulle vilja anmäla en stöld.**
	yaag skeulleh vilya anmairla en sturld
My ... has been stolen from my car.	**Min ... har stulits från min bil.**
	min ... haar steulits frawn min beel
I've been robbed / mugged.	**Jag har blivit rånad / överfallen.**
	yaag haar bleevit rawnad / urverfallen
I've lost my ...	**Jag har förlorat ...**
	yaag haar furloorat
My ... has been stolen.	**Någon har stulit ...**
	nawgon haar steulit
bicycle	**min cykel** *min sewckel*
camera	**min kamera** *min kaamera*
car / rental car	**min bil / hyrbil** *min beel / hewr-beel*
credit cards	**mitt kreditkort** *mit kredeet-koort*
handbag	**min handväska** *min hand-veska*
money	**mina pengar** *meena pengar*
passport / ticket	**mitt pass / min biljett** *mit pus / min bilyet*
purse / wallet	**min portmonnä / plånbok**
	min port-moneh / plawn-book
watch	**min armbandsklocka** *min armbands-klocka*
What shall I do?	**Vad ska jag göra?** *vaad skaa yaag yurra*
I need a police report for my insurance claim.	**Jag behöver en polisrapport för mitt försäkringsbolag.** *yaag behurver en poolees-raport fur mit fursairkrings-boolaag*

Vad är det som saknas?	What's missing?
När blev det stulet?	When was it stolen?
När hände det?	When did it happen?
Var bor ni?	Where are you staying?
Var blev det stulet?	Where was it taken from?
Var var ni då?	Where were you at the time?
Vi ska skaffa en tolk åt er.	We're getting an interpreter for you.
Vi ska undersöka saken.	We'll look into the matter.
Fyll i den här blanketten, tack.	Please fill out this form.

Health

Before you leave home, make sure your health insurance policy covers any illness or accident while you are abroad. EU citizens with Form E111 are eligible for free medical treatment, otherwise you have to pay doctors and dentists on the spot. If you become ill, ask somebody to call a doctor affiliated with **Försäkringskassan** (the national health service). If you are able, go to the out-patient department (**akutmottagning**) at the nearest hospital or to a health center (**vårdcentral**) in rural areas. Take your passport for identification. For emergencies, ☎ 112.

Doctor (general) Läkare (allmänt)

Where can I find a hospital/ dental office [surgery]?
Var finns det ett sjukhus/en tandläkare?
vaar fins det et sjeuk-heus/en tandlairkare

Where's there a doctor/ dentist who speaks English?
Var finns det en läkare/tandläkare som talar engelska? *vaar fins det en lairkare/tandlairkare som talar engelska*

What are the office [surgery] hours?
När är läkarmottagningen öppen?
nair air lairkar-moot-taagningen urpen

Could the doctor come to see me here?
Kan doktorn komma och undersöka mig här? *kun doktorn komma ock eunder-surka may hair*

Can I make an appointment for …?
Kan jag boka en tid …?
kun yaag booka en teed

today/tomorrow
idag/till imorgon *ee daag/til ee morron*

as soon as possible
så snart som möjligt
saw snaart som mur'ligt

It's urgent.
Det är brådskande. *det air broskandeh*

I have an appointment with Doctor …
Jag har tid hos doktor …
yaag haar teed hoos doktor

- Kan jag boka en tid så snart som möjligt?
(Can I make an appointment for as soon as possible?)
- Det är fullbokat idag. Är det brådskande?
(We're fully booked today. Is it urgent?)
- Ja. (Yes.)
- Går det bra kvart över tio (10:15) med doktor Lundgren.
(Well, how about at 10:15 with Doctor Lundgren?)
- Kvart över tio, tack så mycket.
(10:15. Thank you very much.)

Accident and injury   Olycksfall och skada

My … is hurt/injured.	**Min/mitt … är skadad/skadat.**
	min/mit … air <u>skaa</u>dad/<u>skaa</u>dat
husband/wife	**man/fru** man/freu
son/daughter	**son/dotter** sawn/dotter
friend	**vän** ven
child	**barn** baarn
He/She is …	**Han/Hon …** han/hoonn
unconscious	**är medvetslös** air <u>mehd</u>vehts-lurs
(seriously) injured	**är (allvarligt) skadad**
	air (<u>alvaar</u>ligt) <u>skaa</u>dad
bleeding (heavily)	**blöder (kraftigt)** blurder (kraftigt)
I have a(n) …	**Jag har (fått) …** yaag haar (fot)
blister	**en blåsa** en blawsa
boil	**en böld** en burld
bruise	**ett blåmärke** et <u>blaw</u>-mairkeh
burn	**ett brännsår** et <u>brenn</u>-sawr
cut/graze	**ett skärsår/skrubbsår**
	et <u>shair</u>-sawr/<u>skreubb</u>-sawr
insect bite/sting	**ett insektsbett** et <u>insekts</u>-bet
lump	**en knöl** en knurl
rash	**ett utslag** et eut-slaag
strained muscle	**en muskelsträckning**
	en <u>meuskel</u>-streckning
swelling	**en svullnad** en <u>sveull</u>nad
My … hurts.	**Jag har ont i min/mitt …**
	yaag haar oont ee min/mit

Symptoms Symptom

I've been feeling ill for … days.	**Jag har mått dåligt i … dagar.** *yaag haar mot dawligt ee*
I feel faint.	**Jag känner mig yr.** *yaag <u>chenner</u> may ewr*
I have a fever.	**Jag har feber.** *yaag haar <u>fehber</u>*
I've been vomiting.	**Jag har kräkts.** *yaag haar <u>krairkts</u>*
I have diarrhea.	**Jag har diarré.** *yaag haar deeareh*
It hurts here.	**Det gör ont här.** *det yurr oont hair*
I have (a/an) …	**Jag har …** *yaag haar*
backache	**ont i ryggen** *oont ee <u>rewggen</u>*
cold	**en förkylning** *en fur-<u>chewl</u>ning*
cramps	**kramp** *kramp*
earache	**ont i örat** *oont ee urrat*
headache	**huvudvärk** *<u>heuveud</u>-vairk*
sore throat	**ont i halsen** *oont ee <u>halsen</u>*
stomachache	**ont i magen** *oont ee <u>maagen</u>*
sunstroke	**solsting** *soolsting*

Conditions Hälsotillstånd

I have arthritis.	**Jag har artrit.** *yaag haar ar<u>treet</u>*
I have asthma.	**Jag har astma.** *yaag haar astma*
I am …	**Jag är …** *yaag air*
diabetic/epileptic	**diabetiker/epileptiker** *deeaa<u>beh</u>tiker/epi<u>lep</u>tiker*
handicapped	**rörelsehindrad** *rurrelseh-<u>hind</u>rad*
(… months) pregnant	**gravid (i … månaden)** *gra<u>veed</u> (ee … <u>maw</u>naden)*
I have a heart condition.	**Jag har hjärtproblem.** *yaag haar yairt-proo<u>blehm</u>*
I have high/low blood pressure.	**Jag har högt/lågt blodtryck.** *yaag haar hurgt/lawgt blood-trewck*
I had a heart attack … years ago.	**Jag hade en hjärtattack för … år sedan.** *yaag hadeh en yairt-at<u>tack</u> fur … awr sehdan*

163

Doctor's inquiries Läkarens förfrågningar

Hur länge har ni känt er så här?	How long have you been feeling like this?
Är det första gången ni har det här?	Is this the first time you've had this?
Tar ni någon annan medicin?	Are you taking any other medication?
Är ni allergisk mot något?	Are you allergic to anything?
Har ni vaccinerats mot stelkramp?	Have you been vaccinated against tetanus?
Är er aptit bra?	Is your appetite okay?

Examination Undersökning

Jag ska ta er temperatur/ ert blodtryck.	I'll take your temperature/ blood pressure.
Kan ni kavla upp ärmen, tack.	Roll up your sleeve, please.
Kan ni vara snäll och ta av er kläderna på överkroppen.	Please undress to the waist.
Var snäll och ligg ner.	Please lie down.
Öppna munnen.	Open your mouth.
Andas djupt.	Breathe deeply.
Var snäll och hosta.	Cough, please.
Var gör det ont?	Where does it hurt?

Diagnosis Diagnos

Vi måste ta en röntgenbild.	I want you to have an X-ray.
Jag behöver ett blodprov/ett avföringsprov/ett urinprov.	I want a specimen of your blood/stool/urine.
Ni behöver vända er till en specialist.	I want you to see a specialist.
Ni behöver läggas in på sjukhus.	I want you to go to the hospital.
Den/Det är bruten(t)/vrickad(t).	It's broken/sprained.
Den/Det har gått ur led/ den är sträckt.	It's dislocated/torn.

Ni har (fått) …	You have (a/an) …
blindtarmsinflammation	appendicitis
urinvägsinfektion	cystitis
influensa	flu
matförgiftning	food poisoning
benbrott	fracture
magkatarr	gastritis
hemorroider	hemorrhoids
bråck	hernia
inflammation i …	inflammation of …
mässlingen	measles
lunginflammation	pneumonia
ischias	sciatica
halsfluss	tonsilitis
en tumör	tumor
en könssjukdom	venereal disease
Den/det är infekterad(t).	It's infected.
Det smittar.	It's contagious.

Treatment Behandling

Jag ska ge er …	I'll give you a(n) …
ett antiseptiskt medel	antiseptic
något smärtstillande	painkiller
Jag ger er ett recept på …	I'm going to prescribe …
ett antibiotiskt medel	a course of antibiotics
några stolpiller	some suppositories
Är ni allergisk mot någon medicin?	Are you allergic to any medication?
Ta en tablett …	Take one pill …
var … timme	every … hours
… gånger om dagen	… times a day
före/efter varje måltid	before/after each meal
vid smärta	in case of pain
i … dagar	for … days
Besök en läkare när ni kommer hem.	Consult a doctor when you get home.

Parts of the body Kroppsdelar

appendix	**blindtarm** _blind_-tarm
arm	**arm** arm
back	**rygg** rewgg
bladder	**urinblåsa** eu_reen_-blawsa
bone	**ben** behn
breast	**bröst** brurst
chest	**bröstet** _brurstet_
ear	**öra** urra
eye	**öga** urga
face	**ansikte** ansikteh
finger/thumb	**finger/tumme** finger/_teu_mmeh
foot/toe	**fot/tå** foot/taw
gland/tonsils	**körtel/tonsiller** churtel/ton_siller_
hand	**hand** hand
head	**huvud** heuveud
heart	**hjärta** yairta
jaw	**käke** ckairkeh
joint	**led** lehd
kidney	**njure** nyeureh
knee	**knä** knair
leg	**ben** behn
lip	**läpp** lep
liver	**lever** lehver
mouth	**mun** meunn
muscle	**muskel** _meu_skel
neck	**nacke** _nacke_h
nose	**näsa** nairsa
rib	**revben** _rehv_-behn
shoulder	**axel** axel
skin	**hud** heud
stomach	**mage** maageh
thigh	**lår** lawr
throat	**hals** hals
vein	**åder** awdra

Gynecologist Gynekolog

I have …	**Jag har …** *yaag haar*
abdominal pains	**smärtor i buken** *smairtoor ee beuken*
period pains	**menssmärtor** *mens-smairtoor*
a vaginal infection	**en infektion i underlivet** *en infekshoon ee eunder-leevet*
I haven't had my period for … months.	**Jag har inte haft mens på … månader.** *yaag haar inteh haft mens paw … mawnader*
I'm on the Pill.	**Jag tar p-piller.** *yaag taar peh-piller*

Hospital Sjukhus

Please notify my family.	**Var snäll och underrätta min familj.** *vaar snel ock eunder-retta min famil'*
I'm in pain.	**Jag har ont.** *yaag har oont*
I can't eat/sleep.	**Jag kan inte äta/sova.** *yaag kun inteh airta/sawva*
When will the doctor come?	**När kommer doktorn?** *nair kommer doktorn*
Which section [ward] is … in?	**Vilken avdelning ligger … på?** *vilken aavdehlning ligger … paw*
I'm visiting …	**Jag vill besöka …** *yaag vil besurka*

Optician Optiker

I'm near- [short-] sighted/ far- [long-] sighted.	**Jag är närsynt/långsynt.** *yaag air nair-sewnt/long-sewnt*
I've lost …	**Jag har tappat …** *yaag haar tappat*
one of my contact lenses	**en av mina kontaktlinser** *en aav meena kontakt-linser*
my glasses/a lens	**mina glasögon/en lins** *meena glaas-urgon/en lins*
Could you give me a replacement?	**Kan ni ersätta den/dem?** *kun nee airsetta den/dem*

Dentist Tandläkare

I have (a) toothache.	**Jag har tandvärk.**
	yaag haar <u>tand</u>-vairk
This tooth hurts.	**Den här tanden gör ont.**
	den hair tanden yurr oont
I've lost a filling/tooth.	**Jag har tappat en plomb/en tand.**
	yaag har tappat en plomb/en tand
Can you repair this denture?	**Kan ni reparera den här tandprotesen?**
	kun nee repa<u>reh</u>ra den hair <u>tand</u>-protehsen
I don't want it extracted.	**Jag vill inte att ni drar ut tanden.**
	yaag vil inteh at nee draar eut <u>tanden</u>

Jag ska ge er en spruta/ en narkos.	I'm going to give you an injection/an anesthetic.
Ni behöver en plomb/en krona.	You need a filling/cap (crown).
Jag måste dra ut den.	I'll have to take it out.
Jag kan bara laga den tillfälligt.	I can only fix it temporarily.
Ni får inte äta på … timmar.	Don't eat anything for … hours.

Payment and insurance Betalning och försäkring

How much do I owe you?	**Hur mycket är jag skyldig?**
	heur mewcket air yaag <u>shewl</u>dig
I have insurance.	**Jag har försäkring.**
	yaag haar fur<u>sairk</u>ring
Can I have a receipt for my insurance?	**Kan jag få ett kvitto för min försäkring?**
	kun yaag faw et kvittoo fur min fur<u>sairk</u>ring
Would you fill out this insurance form, please?	**Kan ni fylla i den här försäkringsblanketten, tack?** *kun nee fewlla ee den hair fur<u>sairk</u>rings-blan<u>ket</u>ten tuck*

Dictionary
English – Swedish

Most terms in this dictionary are either followed by an example or cross-referenced to pages where the word appears in a phrase. In addition, the notes below provide some basic grammar guidelines.

Nouns

Nouns are either "common gender" or "neuter gender" ➤ 13 and 15. In Swedish, there are five different endings used to form plural nouns.

1. Most **–en** nouns (the majority of which end in **–a**) drop **–a** and add **–or**.
2. **–ar** is the most common plural ending, covering a number of noun groups.
3. Most words taking this ending are foreign in origin, and take **–er/–r** in the plural.
4. Only about 4 percent of nouns take this ending; the singular usually ends in **–e**, the plural in **–n**.
5. The second most common plural ending; these nouns don't have a plural, these are **–ett** words ending in a consonant.

	1 (–or)	2 (–ar)	3 (–er/–r)	4 (–n)	5 (no ending)
	girl	*car*	*family/cow*	*eye*	*house*
Singular	flicka	bil	familj/ko	öga	hus
Plural	flickor	bilar	familjer/kor	ögan	hus

Adjectives

Indefinite form (*a/an;* **en/ett**): adjectives agree in gender (common or neuter) and number with the noun to which they refer. Common (**en**) gender nouns take the base form of the adjective. All adjectives (both **en** and **ett**) modifying plural nouns end in **–a**.

	Singular		Plural	
Common	**en stor kvinna**	a big woman	**två stora kvinnor**	two big women
Neuter	**ett stort hus**	a big house	**två stora hus**	two big houses

Definite form (*the;* **–en/–et**): when an adjective comes before a noun, Swedish uses an "additional definite article", i.e. both a separate word for *the* – **den** or **det** in the singular, **de** in the plural – in front of the adjective and the *the* ending, **–en** or **–et**. The adjective for both genders and singular and plural ends in **–a**.

	Singular		Plural	
Common	**den stora kvinnan**	the big woman	**de stora kvinnorna**	the big women
Neuter	**det stora huset**	the big house	**de stora husen**	the big houses

Verbs

The infinitive of most Swedish verbs ends in **–a**. The present tense of almost all verbs is simple, because it has the same form for all persons and ends in **–r**.

	to be	*to have*	*to come*
Infinitive	**att vara**	**att ha**	**att komma**
Present tense	**är**	**har**	**kommer**

Negation is expressed by using the adverb **inte** (not), usually placed immediately after the verb in a main clause.

a little lite 15
a lot mycket 15
a.m. fm
about *(approximately)* omkring 15
abroad utomlands
accept: to ~ accepterata 136
accident olycka 92, 159
accidentally råka 28
accompany: to ~ följa med 65
accountant revisor 121
acne acne
across *(the road)* över 12
acrylic akryl
actor/actress
skådespelare/skådespelerska
adapter adapter 26, 148
address adress 23, 84, 93, 126
adjoining room angränsande
rum 22
admission charge
inträdesbiljett 114
adult *(noun)* vuxen 81, 100
afraid: I'm ~ *(I'm sorry)* tyvärr 126
after *(time/place)* efter 13, 95, 165
after shave rakvatten 142
after-sun lotion efter-solkräm 142
afternoon: in the ~ på
eftermiddagen 221
aged: to be ~ ålder 159
ago för ... sedan 221; **... years ~**
för ... år sedan 163
agree: I don't ~ det håller jag inte
med om
air luft; **~ conditioning**
luftkonditionering 22, 25;
~ mattress luftmadrass 31;
~ pump luft(slang) 87; **~ sickness
bag** flygsjukpåse 70; **~mail**
flygpost 153; **~port**
flygplats 84, 96
aisle seat plats vid mittgång 69, 74
alarm clock väckarklocka 149

alcoholic *(drink)* alkoholisk
all alla
allergic: to be ~ vara
allergisk 164, 165
allergy allergi
allowance ranson 67
almost nästan
alone ensam: **leave me ~!** lämna
mig ifred! 126
already redan 28
also också 19
alter: to ~ göra ändring 137
alumin(i)um foil
aluminiumfolie 148
always alltid 13
am: I ~ jag är
amazing fantastisk 101
ambassador ambassadör
ambulance ambulans 92
American *(adj.)*
amerikansk 150, 159
American Plan [A.P.] helpension 24
amount *(of money)* summa 42
amusement arcade
spelautomater 113
and och 19
anesthetic narkos 168
animal djur 106
anorak anorak 145
antacid medel mot magsyra
antibiotics antibiotiskt medel 165
antifreeze kylarvätska
antique *(noun)* antikvitet 155
antiseptic antiseptiskt medel 165;
~ cream antiseptisk salva 141
any någon
anyone någon 67; **does ~ speak
English?** talar någon engelska?
anything else? något annat?
apartment lägenhet 28
apologize: I ~ jag ber om ursäkt
appendicitis
blindtarmsinflammation 165

A-Z

be: to ~ vara 17, 121
beach strand 107, 116
beam *(headlights)* helljus 86
beard skägg
beautiful vacker 14, 101
because därför att 15; **~ of** på grund av 15
bed säng 21; **~room** sovrum 29; **~ and breakfast** rum med frukost 24
bedding sängkläder 29
beer öl 40, 157, 158
before *(time)* innan 13, 221; före 165
begin: to ~ börja
beginner nybörjare 117
behind bakom 95
beige beige 143
belong: this belongs to me det här tillhör mig
belt bälte/skärp 144
berth bädd 74, 77
best bästa
better bättre 14
between *(time)* mellan 221; **~ jobs** *(unemployed)* mittemellan jobb 121
bib haklapp
bicycle cykel 75, 83, 160
bidet bidet
big stor 14, 117, 134
bigger större 24
bikini bikini 144
bill nota 42; räkning 32
bin liner soppåse
binoculars kikare
bird fågel 106
birthday födelsedag 219
biscuits kex/småkakor 157, 158
bite *(insect)* bett
bitten: I've been ~ by a dog jag har blivit biten av en hund
bitter beskt 41

bizarre underlig 101
black svart 143; *(coffee)* utan mjölk 40
black and white film *(camera)* svart-vit film 151
bladder urinblåsa 166
blanket täcke 27
bleach klormedel 148
bleeding: he's ~ han blöder 162
blind rullgardin 25
blister blåsa 162
blocked: to be ~ vara stopp i 25
blood blod 164; **~ group** blodgrupp; **~ pressure** blodtryck 163, 164
blouse blus 144
blow-dry föning 147
blue blått 143
board: on ~ ombord 78
boarding card boardingkort 70
boat trip båttur 81, 97
boil böld 162; **boiled** kokt
boiler panna 29
bone ben (i kroppen) 166
book bok 150; **~store** bokhandel 130
booklet of tickets rabatthäfte 79
booted: to be ~ förse med hjullås 87
boots skor, stövlar 115, 145
boring trist 101
born: to be ~ födas 119; **I was ~ in** jag är född i
borrow: may I ~ your ...? får jag låna er ...?
botanical garden botanisk trädgård 99
bottle flaska 37; **~ of wine** en flaska vin 154; **~-opener** flasköppnare 148
bowel tarmar
bowls djupa tallrikar 148
box kartong/påse 110; **~ of chocolates** en chockladask 154

boy pojke 120, 155
boyfriend pojkvän 120
bra behå 144
bracelet armband 149
brakes *(bicycle)* bromsar 83
bread bröd 38, 157
break down: to ~ *(go wrong)* gå
  sönder 88; **the stove has broken
  down** spisen har gått sönder 28
break: to ~ slå sönder 28
breakdown truck
  bärgningsbil 88
breakfast frukost 27
breast bröst 166
breathe, to andas 92, 164
breathtaking hisnande
bridge bro 95, 107
briefs trosor 144
bring, to ta hit/ta med 113, 125
Britain Storbritannien 119
British *(adj.)* engelsk 159
brochure broschyr
broken trasig 137; **to be ~** *(bone)*
  vara brutet 164; vara trasig 25
bronchitis bronkit
brooch brosch 149
brother bror 120
brown brunt 143
browse: to ~ *(in shop)* titta 133
bruise blåmärke 162
bucket hink 155
building byggnad
built: to be ~ byggas 104
bulletin board
  anslagstavla 26
bureau de change
  växelkontor 138
burger hamburgare 40; **~ stand**
  korvstånd, gatukök 35
burn brännsår 162
bus buss 70, 71, 79, 123; **~ route**
  bussfil/busslinje 96; **~ station**
  bussterminal 78; **~ stop**
  busshållplats 65, 96

business affärer/
  affärsvärld 121;
on ~ på affärsresa
  66, 123; **~ class**
  affärsklass 68
busy fullbokat 36; **to be
  ~** *(occupied)* upptagen 125
but men 19
butane gas butangas 30, 31
butcher *(shop)* slaktare/
  charkuteri 130
butter smör 38, 158
button knapp
buy: to ~ köpa 79, 80, 81,
  98, 125, 133
by med 94; **~ bus** med buss 17;
  ~ car med bil 17, 94; **~ train**
  med tåg 17; **~ cash** kontant 17;
  ~ credit card med kreditkort 17;
  (near) nära/vid 36; *(time)*
  vid 221; **~ tomorrow** i
  morgon 13
bye! hej då!

C **cabaret** kabaré 112
  cabin hytt 81
café kafé 35
cagoule vindtät jacka 145
cake kaka 40;
  cakes kakor 158
calendar en kalender 154
call collect: to ~ beställa
  Ba-samtal 127
call for someone: to ~ hämta
  någon 125
call: to ~ *(phone)* ringa 127, 87, 128;
  ringa (efter) 92; **~ the police!** ring
  efter polisen! 92
called: to be ~
  kallas/heta 94
camera kamera 151, 160; **~ case**
  kamerafoldral 151; **~ store**
  fotoaffär 130

A-Z

camp: to ~ tälta, campa; **~site** campingplats 30, 123; **~bed** tältsäng 31

can: I can/I can't jag kan/det kan jag inte 18; **~ I pay** kan jag betala 42

can opener konservöppnare 148

Canada Kanada 119

canal kanal 107

cancel: to ~ avbeställa 68

cancer *(disease)* cancer

candy lite godis 150

cap mössa 144; *(dental)* krona 168

car *(train compartment)* vagn 75

car bil 30, 73, 81, 86, 88, 93, 123, 160; **~ ferry** bilfärja 81; **~ park** parkeringsplats 26, 96; **~ rental** biluthyrning 70; **by ~** med bil 95

carafe karaff 37

caravan husvagn 30

cards kort 121

careful: be ~! var försiktig!

carpet *(rug)* matta

carrier bag: *(in shop)* plastpåse; väska

carry-cot (uttagbar) liggvagn

cart kärra 156

carton påse/kartong 110

case *(suitcase)* väska 69

cash *(money)* kontanter 42; kontant 136; **~ desk** kassa 132; **~ machine** bankomat 139

cash: to ~ lösa in 138

cashier kassa 132

casino kasino 112

cassette kassett 155

castle slott 99

catch: to ~ *(bus)* hinna med

cathedral katedral 99

Catholic katolsk 105

cave grotta 107

CD CD skiva; **~-player** CD spelare

cemetery kyrkogård 99

center of town (i) centrum 21

central heating centralvärme

century talet 155

ceramics keramik

certificate bevis/certifikat 149, 155

chain kedja 149

change *(noun)* växel 84, 87, 136

change: to ~ *(money)* växla 138; *(buses/trains)* byta 75, 79, 80; byta på 39; *(reservation)* boka om, ändra 68

changing facilities skötrum 113

charcoal grillkol 31

charge kostnad/kosta 30; **what is the ~?** vad kostar det? 115, 153

charter flight charterresa

cheap billig 14, 134

cheaper billigare 21, 24, 109, 134

check: please ~ the ... var snäll och kontrollera ...; **to ~ in** checka in 68; **to ~ out** *(hotel)* checka ut 32; **~-in desk** incheckning 69

check book checkbok

cheers! skål

cheese ost 157, 158

chemist apotek 131

cheque book checkbok

chess schack 121; **~ set** schackspel 155

chest bröstet 166

chewing gum tuggummi 150

child barn 159, 162; **~'s cot** barnsäng 22; **~'s seat** barnstol 39

childminder dagmamma (permanent), barnvakt (temporary)

children barn 22, 24, 39, 66, 81, 100, 113, 116, 120, 140

Chinese *(cuisine)* kinesisk 35

chocolate *(flavor)* choklad 40; **~ bar** chokladkaka 150; **~ ice cream [choc-ice]** chokladglass 110

A-Z

cookies kex/småkakor 157, 158
  cooking *(cuisine)* mat; **~ facilities** kokmöjligheter 30
  coolbox fryslåda
copper koppar 149
copy kopia
corkscrew korkskruv 148
correct rätt
cosmetics kosmetika
cost: to ~ kosta 84, 89
cottage stuga 28
cotton bomull 145; *(cotton wool)* bomullsvadd 141
cough: to ~ hosta 141, 164
could I have …? kan jag få …? 18
country *(nation)* land; **~ music** country and western 111
courier *(guide)* guide
course *(medication)* medel, medicin 165; *(meal)* rätt; *(track, path)* led/stig/väg 106
cousin kusin
cover charge kuvertavgift 112
craft shop hantverksaffär
cramps kramp 163
crèche barnpassning
credit card kreditkort 42, 109, 136, 139, 160; **~ number** kreditkortsnummer 109
crib barnsäng 22
crisps chips 157
crockery porslin 29
cross *(crucifix)* kors
cross: to ~ korsa (över) 95
crowded för mycket folk 31
crown *(dental)* krona 168
cruise *(noun)* kryssning
crutches kryckor
crystal *(quartz)* kristall 149
cup kopp 39, 148
cupboard skåp

currency valuta 67, 138; **~ exchange** växelkontor 70, 73, 138
curtains gardiner
customs tull 67, 155
cut skärsår 162; *(hair)* klippa 147; **~ glass** slipat glas 149
cutlery matbestick 29
cycle route cykelled 106
cycling cykel 114
cystitis urinvägsinfektion 165

D **daily** dagligen
  damaged: to be ~ skadad(t) 28, 71
damp *(noun/adj.)* fukt/fuktig
dance *(noun)* dans 111; **to ~** dansa 111; **to go dancing** gå och dansa 124
dangerous farlig
dark mörk 14, 24, 134, 143; **darker** mörkare 143
daughter dotter 120, 162
dawn gryning 221
day dag 23, 97, 122, 221; **~ ticket** dagsbiljett; **~ trip** dagstur
dead *(battery)* vara slut 88
deaf: to be ~ vara döv 163
December december 218
deck chair solstol 116
declare: to ~ förtulla 67
deduct: to ~ *(money)* dra ifrån
deep djup
deep freeze frysbox
defrost: to ~ tina
degrees *(temperature)* grader
delay försening 70
delicatessen delikatessaffär 156
delicious härlig 14
deliver: to ~ leverera
denim denim/jeanstyg 145
Denmark Danmark 119
dental floss tandfloss

dentist tandläkare 131, 168
denture tandprotes 168
deodorant deodorant 142
depart: to ~ *(train, bus)* avgå
department store varuhus 96, 130
departure lounge avgångshall
deposit handpenning 24, 83
describe: to ~ beskriva 159
details detaljer
detergent tvättmedel 148
develop: to ~ *(photos)* framkalla 151
diabetes sockersjuka, diabet
diabetic *(noun)* diabetiker 39; **to be ~** vara diabetiker 163
dialling code landsnummer/ riktnummer 127
diamond diamant 149
diapers blöjor 142
diarrhea diarré 141; **to have ~** ha diarré 163; **I have ~** jag har diarré
dice tärning
dictionary lexikon 150
diesel diesel 87
diet: I'm on a ~ jag håller diet
difficult svår 14
dining: ~ car restaurangvagn 75, 77; **~ room** matsal 26, matrum 29
dinner: to have ~ äta middag 124
dinner jacket smoking
direct *(train, journey, etc.)* direkt 75; **to ~** *(to a place)* visa 18
direction: in the ~ of ... i riktning mot ... 95
director *(company)* direktör
directory *(telephone)* telefonkatalog
dirty smutsig 14, 28
disabled *(noun)* rörelsehindrad 22, 100
discotheque diskotek 112
discount rabatt 24

dish *(meal)* rätt 37, 39; **~cloth** disktrasa 148; **~washing liquid** diskmedel 148
dislocated: to be ~ vara ur led 164
display: ~ cabinet vitrin 149; **~ case** vitrin 134
disposable camera engångskamera 151
distilled water destillerat vatten
disturb: don't ~ stör ej/stör inte
dive: to ~ dyka 116
diving equipment dykarutrustning 116
divorced: to be ~ vara skild 120
dizzy: I feel ~ jag känner mig yr
do: to ~ göra 123; **what ~ you ~?** vad sysslar du med? 121
doctor doktor 92, 167, 131, 155
dollar dollar 67, 138
door dörr 25, ytterdörr 29
double dubbel 81; **~ bed** dubbelsäng 21; **~ room** dubbelrum 21
downtown *(town center)* centrum 83, 99
dozen: a ~ ett dussin 217
dress klänning 144
drink *(noun)* drink 125, 126; **drinks** drinkar 37
drinking water dricksvatten 30
drip: to ~: the faucet [tap] ~s kranen droppar
drive: to ~ köra 93
driver chaufför; **~'s license** körkort 93
drop someone off: to ~ släppa av någon 83
drowning: someone is ~ någon drunknar
drugstore apotek 130
drunk full
dry cleaner kemtvätt 131
dry-clean: to ~ kemtvätta

A-Z

dubbed: to be ~ dubbad 110
dummy *(pacifier)* tröstnapp
during under 221
dustbins sopptunnor 30
duvet täcke

E e-mail e-post 153; ~ **address** e-postadress 153
ear öra 166; **~drops** örondroppar; **~ache** ont i örat 163; **~rings** örhängen 149
early tidig 14, 221; **earlier** tidigare 125, 147
east öster 95
Easter Påsk 219
easy lätt 14
eat: to ~ äta 123, 139, 167
economy class turistklass 68
eggs ägg 157
elastic *(adj.)* elastisk
electric: ~ [electricity] meter elmätare 28; **~ shaver** elektrisk rakapparat
electrical outlets nätuttag 30
electronic elektrisk/elektronisk 69; **~ flash** elektronisk blixt 151; **~ game** elektroniskt spel 155
elevator hiss 26, 132
else: something ~ något annat
embassy ambassad
emerald smaragd
emergency nödsituation 127; **~ exit** nödutgång 132
empty tom 14
enamel emalj 149
end: to ~ sluta 108; **at the ~** i slutet 95
engaged: to be ~ vara förlovad 120
engine motor
engineering teknologi 121
England England 119

English *(language)* engelska 11, 67, 100, 110, 150, 159; **~-speaking** engelsk-talande 98, 159
enjoy: to ~ tycka om 110, 124
enjoyable trevlig 32
enlarge: to ~ *(photos)* förstora 151
enough nog/tillräckligt 15, 42, 136
ensuite bathroom bad på rummet, eget badrum
entertainment guide nöjesguide
entrance fee inträde 100
entry visa visum
envelope kuvert 150
epileptic: to be ~ vara epileptiker 163
equipment *(sports)* utrustning 115
era period 155
error fel
escalator rulltrappa 132
essential som behövs, nödvändig 89
EU EU
Eurocheque eurocheck
evening kväll 109, 124, 132; **in the ~** på kvällen 221
every varje 119; **~ day** varje dag; **~ hour** varje timme 76; **~ week** varje vecka 13
examination *(medical)* undersökning
example: for ~ till exempel
except utom
excess baggage övervikt 69
exchange: to ~ byta 137, växla 138; **~ rate** växelkursen 138
excursion utflykt/rundtur 97
excuse me *(apology)* förlåt mig 10; *(attention)* ursäkta 10; *(getting past someone)* ursäkta mig 10, 94; **excuse me? [pardon?]** förlåt 11

178

exhausted: I'm ~ jag är uttröttad 106
exit utfart 83, 70; utgång 132
expensive dyr 14, 134
experienced ha erfarenhet 117
expiration [expiry] date: when is the ~? när löper det ut? 109
exposure *(photos)* exponering 151
express express 153
extension anknytning 128
extra *(additional)* extra 23; *(adj.)* extra/en … til 27
extract: to ~ *(tooth)* dra ut 168
eye öga 166

F **fabric** tyg 145
face ansikte 166
facial ansiktsbehandling 147
facilities bekvämligheter 22, möjligheter 30
factor … faktor 142
faint: to feel ~ känna sig yr 163
fairground nöjesfält 113
fall höst 219
family familj 66, 74, 120, 167
famous berömd
fan *(air)* fläkt 25
far långt 12, 95, 130; how ~ is it? hur långt är det? 73, 94, 106
far-sighted långsynt 167
farm bondgård 107
fast fort/snabb 17, 93; *(of clock)* fort 221
fast-food restaurant grillbar 35
father far 120
faucet kran 25
faulty: this is ~ det är fel på den
favorite favorit
fax fax 22, 153; ~ machine faxmaskin 153
February februari 218
feed: to ~ mata 39

feeding bottle barnflaska
feel ill: to ~ må dåligt 163
female av kvinnligt kön 159
ferry färja 81, 123
fever feber 163
few få 15
fiancé(e) fästman/fästmö
field äng, fält 107
fifth femte 217
fight *(brawl)* slagsmål, bråk
fill out: to ~ *(a form)* fylla i 168
fill up: to ~ fylla 87
filling *(dental)* plomb(ering) 168
film *(movie)* film 108, 110; *(camera)* 151
filter filter 151
find: to ~ hitta 18
fine fint 19; *(well)* bra 118
fine *(penalty)* böter 93
finger finger 166
Finland Finland 119
fire: there's a ~! det brinner!; ~ alarm brandlarm; ~ department [brigade]; randkåren 92; ~ escape/~ exit brandutgång 132; ~ extinguisher eldsläckare, brandsläckare; ~wood ved
first först(a) 75, 81, 68, 217; ~ class första klass 68, 74; *(floor)* bottenvåning 132
fish fisk: ~ restaurant fiskrestaurang 35; ~ store [fishmonger] fiskaffär 130
fit: to ~ *(clothes)* passa 146
fitting room provrum 146
fix: to ~ laga 168
flashlight ficklampa 31
flat *(tire [tyre])* punktering 83, 88
flavor: what ~s do you have? vad har ni för smaker?

A-Z

flea loppa
flight flyg 68, 70;
  ~ number
  flygnummer 68
flip-flops
  badsandaler 145
floor (*level*) våning 132
florist blomsteraffär 130
flower blomma 106
flu influensa 165
flush: the toilet won't ~ toaletten
  spolar inte
fly (*insect*) fluga
foggy: to be ~ dimmigt 122
folk: ~ art folkkonst, folkhantverk;
  ~ music folkmusik 111
follow: to ~ följa 95; (*pursue*) följa
  efter 159
food mat 39, 119; **~ poisoning**
  matförgiftning 165
foot fot 166; **~ball** fotboll 114;
  ~path fotstig 107
for till, för 94; **~ a day** för en
  dag 86; **~ a week** för en
  vecka 86; **~ two hours** i två
  timmar 13
foreign currency utländsk
  valuta 138
forest skog 107
forget: to ~ glömma 42
fork gaffel 39, 41; **forks** gafflar 148
form blankett 168; formulär 23
formal dress klä sig formellt 111
fortnight två veckor
fortunately lyckligtvis 19
fountain fontänen 99
four-door car bil med fyra
  dörar 86
four-wheel drive (*car*) bil med
  fyrhjulsdrift 86
fourth fjärde 217
foyer (*hotel, theater*) foajé
fracture benbrott 165
frame (*glasses*) ramar

free (*available*) ledig 36, 124;
  (*of charge*) gratis 69
freezer frys 29
French fries pommes frites 38
Frenchdressing vinaigrette
  sås,dressing 38
frequent: how ~? hur ofta? 76;
  frequently ofta
fresh färsk(t) 41
Friday fredag 218
fried stekt
friend vän 123, 125, 162;
  friendly vänlig
fries pommes frites 40
frightened: to be ~ vara rädd
from från 12, 70, 73; **~ ... to**
  (*time*) från ... till 13; från klockan
  ... till 221; **where are
  you ~?** var kommer du
  ifrån? 119
front (*fringe*) framtill 147
frosty: to be ~ vara frost 122
frying pan stekpanna 29
fuel (*gasoline [petrol]*) bensin 86
full full 14; **~ board** helpension 24;
  ~ up (*restaurant, etc.*)
  fullbokat 36; **to be ~** fullbelagt 21
fun: to have ~ ha roligt,
  ha kul
funny roligt 126
furniture möbler
fuse säkring 28; **~ box**
  säkringar 28

G **game** spel 114, 155
  garage bilverkstad 88,
  garage 26
garbage bags soppåsar 148
garden trädgård 35
gas: ~ bottle gascylinder 28;
  I smell ~! det luktar gas!
gas(oline) bensin 88; **~ station**
  bensinstation 87
gastritis magkatarr 165
gate (*airport*) gate, spärr 70

gauze gasbinda 141
gay club gayklubb 112
genuine äkta 134
get: to ~ back *(return)* komma
tillbaka 98; **to ~ off** *(bus, etc.)*
stiga av 79; **to ~ to** anlända 77;
komma till 70; **how do I ~ to ...?**
hur kommer jag till ...? 73, 94;
to ~ *(buy, find)* få tag på 30, 84
gift gåva 67, present 154; **~ shop**
presentaffär 130
girl flicka 120, 155; **~friend**
flickvän 120
give: to ~ ge 136
gland körtel 166
glass glas 37, 39, 148
glasses *(optical)*
glasögon 167
glossy finish *(photos)* glansig,
blank
glove handske
go: to ~ gå 18; *(move)* köra,
åka 93; *(take away)* ta med 40;
~ on fortsätt 19; **~ away!** gå
iväg, ge er iväg!; **to ~ for a walk**
gå på en promenad 124; **to ~ out
for a meal** gå ut och äta 124; **to
~ out** *(in evening)* gå ut; **to
~ shopping**, gå och shoppa 124;
to ~ to gå till 124, resa till 66; **let's
~!** kom, så går vi!; **where does
this bus ~?** vart går den här
bussen?
goggles skyddsglasögon
gold guld 149; **~ plate**
gulddoublé 149
golf golf 114; **~ course**
golfbana 115
good bra 14, 35, god 42;
~ afternoon god middag 10;
~ evening god afton 10;
~ morning god morgon 10;
~ night god natt 10; **to be a
~ value** god valuta 101
good-bye adjö/hej då 10

grandparents
(father's/mother's)
farföräldrar/
morföräldrar
grapes vindruvor 158
grass gräs
gray grått 143
graze skrubbsår 162
great bra 19
green grönt 143
greengrocer
grönsaksaffär 130
grilled grillad
grocer *(grocery store)* matvaruaffär,
livsmedelsaffär
ground *(earth)* mark 31; **~ floor**
(U.S. first floor) bottenvåningen;
~cloth [groundsheet]
tältunderlag 31
group turistgrupp/grupp 66;
groups grupper 100
guarantee garanti 135
guesthouse pensionat 123
guide *(tour)* guide 98; **~book**
guidebok 100, 150
guided: ~ tour guidad tur 100;
~ walk guidade vandringar 106
guitar gitarr
gum *(teeth)* tandkött; *(material)*
gummi
guy rope tältlina 31
gynecologist gynekolog 167

H **hemorrhoids** hemorroider
hair hår 147; **~ mousse**
hårmousse 142; **~ spray**
hårspray 142; **~cut** klippning;
~dresser *(women/men)*
damfrisör/herrfrisör 131, 147
half: a ~ en halva 217; **~ board**
halvpension 24; **~ past seven**
halv åtta 220
ham skinka 157
hammer hammare 31

A-Z

A-Z

hand hand 166; **~ baggage** handbagage 69; **~ washable** handtvätt 145; **~bag** handväska 144, 160
handicap *(golf)* handikapp
handicapped: to be ~ vara rörelsehindrad 163
handicrafts hantverk
handkerchief näsduk
hanger hängare 27
hangover *(noun)* baksmälla 141
happen: to ~ hända 93
happy: I'm not ~ with the service jag är inte belåten med betjäningen
harbor hamn
hard hård 31; *(difficult)* svår/jobbig 106
hat hatt 144
have: to ~ få/ha 70, 133; na 120; *(food)* äta 42; **can I ~ ...?** kan jag få ...? 18; **I ~ two children** jag har två barn 18; **could I ~ ...?** kan jag få ...? 38; **does the hotel ~ (a/an) ...?** finns det ... på hotellet? 22; **I'll ~ ...** jag tar ... 37
hay fever hösnuva 141
head huvud 166; **~ waiter** hovmästaren 41; **~ache** huvudvärk 163
heading: to be ~ *(in a direction)* vara på väg 83
health: ~ food store hälsokostaffär 130; **~ insurance** hälsoförsäkring 168
hear: to ~ höra
hearing aid hörselapparat
heart hjärta 166; **~ attack** hjärtattack 163; **hearts** *(cards)* hjärter
heat värme 25; *(heating)* (central)värme 25

heater element
heavy tung 14, 69, 134; *(snow)* djup 117
height hur lång/längd 159
hello hej 10, 118
help: can you ~ me? kan ni hjälpa mig? 18, 92, 133
hemorrhoids hemorroider 165
here här 17, 31, 35, 77, 106, 119; *(to here)* hit 12
hernia bråck 165
hers hennes 16; **it's ~** den är hennes
hi! hejsan! 10
high hög 122, 163
highlight: to ~ *(hair)* göra blonda slingor 147
highway motorväg 88, 92, 94
hiking fotvandra, luffa; **~ gear** vandringsutrustning
hill kulle 107
him honom 16
hire hyra 83
his hans 16; **it's ~** den är hans
historic site historisk plats 99
HIV-positive HIV positiv
hobby *(pastime)* hobby/intresse 121
hold on: to ~ *(wait)* vänta 128
hole *(in clothes)* hål
holiday semester 123; **~ resort** semesterort; **on ~** på semester 66
home hem 126; **we're going ~** vi ska åka hem
homosexual *(adj.)* homosexuell
honeymoon: we're on ~ vi är på bröllopsresa
hopefully förhoppningsvis 19
horse häst; **~-racing** hästkapplöpning 114
hospital sjukhus 96, 131, 164, 167

hot hett 14, 122; **~ dog** varm korv 110; **~ water** varmvatten 25

hotel hotell 21, 123

hour timme 97, 116; **in an ~** om en timme 84

house hus; **~wife** hemmafru 121

hovercraft svävare 81

how? hur 17; **~ are things?** hur är det? 19; **how long ...?** *(time)* hur länge ...? 23, 68, 75, 76, 78, 88, 94, 98, 106, 135; **~ many times ...?** hur många gånger ...? 140; **~ many ...?** hur många ...? 15, 79, 80; **~ much** hur mycket 15, 21, 65, 68, 79, 89, 100, 109, 136, 140; **~ old** hur gammal 120, 155; **~ are you?** hur står det till? 118

hundred hundra 217

hungry: I'm ~ jag är hungrig

hurry: I'm in a ~ jag har bråttom

hurt: to ~ göra ont 164; **to be ~** bli skadad 92, 162; **my ... ~s** jag har ont i min/mitt ... 162

husband man 120, 162

I **I'd like ...** jag skulle vilja ... 18

I've lost jag har tappat

ice is 38; **~ cream** glass/glace 40; **~-cream parlor** glasstånd 35

icy med skare 117; **to be ~** fruset 122

identification ID-kort, identifikation

ill: I'm ~ jag är sjuk

illegal: is it ~? är det olagligt?

imitation imitation 134

in *(place)* i 12, 88; *(within period of time)* om 13; **~ front of** framför 125

include ingå i/inkludera 24; **to be included** inräknad 42; **is ... included?** är ... inkluderad? 86, 98

incredible otrolig 101

indicate: to ~ visa, ange

indigestion dålig matsmältning

indoor pool inomhusbassäng 116

inexpensive billigare 35

infected: to be ~ vara infekterat 165

infection infektion 167

inflammation inflammation 165

informal *(dress)* vardagsklädsel

information information 97; **~ desk** information 73; **~ office** informationskontor/turistbyrå 96

injection spruta 168

injured: to be ~ bli skadad 92, 162

innocent oskyldig

insect insekt 25; **~ bite/sting** insektsbett 141, 162; **~ repellent** insektsmedel 141

inside inne i 12

insist: I ~ jag insisterar

insomnia sömnlöshet

instant coffee snabb-kaffe 158

instead of istället för 38

instructions bruksanvisning 135

instructor instruktör, lärare

insulin insulin

insurance försäkring 86, 89, 93, 160, 168; **~ card [certificate]** försäkringsbrev 93; **~ claim** försäkringskrav 160

interest *(hobby)* hobby/intresse 121; **to be interested in** vara intresserad av 111; **interesting** intressant 101

International Student Card internationellt studentkort 29

Internet Internet 153

interpreter tolk 160

intersection korsning 95

A-Z

into in till 70
introduce oneself: to ~
presentera sig 118
invite: to ~ bjuda 124
iodine jodin
Ireland Irland 119
is: ~ it …? är det …? 17;
~ there …? är det …? 17;
it ~ … det är … 17
Italian *(cuisine)* italiensk 35
itch: it itches det kliar
item artikel 69
itemized bill specificerad
räkning 32

J
jacket jacka 144
jam sylt 157
jammed: to be ~ sitta fast 25
January januari 218
jaw käke 166
jazz jazz 111
jeans jeans 144
jellyfish manet
jet lag: I'm lagged jag lider av
jetlag
jet-ski jet-ski 116
jeweler juvelerare 130,
guldsmed 149
job: what's your ~? vad sysslar
ni/du med?
join: to ~ vara med, gå i 117; **to
~ in** vara med 115; **can we ~ you**
får vi följa med/göra sällskap 124
joint *(noun)* led 166; **~ passport**
gemensamt pass 66
joke skämt
journalist journalist
journey resa 76, 78
jug *(of water)* kanna
July juli 218
jump leads startkablar
jumper jumper, tröja

junction *(intersection)* vägkorsning;
korsning 95
June juni 218

K
keep: to ~ behålla 84;
~ the change! behåll växeln!
kerosene fotogen; **~ stove**
primuskök 31
ketchup ketchup, tomatsås
kettle vattenkokare 29
key nyckel 27, 28, 88; **~ ring**
nyckelring 154
kiddie pool barnbassäng 113
kidney njure 166
kilometer kilometer 88
kind *(pleasant)* snäll, trevlig
kind: what ~ of … vad för slags …
kiss: to ~ pussa, kyssa
kitchen kök 29
knapsack ryggsäck 31, 145
knee knä 166
knickers trosor
knife kniv 39, 41; **knives**
knivar 148
know: to ~ känna till 146
kosher koscher
krona kronor 67

L
label etikett
lace spets 145
ladder stege
lake sjö 107
lamp lampa 25, 29
land: to ~ *(airplane)* landa 70
language course språkkurs
large stor 40, 69, 110; **larger**
större 134
last sista 14, 68, 75, 80, 81; *(Tuesday,
etc.)* förra 218
last: to ~ räcka
late *(delayed)* försenat 70; sen 14,
221; **later** senare 125, 147

laundromat snabbtvätt 131
laundry: ~ facilities
  tvättmöjligheter 30; **~ service**
  tvättservice 22
lavatory toalett
lawyer advokat 159
laxative laxativ
lead: to ~ *(in a direction)* gå till,
  leda till 94
lead-free blyfri 87
leader *(group)* gruppledare
leak: to ~ *(roof, pipe)* läcka
learn: to ~ *(language)* lära sig
leather läder 145
leave: to ~ *(av)*gå 41, 70, 73, 76,
  81, 126; åka/fara 98; resa
  (till) 32, 70; lämna 41; **I've left my
  bag** jag har lämnat min väska;
  (plane) flyga 68
left: on the ~ till vänster 76, 95
left-luggage office
  effektförvaring 71, 73
leg ben 166
legal: is it ~? är det lagligt?
leggings tights 144
lemon citron 38
lemonade sockerdricka 158
lend: could you ~ me ...? kan
  ni/du låna mig ...?
length längd
lens objektiv 151; **~ cap** linsskydd
  151; *(in glasses)* lins 167;
lesbian club lesbisk klubb
less mindre 15
lesson lektion 115
let: ~ me know! hör av dig, låt mig
  få veta!
letter brev 152; **~box** postlåda
level *(adj.)* jämn 31
library bibliotek
lie down: to ~ ligga ner 164
life liv; **~belt** livbälte; **~boat**
  livbåt; **~guard** livräddare 116;
  ~jacket livväst

lift *(hitchhiking)*
  lifta 83
lift hiss 26, 132;
  ~ pass liftpass 117
light: *(lamp/color)*
  ljus 14, 25, 83,
  134, 143; *(weight)* lätt 14, 134;
  ~ bulb glödlampa 148; **lighter**
  ljusare 143, 150
like: to ~ tycka om 101, 119,
  121, 125, 135, gilla 101, trivas 119;
  I'd ~ ... jag skulle vilja...
  37, 40, 141, 157, jag vill ha ... 141;
  don't ~ it jag tycker inte om det;
  I ~ it jag tycker om det
like this *(similar to)*
  som den här
limousine limousine, lyxbil
line *(subway)* linje 80
linen linne 145
lip läpp 166; **~stick** läppstift
liqueur likör
liquor store systembolag 131
liter liter 87
little *(small)* liten
live: to ~ bo 119; **~ together**
  bo ihop 120
liver lever 166
living room vardagsrum 29
lobby *(theater, hotel)* foajé
local regional 35; för den här
  regionen 37
lock: to ~ låsa 88; *(noun)* lås 25; **to
  ~ oneself out** låsa ut sig 27
log on: to ~ logga in 153
long lång 144, 146; **~-distance bus**
  långfärdsbuss 78; **~-sighted**
  långsynt 167
look: to ~ for leta efter 18, 133; **I'm
  ~ing for ...** jag söker ... 143; **to
  ~ like** se ut 71; **I'm just ~ing** jag
  tittar bara
loose lös 146
lorry lastbil

lose: to ~ förlora 28, 138, 160, tappa 138, 160; **I've lost ...** jag har förlorat ... 71; **lost-and-found [lost property office]** hittegodsexpedition 73; **lost: I'm lost** jag har kommit vilse 106; **lost: I've lost ...** jag har förlorat/ jag har tappat ... 100, 160

lots of fun mycket rolig

louder högre 128

love: to ~ tycka om 119; **I ~ you** jag älskar dig

lovely härlig 122, underbar 125

low låg 122, 163; **~-fat** mager

lower (berth) underbädd 74

luck: good ~ lycka till 219

luggage bagage 32, 69, 71; **~ carts [trolleys]** bagagekärror 71

lump knöl 162

lunch lunch 98, 152

lung lunga

M machine washable maskintvätt 145

madam damen

magazine veckotidning 150

magnificent storslagen 101

maid städerska 27, 28

mail (noun) post 27, 152; **by ~ post** per post 22; **to ~** posta 27; **~box** postlåda 152

main största/förnämsta 130; **~ street** huvudgata 95

make up: to ~ göra iordning 140

make-up makeup

male av manligt kön 159

mallet klubba/trähammare 31

man man

manager chef 41, 137; direktör 25

manicure manikyr 147

manual (car) med växel

many många 15

map karta 94, 106, 150

March mars 218

margarine margarin 158

market torg 99

married: to be ~ vara gift 120

mascara maskara

mask (diving) mask

mass gudstjänst 105

massage massage 147

mat finish (photos) matt

match (sport) match 114

matches tändstickor 31, 148, 150

matinée matiné 109

matter: it doesn't ~ det spelar ingen roll; **what's the ~?** vad står på/vad har hänt?

mattress madrass

May maj 218

may I får jag 18

maybe kanske

me mig 16

meal varmrätt 38; måltid 42, 70, 125, 165,

mean: what does this ~? vad betyder det här? 11

measles mässlingen 165

measure: to ~ mäta 146

measurement mått

meat kött 41

mechanic mekaniker 88

medication medicin 164, 165

medicine medicin 141

medium mitt emellan 122, vanlig/medium 40

meet: to ~ träffas 125; **pleased to ~ you** trevligt att träffas 118

meeting place [point] mötesplats 12

member (club) medlem 88, 112, 115

men (toilets) herrtoalett

mention: don't ~ it ingen orsak 10

menu meny

message meddelande 27

metal metall

metro: ~ map tunnelbanekarta 80;
~ station tunnelbanestation
80, 96

microwave *(oven)* mikrougn

midday mitt på dagen

midnight midnatt 13, pånatten 220

migraine migrän

milk mjölk 157

milk: with ~ med mjölk 40

million million 217

mind: do you ~? har du/ni något
emot? 77, 126

mine min 16; **it's ~!**
den är min!

mineral water
mineralvatten

mini-bar mini-bar 32

minimart närbutik 156

minute minut

mirror spegel

missing: to be ~ komma
bort/saknas 137, 159

mistake fel 32, 41, 42

misunderstanding: there's been a ~
det har blivit ett missförstånd

mobile home mobilt hus

Modified American Plan [M.A.P.]
halvpension 24

moisturizer *(cream)*
fuktighetskräm

monastery kloster 99

Monday måndag 218

money pengar
139, 160; **~ order** postanvisning

month månad 218

moped moped 83

more mer 15, 67, 94; **I'd like
some ~ …** jag skulle vilja ha
lite mer … 39

morning: in the ~ på morgonen 221

mosque moské 105

mosquito bite myggbett

mother mor 120

motion sickness
åksjuka 141

motorbike
motorcykel 83

motorboat
motorbåt 116

motorway motorväg 94, 92

mountain berg 107; **~ bike**
mountainbike; **~ pass**
bergspass 107; **~ range**
bergskedja 107

moustache mustasch

mouth mun 164, 166; **~ ulcer**
munsår

move: to ~ flytta 25, 92; **don't
~ him!** flytta honom inte! 92

movie film 108; **~ theater**
bio(graf) 110

Mr. herr

Mrs. fru

much mycket 15

mugged: to be ~ bli överfallen 160

mugging överfall 159

mugs muggar 148

mumps påssjukan

muscle muskel 166

museum muséum 99

music musik 112, 121

musician musiker

must: I ~ jag måste

mustard senap 38

my min 16

myself: I'll do it ~ jag gör det själv

N **name** namn
22, 36, 93,
118, 120; **my ~ is** mitt namn
är/jag heter 118; **what's your ~?**
vad heter ni/du? 118

napkin servett 39

nappies blöjor 142

narrow smal 14

national *(adj./citizen)*
lands-/medborgare

nationality nationalitet 23
nature: ~ reserve naturreservat 107; **~ trail** naturstig 107
nausea illamående
near nära 12, 84; **~ here** i närheten 35; **~-sighted** närsynt 167; **~by** här intill 21, i närheten 87, 115; **~est** närmaste 80, 88, 92, 127, 130, 140
necessary: is it ~? behöver man? 112
neck nacke 147, 166; **~lace** halsband 149
need: I ~ to … jag behöver … 18
nephew *(brother's/sister's)* brorsson/systerson
nerve nerv
nervous system nervsystem
never aldrig 13; **~ mind** det spelar ingen roll 10
New Year Nyår 219
New Zealand Nya Zealand 119
new ny 14
news: ~paper tidning 150; **~stand [~agent]** tidningskiosk/tidningsaffär 131, 150
next näst(a) 14, 68, 75, 78, 80, 81, 94, 100; på 218; **~ stop!** nästa hållplats! 79; **~ to** bredvid/intill 12, 95
nice trevlig 14, rar
niece *(brother's/sister's)* brorsdotter /systerdotter
night: at ~ på natten 221; **for two ~s** *(in hotel)* för två nätter 22; **~club** nattklubb 112
no way! uteslutet! 19
no nej 10; **~ one** ingen 16, 92
noisy bullrigt 24, störande 14
non-alcoholic utan alkohol
non-smoking icke-rökare 36, 69

none ingen 15
nonsense! dumheter! 19
noon klockan tolv på dagen 220
normal tillåten/normal 67
north norr 95
Norway Norge 119
nose näsa 166
not inte; **~ bad** inte dåligt 19; **~ yet** inte ännu 13
nothing ingenting 16; **~ else** inget annat 15
notify: to ~ underrätta 167
November november 218
now nu 13, 32, 84
number nummer 138; **~ plate** nummerskylt; **sorry, wrong ~** förlåt, jag har fått fel nummer
nurse sjuksköterska
nylon nylon

O o'clock: it's … ~ klockan är … 220
occasionally ibland
occupied upptagen 14
October oktober 218
odds *(betting)* vinstchans 114
of course naturligtvis 19
off-licence systembolag 131
off-peak lågsäsong
office kontor
often ofta 13
oil olja 38
okay okej 10, 19
old gammal 14; **~ town** gamla stan 99
olive oil olivolja
omelet omelett 40
on *(day, date)* på 13; **~ foot** till fots 17, 95; **~ the left** till vänster 12; **~ the right** till höger 12; **to be ~** *(film, etc.)* på 110

on/off switch av/på kontakt
once en gång 217; **~ a day** en gång om dagen 76
one like that en sån där 16
one-way ticket enkel biljett 65, 68, 74, 79
open öppen 14; **to ~** öppna 77, 100, 132, 140, 152, 164,
open-air pool utomhusbassäng 116
opening hours öppet/ öppettider 100
opera opera 108, 111; **~ house** opera 99
operation operation
opposite mitt emot 12, 95
optician optiker 131, 167
or eller 19
orange *(color)* orange 143; **oranges** apelsiner 158
orchestra orkester 111
order: to ~ beställa 32, 37, 41, 135, skaffa
organized hike/walk organiserad vandring
our vår 16
outdoor utomhus
outrageous alldeles för dyrt 89
outside utanför 12, ute 36
oval oval 134
oven ugn
over: ~ here här 157; **~ there** där borta 36, 157; **I've been ~charged** ni har tagit för mycket betalt; **~done** för mycket stekt 41; **~heat** för hög värme; **~night** över natten 23
owe: to ~ vara skyldig 168; **how much do I ~?** hur mycket blir jag skyldig?
own: I'm on my ~ jag är ensam 66; **on my ~** ensam 65, 120
owner ägare

P **p.m.** em
pacifier tröstnapp
pack: to ~ packa 69
package paket 153
packed lunch matsäck
paddling pool barnbassäng 113
padlock hänglås
pail hink 155
pain: to be in ~ ha ont 167; **~killer** smärtstillande medel 141, 165
paint: to ~ måla; **~er** målare; **~ing** målning
pair: a ~ of ett par 217
palace slott 99
palpitations hjärtklappning
panorama panorama 107
pants *(U.S.)* (lång)byxor 144
panty hose strumpbyxor 144
paper napkins pappersservetter
paracetamol värktabletter
paraffin paraffin 31
paralysis förlamning
parcel paket 153
parents föräldrar 120
park park 96, 99, 107
parking: ~ lot parkeringsplats 26, 87, 96; **~ meter** parkeringsmätare 87
parliament building riksdagshus 99
partner *(boyfriend/girlfriend)* sambo (pojkvän/flickvän)
party *(social)* fest 124
pass: to ~ *(a place)* passera 77
passport pass 23, 66, 69, 160; **~ number** passnummer 23
pasta pasta 38
pastry store konditori 131
patch: to ~ laga 137
patient *(noun)* patient

pavement: on the ~ på trottoaren

pay phone allmän telefon

pay: to ~ betala 42, 136; **can I ~ in ...** kan jag betala med 67

payment betalning

peak topp 107

pearl pärla 149

pebbly *(beach)* stenig 116

pedestrian: ~ crossing övergångsställe 96; **~ zone [precinct]** gågata 96

pen kulspetspenna 150

people människor 119, någon (människa), några 92

pepper peppar 38

per: ~ day per dag 30, 83, 86, 87, 115; **~ hour** i timme 87, per timme 115, 153; **~ night** per natt 21, 24; **~ round** *(golf)* per runda 115; **~ week** per vecka 24, 30, 83, 86

perhaps kanske 19

period *(menstrual)* mens(truation) 167; **~ pains** menssmärtor 167

perm: to ~ permanenta 147

person person 93

petrol bensin 88; **~ station** bensinstation 87

pewter tenn 149

pharmacy apotek 131, 140, 156

phone: ~ call (telefon)samtal 159; **~ card** telefonkort 127, 153; **to ~** ringa

photo: to take a ~ ta ett foto; **~graph** foto 98; **~grapher** fotograf

photocopier kopiator 153

phrase uttryck 11; **~ book** språkguide 11

pick up: to ~ hämta 28

picnic picknick; **~ area** picknickområde/rastplats 107

piece *(item)* stycke 69

piece: a ~ of ... en bit ... 40

pill *(contraceptive)* p-piller 167; tablett 165

pillow kudde 27; **~ case** örngott

pilot light tändlåga

pink rosa 143

pipe *(smoking)* pipa

pitch *(camping)* tältplats

pizza pizza 40

pizzeria pizzeria 35

place a bet: to ~ spela totto 114

plane plan, flygplan 68, 123

plans planer 124

plant *(noun)* planta, växt

plaster plåster 141

plastic: ~ bags plastpåsar; **~ wrap** plastfolie 148

plate tallrik 39, 148

platform plattform 73, 76, 77

platinum platina 149

play teaterpjäs 108; **to ~** spela 110, 111, 114, 121; **~ground** lekplats 113; **~group** lekgrupp 113; **~ing field** lekplats 96; **to be ~ing** *(movie, etc.)* visas 110

playwright författare 110

pleasant angenäm 14

please ... tack 10

plug *(bathroom, kitchen)* propp 148; *(electric)* stickkontakt 148

pneumonia lunginflammation 165

point to: to ~ peka på 11

poison gift

police polisen 92, 159; **~ report** polisrapport 160; **~ station** polisstation 96, 131, 159

pollen count pollenhalt 122

polyester polyester

pond damm 107
pop *(music)* popmusik 111
popcorn popcorn 110
popular populär 111, 155
port *(harbor)* hamn
porter bärare 71
portion portion 39, 40
possible: as soon as ~
så snart som möjligt
post *(noun)* post; **~ office**
post 96, 131, 152; **to ~** posta;
~age porto 152; **~box**
postlåda 152; **~card**
vykort 152, 154
potato chips chips 157
potatoes potatis 38
pottery *(material/place)*
keramik/krukmakeri
pound *(sterling)* engelska
pund 67, 138
powdery *(snow)* nysnö 117
power: ~ cut strömavbrott;
~ points nätuttag 30
pregnant: to be ~ vara
gravid 163, 167
premium *(gas)*
premiumbensin 87
prescribe: to ~ skriva recept 165
prescription recept 140, 141
present *(gift)* gåva, present
press: to ~ stryka 137
pretty söt
price pris 24
priest präst
prison fängelse
produce store
livsmedelsaffär 131
profession yrke 23
program programm 108, 109
pronounce: to ~ uttala
Protestant protestantisk 105
pub pub, bar
public *(noun)* allmänheten 100

pump pump 83; *(gas station)* tank 87
puncture
punktering 83, 88
puppet show dockteater
pure ren 145
purple lila 143
purse portmonnä 160
push-chair barnvagn, sittvagn
put up: can you put me up for the night? kan jag få husrum här inatt?
put: to ~ *(to place)* ställa 22
put: where can I ~ ...?
var kan jag lägga ...

Q **quality** kvalitet 134
quarter: a ~ en
fjärdedel 217; **~ past** kvart
över 220; **~ to** kvart i 220
queue: to ~ köa 112
quick snabb 14; **what's the ~est way?** vad är snabbaste vägen?;
~ly snabbt 17
quiet tyst 14; **~er** lugnare 126,
tystare 24

R **rabbi** rabbin
racetrack [race course]
kapplöpningsbana 114
racket *(tennis, squash)* racket 115
railway järnväg
rain: to ~ regna 122; **~coat**
regnrock/regnkappa 144
rape våldtäckt 159
rapids forsar 107
rare *(steak)* blodig; *(unusual)*
ovanlig
rash utslag 162
razor rakhyvel; **~ blades**
rakblad 142
reading att läsa 121

room rum 21, 25
rope rep
round rund 134; **~ neck** rund i halsen 144; **~-trip ticket** returbiljett 65, 68, 74, 79
route led/rutt/väg 106
rubbish *(trash)* sopor 28
rucksack ryggsäck
rude: to be ~ ohövlig, otrevlig
ruins ruiner 99
run into: to ~ *(crash)* köra på 93
run out of: to ~ *(fuel)* vara slut 88
rush hour rusningstimmen

S **safe** *(noun)* kassaskåp 27; **safe** *(adj.)* utan risk 116; **to feel ~** trygg/säker 65
safety säkerhet; **~ pins** säkerhetsnålar
salad sallad 38
sales *(job)* försäljning 121
sales tax moms 24
salt salt 38, 39; **salty** salt
same samma 75
sand sand
sandals sandaler 145
sandwich smörgås 40
sandy *(beach)* sandig 116; **~ beach** sandstrand
sanitary napkin [towel] bindor 142
satellite TV satellit TV 22
satin satäng, satin
satisfied: I'm not ~ with this jag är inte nöjd med det här
Saturday lördag 218
sauce sås 38
sauna bastu 22
sausage korv 158
say: how do you ~ ...? hur säger man ...?
scarf halsduk 144; scarf 154
scheduled flight reguljärflyg
sciatica ischias 165

scissors sax 148
scooter skoter
Scotland Skottland 119
screwdriver skruvmejsel 148
sea hav 107; **~front** strandpromenad, sjösida; **I feel ~sick** jag är sjösjuk
season ticket säsongsbiljett
seat plats 74, 77, 108, 109
second andra 217; **~ class** andra klass 74; **~ floor** *(U.S.)* första våningen 132; **~-hand** sekunda
secretary sekreterare
sedative lugnande medel
see: to ~ se 37, 124, titta på 18; *(inspect)* se på 24; *(observe)* se/observera 93; *(witness)* vittne 93; **~ you soon!** hoppas vi ses snart! 126
self-employed: to be ~ egen företagare 121
self-service *(gas station)* själv-service 87
sell: to ~ sälja 133
send: to ~ skicka 153
senior citizen pensionär 74, 100
separated: to be ~ vara separerad 120
separately var för sig 42
September september 218
serious allvarlig
service gudstjänst 105; *(tip)* serveringsavgift 42
serviette servett 39
set menu meny 37
sex samlag, sex
shade nyans 143
shady skuggigt 31
shallow grund
shampoo schampo 142; **~ and set** tvätt och läggning 147
share: to ~ *(room)* dela
sharp vass 69

shaving: ~ **brush** rakborste; ~ **cream** rakkräm

she hon

sheath (contraceptive) kondom

sheet (bed) lakan 28

ship båt 81

shirt (men's) skjorta 144

shock (electric) (elektrisk) schock

shoe: ~**s** skor 145; ~ **repair** skomakare; ~ **store** [~ **shop**] skoaffär 131

shop assistant expedit, försäljare

shopping: ~ **area** affärscentrum 99; ~ **basket** shoppingkorg; ~ **mall** [**centre**] shoppingcentrum/ affärscentrum 130; ~ **trolley** shoppingvagn; **to go** ~ gå och shoppa, gå och handla

short kort 14, 144, 146, 147; ~**-sighted** närsynt 167

shorts shorts 144

shoulder skuldra/axel 166

shovel spade 155

show: to ~ visa 18, 94, 134; **can you** ~ **me?** kan ni visa mig? 106

shower dusch 21; ~**s** duschar 30; ~ **room** duschrum 26

shut stängd 14; **to** ~ stänga 132; **when do you** ~**?** när stänger ni?

shutter persienn 25

sick: I'm going to be ~ jag vill kräkas

side order extra portion 38

side street sidogata 95

sides (of head) sidor 147

sights sevärdheter

sightseeing: ~ **tour** sightseeingtur 97; **to go** ~ gå på sightseeing

sign (road) (väg)skylt 93, 95; ~**post** vägskylt

silk silke

silver silver 149; ~ **plate** nysilver 149

singer sångare/sångerska 155

single enkel 81; ~ **room** enkelrum 21; ~ **ticket** enkel biljett 65, 68, 74; **to be** ~ vara gift 120

sink handfat 25

sister syster 120

sit: to ~ sitta 36, 77, 126, 146; ~ **down, please** varsågod och sitt

skates skridskor 117

ski: ~**boots** skidpjäxor 117; ~ **poles** stavar 117

skin hud 166

skirt kjol 144

skis skidor 117

sleep: to ~ sova 167

sleeping: ~ **bag** sovsäck 31; ~ **car** sovvagn 74, 77; ~ **pill** sömntablett

sleeve ärm 144

slice: a ~ **of ...** en skiva ... 40

slippers tofflor 145

slow långsam 14; **to be** ~ vara långsam; (clock) sakta 221; ~ **down!** sakta farten, sakta ner!; **slowly** (speak) långsamt 11; långsammare 94, 128; sakta/långsamt 17

SLR camera kamera med enkellinsreflex 151

small liten 14, 24, 40, 110, 117, 134; ~**er** mindre 134; ~ **change** växel 138

smell: there's a bad ~ det luktar illa

smoke: to ~ röka 126

smoking (adj./area) rökare 36, 69

snack bar barservering 73,

snacks matbit, lätt mål

sneakers sportskor

snorkel snorkel

snow snö 117; **to** ~ snöa 122

soap tvål 27, 142; ~ powder tvättmedel
soccer fotboll 114
socket kontakt
socks sockar 144
soft drink läskedryck 110, 157
sole *(shoes)* sula
soloist solist 111
soluble aspirin vattenlösliga aspirin
some några
something något 16; ~ to drink något att dricka 70; ~ to eat något att äta 70
sometimes ibland 13
son son 120, 162
soon snart 13
sore: ~ throat halsont 141, ont i halsen 163; it's ~ det gör ont
sorry! förlåt mig!
soul music blues och soulmusik 111
sour surt 41
South Africa Sydafrika
South African *(person)* sydafrikansk
south söder 95
souvenir souvenir 98, 154; ~ guide souvenirguide 154; ~ store souvenirbutik 131
space plats 30
spade spade 155
spare extra 28
speak: to ~ tala 11, 41, 67, 128, tala med 18; to ~ to someone tala med 128; do you ~ English? talar ni engelska? 11
special särskild 86; ~ delivery express 153
specialist specialist 164
specimen prov 164
spectacles glasögon
spell: to ~ stava 11
spend: to ~ spendera, göra av med
spicy kryddstark, kryddad
sponge svamp 148

spoon sked 39, 41; ~s skedar 148
sport sport 121; ~s club sportklubb 115; ~s ground idrottsplats 96; ~ing goods store sportaffär 131
spot *(place, site)* plats 31
sprained: to be ~ vara vrickad 164
spring vår 219
square *(adj.)* fyrkantig 134
square *(noun)* fyrkant 134
stadium stadion 96
staff personal 113
stain fläck
stainless steel rostfritt stål 149
stairs trappor 132
stamp frimärke 152; ~s frimärken 150
stand in line: to ~ vänta, köa 112
standby ticket avbeställd biljett
start: to ~ *(car, etc.)* starta 88; börja 108, 112
statement *(to police)* rapport(era) 93
stationer's bok- och pappershandel
statue staty 99
stay *(noun)* vistelse 32; to ~ *(remain)* stanna 23, stanna kvar 65, bo 123,
steak house stekhus 35
sterilizing solution steriliseringsvätska 142
stiff neck stel nacke
still: I'm ~ waiting jag väntar fortfarande
stockings strumpor 144
stolen: to be ~ bli stulen 160, stulen(t) 71
stomach mage 166; ~ ache ont i magen 163
stool *(faeces)* avföring 164
stop: to ~ stanna 77, 98; to ~ at stanna 76; *(noun)* hållplats 79, 80

stopcock avstängningskran 28
store guide information 132
stormy: to be ~ stormigt 122
stove spis 28, 29
straight ahead rakt fram 95
strained muscle muskelsträckning 162
strange konstig 101
straw (drinking) strå
strawberry (flavor) jordgubbs 40
stream å 107
streetcar spårvagn 79
strong (potent) stark
student studerande 74, 100, 121
study: to ~ studera 121
style stil 104
subtitled: to be ~ med undertitlar 110
subway: ~ map tunnelbanekarta 80; ~ station tunnelbanestation 80
sugar socker 38, 39
suggest: to ~ föreslå 123
suit (man's/woman's) kostym/dräkt 144
suitable lämplig(t) 140; ~ for lämpligt till
summer sommar 219
sun: ~ block solkräm med extra skydd 142; to ~bathe solbada; ~burn solbränna 141; ~glasses solglasögon; ~ny soligt 31; ~shade solparasol 116; ~stroke solsting 163; ~tan lotion solkräm 142
Sunday söndag 218
super (gas) premiumbensin 87
superb fantastisk 101
supermarket snabbköp 156
supervision/be supervised uppsikt/vara under uppsikt 113
supplement tillägg 68, 69

suppositories stolpiller 165
sure: are you ~? är du säker på det?
surfboard surfbräde 116
surname efternamn
sweater tröja 144
sweatshirt sweatshirt 144, tröja
Swedish (language) svenska 11, 126
sweet (taste) sött
sweets lite godis 150
swelling svullnad 162
swim: to ~ simma 116; ~suit baddräkt 144
swimming simning 114; ~ pool simbassäng 22, 26, 116; ~ trunks badbyxor 144
swollen: to be ~ svullen
symptom symptom 163
synagogue synagoga 105
synthetic syntetisk 145

T T-shirt T-skjorta 144, 154
table bord 36, 112
take: to ~ ta 24, 40, 71, 78,86, 140, 165; to ~ away ta med 40; to ~ out (extract tooth) dra ut 168; to ~ photographs fotografera, ta foto 98, 100; I'll ~ it (room) jag tar det 24, 135; is this seat ~n? är det här platsen upptagen? 77; ~ me to kör mig till 84
talk: to ~ tala med
tall lång 14
tampons tamponger 142
tan solbränna
tap kran 25
taxi taxi 32, 70, 71, 84; ~ stand [rank] taxi 96
tea té 40; ~ bags thépåsar 158; ~ towel diskhandduk 154
teacher lärare
team lag 114
teaspoons teskedar 148
teddy bear nalle 155

telephone telefon 22, 92, 127; ~ bill
telefonräkning 32; ~ booth
telefonkiosk 127; ~ call
telefonsamtal 32; ~ number
telefonnummer 127

tell: to ~ säga 18; can you ~ me ...?
kan ni tala om för mig ...? 79

temperature *(body)*
temperatur 164

temple tempel 105

temporarily tillfälligt 168

tennis tennis 114; ~ court
tennisbana 115

tent tält 30, 31; ~ pegs
tältpinnar 31; ~ pole
tältstake 31

terminus *(bus, etc.)* bussterminal/
busshållplats 78

terrace terrass 35

terrible dåligt/
hemskt 19, 101, 122

terrific fantastiskt 19

tetanus stelkramp 164

thank you tack 10, 118

that *(object)* det 94; ~ one den
där 16, 134, 157

that's true! det är sant! 19

that's all det var allt 133

theater teater 96, 99, 110, 111

theft stöld 160

theirs deras 16

them dem 16

theme park sommarland, nöjesfält

then *(time)* då 13

there där 17; *(to there)* dit 12; ~ are
... det finns/det är ... 17; over ~
där borta 76

thermometer termometer

thermos flask
termosflaska

these de där 134, de här 157

they de

thick tjock 14

thief tjuv

thigh lår 166

thin smal , tunn 14

think: I ~ jag tror 42;
to ~ about something
tänka på det 135

third tredje 217; a ~ en
tredjedel 217; ~ party insurance
trafikförsäkring (ansvarig mot
tredje man)

thirsty: I am ~ jag är törstig

this den här 84; *(Tuesday, etc.)*
nästa 218; ~ evening ikväll 36;
~ one den här 16, 134, 157

those de här 134, 157

thousand tusen 217

throat hals 166

thrombosis trombos

through genom

thumb tumme 166

Thursday torsdag 218

ticket biljett 74, 65,
68, 69, 75, 79, 80, 81,
100, 109, 114, 160; ~s biljetter 108;
~ office biljettkontor 73

tie slips 144

tight trång 146

tights strumpbyxor 144

till receipt kassakvitto

time: is it on ~? gårdet i tid? 76;
free ~ ledig tid 98; what's the ~?
hur mycket är klockan? 220;
~table tidtabell 75

tin opener
konservöppnare 148

tire *(noun)* däck 83

tired: I'm ~ jag är trött

tissue pappersnäsdukar 142

to *(place)* till 12

tobacco tobak 150; ~nist
tobaksaffär 130

today idag 89, 124, 218

toe tå 166

toilet toalett 25, 26, 29, 78, 98, 113;
~ paper toalettpapper 25, 142

tomatoes tomater 157

A-Z

tomorrow imorgon 36, 84, 122, 124, 218
tongue tunga 166
tonight ikväll 108, 110, 124
tonsilitis halsfluss 165
tonsils tonsiller 166
too *(extreme)* för 17, 41, 93, 117, 135, 146; ~ **much** för mycket 15
tooth tand 168; **~brush** tandborste; **~ache** tandvärk; **~paste** tandkräm 142
top *(of head)* topp 147
torch ficklampa 31
torn: to be ~ *(muscle)* vara sträckt 164; **this is ~** det är slitet
tough *(food)* för segt 41
tour tur 98; **~ guide** reseledare 27; **~ operator** reseledare 26
tourist turist; **~ office** turistbyrå 97
tow truck bärgningsbil 88
towel handduk
tower torn 99
town stad 70, 94; **~ hall** stadshus 99
toy leksak 155
traditional restaurant värdshus 35
traffic trafik; **~ jam** trafikstockning; **~ light** trafikljus 95; **~ violation [offence]** trafiköverträdelse
trailer husvagn 30, 81
train tåg 13, 73, 75, 77, 123; **~ station** järnvägsstation 73, 84, 96
trained utbildad 113
tram spårvagn 79
transfer transfer
transit: in ~ på genomresa, i transit
translate: to ~ översätta 11
translation översättning
translator översättare
trashcans sopptunnor 30

travel: ~ agency resebyrå 131; **~ sickness** åksjuka 141; **~er's check [cheque]** resecheckar 136, 138
tray bricka
tree träd 106
trim klippa/klippning av topparna 147
trip resa 76, 78
trolley kärra 156
trousers byxor 144; **trouser press** byxpress
truck *(U.S.)* lastbil
true: that's not ~ det är inte sant
try on: to ~ *(clothes)* prova 146
Tuesday tisdag 218
tumor tumör 165
tunnel tunnel
turn: to ~ down *(volume, heat)* stänga/skruva ner; **to ~ off** stänga av 25; **to ~ on** sätta på 25; **to ~ up** sätta/skruva upp
TV TV 22
tweezers pincett
twice två gånger 217; **~ a day** två gånger om dagen 76
twin beds två sängar 21
twist: I've ~ed my ankle jag har vrickat min fotled/ankel
two-door car bil med två dörrar 86
type typ 109; **what ~ of ...?** vilken slags ...? 112
typical typisk 37
tyre däck 83

U **U.K.** Storbritannien 119
U.S. U.S.A. 119
ugly ful 14, 101
ulcer sår; *(stomach)* magsår
umbrella *(for sun/rain)* solparasol/paraply 116
uncle *(paternal/maternal)* farbror/morbror 120

uncomfortable obekväm 117
unconscious: to be ~
medvetslös 92; **he's ~** han är
medvetslös 162
under under; **~done** blodig, inte
genomstekt 41
underpants kalsonger 144
understand: to ~ förstå 11; **do you
~?** förstår ni? 11; **I don't ~** jag
förstår inte 11, 67
undress: to ~ klä av sig 164
uneven (*ground*) ojämn 31
unfortunately tyvärr 19
uniform uniform
unit (*phone card*) enheter 153
United States USA, Förenta
Staterna
unleaded petrol blyfri bensin
unlimited mileage obegränsat
miltal
unlock: to ~ låsa upp
unpleasant otrevlig 14
unscrew: to ~ skruva av, skruva ur
until tills 221
up to fram till 12
upper (*berth*) överbädd 74
upset stomach ont i magen 141
urine urin 164
USA USA
use: to ~ använda 139; **for my
personal ~** för mitt personliga
bruk 67

V **V-neck** V-ringad 144
vacant ledig 14
vacation semester 123; **on ~** på
semester 66
vaccinated against: to be ~ vara
vaccinerad mot 164
vaginal infection
underlivsinfektion 167
valet service
biltvätt (for car)

valid gälla 75
validate: to ~
giltigförklara,
validera
valley dal 107
valuable värdefull
valve avstängningskran 28
vanilla (*flavor*) vanilj 40
VAT MOMS 24; **~ receipt** MOMS
kvitto
vegan: to be ~ vara vegan
vegetables grönsaker 38
vegetarian vegetariansk 35, 39
vein ven, ådra 166
venereal disease könssjukdom 165
ventilator ventil
very mycket 17; **~ good** mycket
bra 19
video: ~ game videospel;
~ recorder videomaskin;
~cassette videofilm 155
view: with a ~ of the sea med
sjöutsikt; **~point**
utsikspunkt 99, 107
village by 107
vinaigrette vinaigrettesås,
dressing 38
vinegar vinäger 38
visa visum
visit (*noun*) besök 66, 119; **to
~** (*hospital*) besöka 167; (*places*)
besöka (sevärdheter) 123
visiting hours besökstider
vitamin tablet vitamintablett 141
volleyball volleyboll 114
voltage volt
vomit: to ~ kräkas 163

W **wait: to ~** vänta 36, 41, 140;
to ~ for vänta (på) 76 89; **~!**
vänta! 98; **waiter!** (*male/female*)
ursäkta! 37
waiting room väntrum 73

wake väcka 70; **to ~ someone** väcka 27; **~-up call** väckning
Wales Wales 119
walk home: to ~ promenera hem 65
walking: ~ boots vandrarkängor 145; **~ gear** vandringsutrustning; **~ route** vandringsled 106
wallet plånbok 42, 160
war memorial krigs monument 99
ward (hospital) avdelning 167
warm varm 14; (weather) varmt 122; **~er** varmare 24
washbasin tvättställ
washing: ~ machine 29; **~ powder** tvättmedel 148; **~-up liquid** diskmedel 148
wasp geting
watch armbandsklocka 149, 160
water vatten 87; **~ bottle** varmvattensflaska; **~ heater** varmvattenberedare 28; **~ skis** vattenskidor 116; **~fall** vattenfall 107
waterproof vattentät; **~ jacket** vattentät jacka/anorak 145
wave våg
waxing benvaxning 147
way: I've lost my ~ jag har gått (åkt) vilse 94; **it's on the ~ to ...** det är på vägen till 83
we vi; **~'d like ...** vi skulle vilja ... 18
wear: to ~ vara klädd i 159
weather väder 122; **~ forecast** väderleksrapporten 122
wedding bröllop, vigsel; **~ ring** vigselring
Wednesday onsdag 218
week vecka 23, 97, 218
weekend veckoslut 24, helg 218; **~ rate** helgrabatt 86

weight: my ~ is ... jag väger...
welcome to ... välkommen till ...
well-done (steak) genomstekt
west väster 95
wet (snow) blötsnö 117
wetsuit våtdräkt
what? vad? 94, 104; **~ is the charge** vad kostar det 30; **~ kind of ...?** vad för slags ...? 37, 106; **~ time?** när? 32, hur dags ...? 68, 76, 78, 81
wheelchair rullstol
when? när? 13, 68, 78, 104
where? var? 12, 73, 76, 78, 84, 88, 98; **~ is the ...?** var ligger/finns...? 99; **~ is ...?** var är ...? 80, 94; **~ were you born?** var är du född? 119
which? vilken? 16
white vitt 143
who? vem? 16, 104
whose vems 16
why? varför? 15; **~ not?** varför inte? 15
wide bred 14
wife fru 120, 162
wildlife naturliv
windbreaker vindtät jacka 145
window fönster 25, 77; (shop) (skylt)fönster 134, 149; **~ seat** plats vid fönster 69, 74
windscreen vindruta
windy: to be ~ blåsigt 122
wine vin 158; **~ list** vinlistan 37
winter vinter 219
wishes: best ~ varma lyckönskningar 219
with med 17
withdraw: to ~ ta ut 139
within (time) om 13
without utan 17, 38, 141

ENGLISH ➤ SWEDISH

witness bevittna, se 93
wood skog 107
wool ull 145
work: to ~ *(function)*
  fungera 28, 83; **it doesn't ~** det
  fungerar inte 25, 137
worse sämre 14; **worst** sämst,
  värst
write down: to ~
  skriva (ner) 136
writing paper brevpapper 150
wrong fel 14, 88, 95, 136;
  ~ number fel nummer 128;
  there's something ~ with ...
  det är något fel med ...

X Y Z **x-ray** röntgenbild 164
      yacht segelbåt
year år 119, 218
yellow gult 143
yes ja 10
yesterday igår 218
yogurt yoghurt 158
you *(formal/informal)* ni/du
young ung 14
your *(formal/informal)* er/din 16
youth hostel vandrarhem 29, 123
zebra crossing övergångsställe
zero noll
zip(per) dragkedja
zoo djurpark 113

A-Z Dictionary
Swedish – English

This Swedish–English Dictionary covers all the areas where you may need to decode written Swedish: hotels, public buildings, restaurants, stores, ticket offices, and on transportation. It will also help with understanding forms, maps, product labels, road signs, and operating instructions (for telephones, parking meters, etc.).
If you can't locate the exact sign, you may find key words or terms listed separately.

A 5A five amps
advokat lawyer *(title)*
affären upphör going-out-of-business sale
affär med sekunda varor secondhand store
affärscentrum shopping mall [centre]
aftonsång evening service *(church)*
Aktiebolag (AB) Inc. [Ltd.] *(company)*
allmän byggnad public building
allmän helgdag National Holiday
allmän toalett automated public toilet
allt för trädgården garden center
alpin skidåkning downhill skiing
alternativ väg alternate route
ambassad embassy
ambulans ambulance
ankomst arrivals
ankring förbjuden no anchorage
Annandag Påsk Easter Monday
annullerad canceled
antikaffär antique store
anvisningar directions *(map)*
använd gångtunneln use the underpass
använd helljus use headlights
använd innan … use-by date
använd kedjor eller vinterdäck use chains or snow tires
använda biljetter used tickets
apotek pharmacy

apotek med nattöppet all-night pharmacy
april April
att hyra for rent [for hire]
augusti August
automatiska dörrar automatic doors
avdelning department
avsändare sender

B **babykläder** babieswear
backe(piste) för mellanstadium intermediate slope (skiing)
backe(piste) för nybörjare piste for beginners
bad baths
badrum bathroom
bagageutlämning baggage claim
bagare baker
bageri bakery
baktrappa backstairs
bank bank
Bankomat ATM (automated teller)/ cash machine
bankutgifter bank charges
bara only
bara frakt freight only
barn children
barnbassäng children's pool
barnsäkert lock childproof cap *(on bottle, etc.)*
bastu sauna

ba samtal collect call [reverse-charge call]

begränsad last load limit

behandlingsrum treatment room

behåll kvittot/biljetten keep your receipt/ticket

behåll kvittot för byte eller pengar tillbaka keep your receipt for exchange or refund

bensin gasoline [petrol]; **95 oktan ~** regular; **98 oktan ~** premium [super]

bensinstation gas [petrol] station

berg mountain

bergsklättring rock climbing

beroende på tillgänglighet subject to availability

beställningssytt made to order

besökstider visiting hours

betala innan ni fyller tanken pay for gas before fuelling

betala kontant pay cash

betala parkeringen pay parking lot [car park]

betala vid disken pay at counter

betala vid ingången pay on entry

betala vid mätaren pay at the meter

betalas till ... payable to ...

betalt paid (with thanks)

betjäning service (*shop, restaurant*)

beträd ej gräset, förbjudet att beträda gräset keep off the grass

bevara på kallt ställe keep in a cool place

bibliotek library

bijetter till i kväll tickets for tonight

bildäck car deck (*ferry*)

biljett ticket

biljettagentur ticket agency

biljetten gäller för tunnelbana ticket valid for subway [metro]

biljettkontor box office/ ticket office

bilregistreringsnummer car registration number

biluthyrning car rental

biskop bishop

biväg secondary road

biverkningar side effects

blockera inte ingången do not block entrance

blodgupp blood type [group]

blomsterhandel florist

blybensin leaded (*fuel*)

blyfri bensin unleaded (*gasoline*)

blötsnö wet snow

boardingkort boarding pass (*airport*)

bokhandel bookstore

bollspel förbjudet, inget bollspel no ball games

bondgård farm

bostadsområde housing estate

bottenvåning basement

bottenvåningen first floor [ground floor]

boules bowls

branddörr fire door

brandkår fire department [brigade]

brandsläckare fire extinguisher

brandstation fire station

brandutgång fire exit

bromskrafter brake power

bruksanvisning instructions for use

brygga bridge (*ship*)/jetty (*by shore*)

bröd bread

bungee-hopp bungee-jumping

bussfil bus lane

busshållplats bus shelter/bus stop/request stop

bussväg bus route

byt vid ... change at ...

båt boat

båtkryssningar cruises, boat trips

båtturer pleasure steamers, riverboats

bäck stream

bär badmössa bathing caps must be worn

bärgningsbil breakdown services

bäst före ... best before ... (*date*)

bön prayers

A-Z

A-Z

börjar klockan …
begins at …
börjar … commencing …
börsen stock exchange

C checka in check-in
(*airport*)

chef, direktör manager
cykelbana cycle lane/path

D dagens rätt dish/specialty of
the day

dagens meny menu of the day
damer ladies restroom [toilets]
damfrisör hairdresser
damkläder ladieswear
damm pond
damtidning women's magazine
damtoalett ladies restroom [toilets]
datorer computers
delikatessaffär delicatessen
den här bussen går till … this bus is
going to …
den här maskinen ger växel this
machine gives change
detta tåg stannar vid … this train
stops at …
diesel diesel
diet diet
dimma fog
dimrisk risk of fog
direktservice direct service
diskmaskinsfast dishwasher-proof
djupt deep end (*swimming pool*)
djupfryst frozen
djupfryst mat frozen foods
doktorns rum consulting room
(*doctor's*)
domstolsbyggnad courthouse
donation donations
dörrarna stängs … minuter efter
föreställningens början doors close
… minutes after performance begins
dosering dosage
dra här tear here

drag i nödsituation/nödbroms
pull for alarm
dricks tip
dricksvatten drinking water
drinkar drinks
droppar drops (*medication*)
dubbad dubbed
dusch showers
dykning förbjuden no diving
dyktrampolin diving board
däckstol deck chair
dålig väg poor road surface
där uppe upstairs

E effektförvaring baggage check
efter-sol kräm after-sun lotion

efternamn last name
ej dricksvatten do not drink the water
ej allmän väg service road
ej ingång no entrance
ej retur non-returnable
ej tillträde no access
ej tillåtet att springa no running
ej tillåtna bilar bogseras bort
unauthorized vehicles will be towed
ekologiskt område
conservation area
elektricitetsmätare electricity meter
elektriska varor electrical goods
em p.m.
endast barn med målsman no
unaccompanied children
endast för biljettinnehavare ticket
holders only
endast för boende residents only
endast för dem med säsongbiljetter
season ticket holders only
endast handtvätt handwash only
endast ingång access only
endast ingång för boende
access to residents only
endast lastbilar truck route
endast leverans deliveries only
endast på veckodagar
weekdays only

endast rakapparater razors [shavers] only

endast tidningar newspapers only

engelska English

engelska pund pound sterling

enkel biljett one-way trip [journey]

enkelriktad gata one-way street

enplansvilla bungalow

entré entrance, way in

entré genom bakdörren/framdörren enter by the rear/front door

EU medborgare EU citizens

exakt belopp, ingen växel exact fare, no change given

exakt växel exact change

expresspaket express parcel post

expresspost express mail

extrapris prices slashed

F facklitteratur non-fiction (section in bookstore)

fara danger

februari February

fet hud oily skin

fettfri fat-free

fettinnehåll fat content

film i orginalversion film in original version

fiskdisk/fiskaffär fish stall

fiske förbjudet/ej tillåtet no fishing

fiske angling

fiske tillåtet fishing permitted

flaskbank bottle bank

flerpacketerat multipack

flicknamn maiden name

flod river

flodrand/flodstrand river bank

flyginformation flight information

flygnummer flight number

flygplan plane

flygplats airport

flygsteward flight attendant (male)

flygterminal air terminal

flygvärdinna flight attendant (female)

fm a.m.

formell klädsel formal wear

fotgängare pedestrians

fotstig footpath

fri(tt) free

fri höjd ... headroom ... (height restriction)

frimärken stamps

fritt inträde free admission

fritt porto freepost

fru Mrs.

frukost breakfast

frukostrum breakfast room

fruktjuice, fruktjos fruit juices

frusen frozen

fråga om hjälp please ask for assistance

fråga vid receptionen ask at reception

från ... till ... from ... to ...

fröken Miss

fullbelagt full up

fyrkant square (geometric)

fyrverkeri fireworks

fryst mat frozen foods

får ej vidröras do not touch

får inte tas invärtes not to be taken internally

får inte tas oralt not to be taken orally

fält field

färghållbart colorfast

färsk fresh

födelsedatum date of birth

födelseort place of birth

fönsterplats window seat

för avancerade skidåkare for advanced skiers

för fett/normalt/torrt hår for greasy/normal/dry hair

för förfrågningar, ... for inquiries, see ...

för nybörjare for beginners (skiers)

för två for two

förbättrad(t) improved

... förbjuden(t) ... forbidden

A-Z

förbjudet att parkera no parking
förbjudet att röka no smoking
förbjudet att röka/rökning ej tillåtet på bildäck no smoking on car decks
förbjudet att slänga sopor don't dump trash
förbjudet att elda och grilla no fires/barbecues
förbjudet att fotografera no photography
förbjudet att stanna no stopping
före ... before ...
före måltiden before meals
Förenta Staterna United States
föreställning performance/show
föreställning utan uppehåll continuous showings
förfriskningar refreshments available
förhandsbokning advance reservations [bookings]
förkörsrätt right of way
förorter suburbs
försäkringsbrev national insurance card
försäljningsdatum sell-by date
församling parish
försenad(t) delayed
första hjälpen first aid
första klass first class
första raden dress circle
första våningen second floor [first floor]
förvaras oåtkomligt för barn keep out of reach of children
förvaringsskåp luggage lockers

G galleri gallery
gata street
gate gate *(boarding)*
gjord i ... made in ...
glutenfritt gluten free
glöm inte att ... don't forget to ...

glöm inte att bekräfta er biljett don't forget to validate your ticket
glöm inte dricksen till guiden remember to tip your guide
Gör-det-själv varuhus DIY store
gräsmark grass *(camping site)*
gratis present free gift
gratis free of charge
gravplats cemetery
gränd lane
grönsaker vegetables
grönsaksaffär greengrocer
grönt försäkringskort green (insurance) card
grotta cave
grunt shallow end *(swimming pool)*
grupper välkomna parties welcome
gula sidorna yellow pages
guld gold
gymnasium *(16-19 yrs.)* high school [secondary school]
gågata traffic-free zone
... gånger om dagen ... times a day
gångstig walkway, path
gåvor donations

H hall hall
halva priset half price
halvpension Modified American Plan (M.A.P.) [half board]
halvö peninsula
hamn docks/port
hamnområde harbor
handgjord handmade
handsydd hand-sewn
hastighetsbegränsning speed limit
hav sea
havsytan sea level
helpension American Plan (A.P.) [full board]
helt ny brand-new
hemadress home address
hemgjord homemade
heminredning home furnishings
herr Mr.

herrfrisör barber
herrkläder menswear
herrtoalett gentlemen restroom [toilets]
hiss elevator [lift]
hittegodsexpedition lost-and-found [lost property] office
hjälm är obligatoriskt helmets required
hjälplinje help line
hotellfoajé lounge
hudkräm moisturizer
hur maten serveras serving suggestions
hus att hyra house for rent
hushållslinne household linen
huvudled main road
hyreshus apartment
hyttdäck cabin decks
håll avstånd keep your distance
håll grinden stängd keep gate shut
håll till höger stay to the right
håll till vänster stay to the left
hårfrisör stylist
hårtork hairdryer
häfte booklet (*tickets*)
hälsokost health food
hälsokostaffär healthfood store
händelse event
här here
hästkapplöpningsbana racetrack [race course]
högerkörning drive on the right
höghus apartment building
högspänning(sledning) high voltage
högstadieskola (*13–16 yrs.*) junior high school [secondary school]
höjd över havet height above sea level
höst fall [autumn]

I **i centrum** downtown area
icke-rökare no smoking
i ... dagar for ... days
ID-kort ID card

idag today
i eftermiddag this afternoon
ikväll this evening
i morgon tomorrow
i morse this morning
incheckning check-in desk (*airport*)
industriområde business district/industrial estate
infart expressway entrance
information information desk
inga barn under ... no children under ...
inga EU-medborgare non-EU citizens
inga kreditkort no credit cards
ingen avstjälpningsplats no dumping
ingen dykning no diving
ingen genomfart no passing
ingen genomfartsväg no outlet [no through road]
ingen parkering no parking
ingen paus no intermissions [intervals]
ingen rabatt no discounts
ingen söndagsgudstjänst no Sunday service
ingen trafik traffic-free zone
ingen utgång no exit
ingen vägren end of hard shoulder
ingen åkning utanför pisten no off-trail skiing
inget att deklarera nothing to declare
inget tillträde no entry/no access
inget tillträde för cyklar eller motorcyklar no access to cyclists and motorcyclists
inget tillträde till bildäck under resan no access to car decks during crossing
inkluderat included (*in the price*)
inklusive betjäning/inklusive serveringsavgift service included
innan ... before ...
innehåller ej ... contains no ...
inomhusbassäng indoor swimming pool

A-Z

instruktör instructor
inte inkluderat not included *(in the price)*
inte kopplad disconnected
inte mer än 5 saker 5 items or less
intensivvård intensive care
intercity tåg intercity trains
i nödsituation slå sönder glaset break glass in case of emergency
i nödsituation ring ... emergency number ...
isigt väglag icy road
i övermorgon the day after tomorrow

J **jakt** hunting
januari January
jetski jet-ski
Jul Christmas
juli July
juni June
juvelerare jeweler
järnhandel hardware store
järnvägsstation train station
järnvägsövergång railroad [level] crossing

K **kabinlift** cable car
KAK Kungliga Automobilklubben Swedish Automobile Association
kallt cold
... kan köpas här ... on sale here
kan tillagas i mikro microwaveable
kan tuggas chewable *(tablets, etc.)*
kanalbåtar river boats
kapslar capsules *(medication)*
kapslar lätta att öppna easy-to-open ampules
kassa, betala här checkout, please pay here
kassör cashier
katalog directory
kemtvätt dry-cleaner
klinik clinic

klippa cliff
klippklättring rappeling [abseiling]
klubbhus clubhouse
knacka och stig in knock and enter
konditori coffee/pastry shop
konduktör/biljett-kontrollant subway ticket inspector
konferensrum conference room
konflikt med annan medicin interference with other drugs
kongresshall convention hall
konserveringsmedel preservatives
kontakta doktor innan användning consult your doctor before use
kontant cash
korsa inte do not cross
korsning intersection [junction]
kort tidsparkering short-term parking
krigsmomument war memorial
kriminalpolisen criminal investigation deptartment
krona *(sing.)***/kronor** *(plur.)* krona/kronor
kulle hill
kundinformation customer information
kundparkering customer parking lot
kundservice customer service
kust coast
kvalitetsstandard quality standard
kvicksand quicksand
kyrka church
kärr swamp
kärror carts
kök kitchen
köp 2, få 1 gratis buy 2, get 1 free
köp en polett vid disken buy a token at cash desk
kör försiktigt drive carefully
körkort driver's license
kör på höger sida drive on the right
kör sakta slow down

L landsväg A-road
lastbil truck [heavy goods vehicle (HGV)]
ledig for rent
lediga rum vacancies
ledigt vacant
leksaker toys
leksaksaffär toy store
linne linen
liten small
liten väg alley
livbåtar life boats
livbälte preserver [belt]
livsfara danger of death
livsmedelsbutik grocery store [grocer]
livvakt lifeguard
livvästar life jackets
logi accommodation (available)
loppmarknad flea market
lotteri lottery
luffa walking/hiking
luft air pump/air (*gas station*)
luftkonditionerat air conditioned
luta er inte ut genom fönstret do not lean out of windows
lutning incline (*road sign*)
lyft telefonluren lift receiver (*telephone*)
långfärdsbuss long-distance bus [coach]
långsam trafik slow traffic
långt fordon long vehicle
långtidsparkering long-term parking
låt passagerarna gå av först let passengers off first
läder leather
lägenhet med självhushåll self-catering apartment
läkarcentral general practitioner (*doctor*)
lämna bilen i ettans växel leave your car in first gear
lämna ert bagage här leave your bags here

lämna inte ert bagage utan uppsikt do not leave baggage unattended
lämna inte värdesaker i bilen do not leave valuables in your car
lämna nycklarna vid receptionen leave keys at reception
lämpligt för vegetarianer/veganer suitable for vegetarians/vegans
län administrative district
längdåkning cross-country skiing
lätt att laga fast cooking
lördag Saturday
lös i vatten dissolve in water

M maj May
makas/makes namn name of spouse
marklägenhet garden apartment
marknad market
mars March
maskintvätt machine washable
matbutik produce store [grocer]/general store
matsal dining room
med bad with bathroom
med dusch with shower
med måltider with food/meals
med sjöutsikt with sea view
mejeri dairy
mejeriprodukter dairy products
mellan klockan ... och klockan... between ... and ... (*time*)
mellannivå intermediate level
meny för bantare diet menu
meny (för) ... kronor set menu for ... kronor
metspö fishing rod
midnatt midnight
minimipris minimum charge
minimum minimum (*requirement*)
... minuter försenat ... minutes delay
mitt på dagen noon
mor mother

A-Z

moské mosque
motorväg highway [motorway]
motorvägskorsning highway interchange [motorway junction]
motorvägspolis highway police
mottagaren betalar samtalet collect call [reverse-charge call]
mur wall
muséum museum
mycket långsamt dead slow
måndag Monday
mäklare real estate agent
möbler furniture
möjliga förseningar delays likely
mötesplats meeting place [point]

N natt night
nattklocka night bell
nattportier night porter
nere downstairs
nettovikt net weight
non-stop till ... nonstop to ...
nord(lig) north(ern)
normal hud normal skin
notera ert parkeringsplatsnummer note your parking space number
noterad (historisk) byggnad listed (historic) building
nudiststrand nudist beach
nummerplåt registration number plate (car)
nya titlar new titles
nya utgåvor new releases
nyheter news
nymålat wet paint
nysnö powdery snow
Nyår New Year
Nyårsafton New Year's Eve
Nyårsdagen New Year's Day
nära affär within easy reach of shopping
nära havet within easy reach of the sea
närbutik general store

nästa avhämtning ... next collection at ...
nätverk network
nödbroms emergency brake
nödsituation emergency
nödutgång emergency exit/service stairs
nöjesfält amusement park/fair

O ojämn väg uneven road surface
olja oil (car)
olyckfallsavdelning emergency medical service
omfartsled bypass (road)
onsdag Wednesday
optiker optician
ordinering prescription
ost cheese

P paket parcel
palmsöndagen Palm Sunday
pant returnable
pappershandel stationer
paraply umbrellas [sunshades]
parkering för tågresenärer parking for train users
parkeringsböter parking ticket
parkering tillåten parking permitted
parkering tillåten på jämnt/ojämnt datum parking allowed on even/odd days
parkeringshus multistory parking lot [car park]
parkeringsmätare parking meter
parkett orchestra [stalls] (theater)
paviljong pavilion
pensionat guest house
per dag/vecka per day/week
picknickområde picnic area
plantskola garden center
platser uppe seats upstairs
plats för handikappad please give up this seat to the elderly/disabled
platsnummer seat number

plattform platform
pocketbok paperback *(book)*
poliklinik outpatients *(hospital)*
polis police
polisstation police station
postanvisning money orders
post(kontor) post office
presenter gifts
pris per liter price per liter
pris per rum room rate
privat private
privat område private property
provrum fitting room
Påsk Easter
Påskdagen Easter Sunday
på övervåningen upstairs

R rabatt discount
rabattvaruhus discount store
rad row/tier
ramper ramps
rastplats picnic area/rest area
reavaror bytes ej sale goods cannot be exchanged
recept prescription
receptionen reception *(hotel)*
reducerade priser reduced prices
rekommenderad recommended
rekommenderat brev registered letter
rekommenderad tillagning cooking recommendations
reparationer repairs *(car)*
reparationsverkstad body shop/mechanic
resans tidschema holiday timetable
resebyrå travel agent
reserverad reserved
reserverad fil reserved lane
reservoar reservoir
retur returnable
returglas returnable bottle
ridning horseback riding
ridån går upp curtain up *(theater)*
rinnande vatten running water
romaner fiction *(section in bookstore)*

rondell roundabout *(circulatory traffic system)*
rum att hyra rooms for rent
rum med frukost bed and breakfast
rummet måste lämnas före klockan ... vacate your room by ...
rumservice room service
rundtur round-trip [return]
rökning smoking

S salt salt
sandmark sand *(camping site)*
secondhand-affär secondhand store
segelflyg hanggliding
segelklubb sailing club
seglingsinstruktör sailing instructor
sekunda secondhand store
semesterschema holiday timetable
semesterstängt closed for vacation [holiday]
senaste tillträde klockan ... latest entry at ... p.m.
serietidningar comic books *(magazines)*
serveras bäst kall best served chilled
servering pågår service in progress
serveringsavgift service charge
serveringsavgift inte (ej) inkluderad service not included
service ej inräknad no service charge included
shoppingcenter shopping mall [centre]
shoppingkorg shopping basket
silke silk
simning swimming
simning med bevakning supervised swimming
sista bensinstationen innan motorvägen last gas station before the highway [motorway]
sista uppropet last call
sittplats vid gången aisle seat

A-Z

sjukhus hospital/infirmary
själv-service restaurang self-service restaurant
sjö lake
skala: 1:100 scale: 1:100
skepp ship
skidspår ski trail
skog wood/forest
skola school
skomakare shoe repair
skor shoes
skridskor skates
skräddarsytt made to measure
skräpa inte ner no littering
skyttelservice shuttle service
skönhetsbehandling beauty care
skönlitteratur fiction (section in bookstore)
sköterskor nurses
slaktare butcher
slott castle
slut på vägarbete end of construction (road)
slå dial
slå in PIN numret enter your PIN
slå nummer ... dial number ...
slå ... till linjen dial ... for an outside line
slå ... till receptionen dial ... for reception
släp trailer
smaksättning flavoring
smal väg narrow road
snabbkassa express checkout
socker sugar
sockerfritt sugar-free
solblockskräm sun-block cream
soldäck sun deck
solkiga varor spoiled goods
som föreslås recommended
sommar summer
sommar tidtabell summer timetable
sopor trash [rubbish]/garbage disposal

sparbank savings bank
spelarkad/spelautomater amusement arcade
spelrum game room
spädbarnskläder babieswear
stadion stadium
stadshus town hall
stadsmur city wall
stadspark public gardens/park
standardpris standard charge
stenmark stone (camping site)
stig footpath
stigning incline (road sign)
Storbritannien United Kingdom
stormarknad factory outlet
stormvarning gale/storm warning
stryk ej do not iron
student student
studio studio
stuga med självhushåll self-catering cottage
surfbräde surfboard
stål steel
städa rummet this room needs making up
stämpla biljetten validate/punch your ticket
stäng av turn off
stäng av motorn turn off your engine
stäng dörren close the door
stängd för trafik closed to traffic
stängt closed
stängt för reparation closed for repairs/renovations
stör ej do not disturb
störthjälm (crash) helmet
stötsäker shockproof
ström stream
sumpmark marsh
svävare hovercraft
syd(lig) south(ern)
säsongsbetonat according to season
sätta in och ta ut pengar deposits and withdrawals

sätt biljetten på vindrutan place ticket on windshield [windscreen]

sätt fast bältet fasten your seat belt

sätt i biljetten insert ticket

sätt i kortet insert (credit) card

sätt i myntet insert coins

sätt i pengar i maskinen och ta en biljett insert money (in machine) and take ticket

sätt på helljus turn on headlights

säsongbiljett season ticket

söndag Sunday

T **ta biljetten** take ticket

tabletter pills, tablets

ta efter måltid take after meals (*medication*)

tack för ert bidrag thank you for your contribution

take-away mat take-away food

tala inte med föraren do not talk to the driver

tandläkare dental office [surgery]

ta pengarna/kortet take your money/card

tappar inte formen will not lose its shape

tax-fri affär duty-free shop

tax-fria varor duty-free goods

taxi taxi stand

taxifil taxi lane

telefonist operator (*telephone*)

telefonkiosk pay phone

telefonkort phone card

textad film subtitled

tid för avhämtning times of collection

tidningar magazines

tidningskiosk newsstand

tidskrifter periodicals

tillaga från fruset cook from frozen

till exempel e.g.

tillfällig trafikomläggning temporary detour [diversion]

tills until

tillstånd behövs permit-holders only

tillträde förbjudet keep out/no trespassing

tillåtet bagage luggage allowance

… timmar försenat … hours delay

timme hour

tisdag Tuesday

tjäle potholes

tomt vacant

torg square (*town feature*)

torr hud dry skin

torsdag Thursday

trafikfree zon traffic-free zone

trafik från motsatt riktning traffic from the opposite direction

trafikomläggning detour [diversion]/new traffic system in operation

trafikpolis traffic police

trafikstockning: försening traffic jams: delays likely

transportdepot haulage depot

trapphus service stairs

trottoar sidewalk [pavement]

tryck push

tryck och öppna press to open

trä wood

tull customs/toll

tullkontrol customs control

tungt snöfall heavy snow

tunnel underpass

tunnelbana subway

turistattraktion tourist attraction

turistbyrå tourist office

turkiskt bad Turkish bath

tuta ej use of horn prohibited

två-filig väg two-lane highway

tvätt laundry

tvätta separat wash separately

tvättfat wash basin

tåget stannar i … local [stopping] service (*train*)

tävling contest

U ull wool
under byggnad under construction
underjordsgarage underground garage
underkläder lingerie/underwear
ungdom young adult/youth
uppdaterad updated
uppför trappan upstairs
upplysningar information desk
ur funktion out of order
urmakare watchmaker
utan måltider food not included
ute- open air
utebassäng outdoor swimming pool
utfart highway exit
utfart lastbil truck exit
utförsäljning going-out-of-business/clearance sale
utgång exit, way out
utgång genom bakdörren/framdörren exit by the rear/front door
utländsk foreign
utländska språk foreign languages
utländsk valuta foreign currency
utlöpande datum expiration [expiry] date
utom på ... except on ...
utsiktspunkt view point
utsålt sold out
utsätt inte för solljus do not expose to sunlight
uttag withdrawals

V valuta exchange
valuta köpt vid ... currency bought at ...
valuta såld vid ... currency sold at ...
valutanotering exchange rate
valutaväxling currency exchange
vandra walking, hiking
vandrarhem youth hostel
var god vänta please wait
varje månad monthly

varje vecka weekly
varmt hot *(water, faucet [tap])*
varning caution/warning
varning för fallande sten falling rocks
varning för hunden beware of dog
varor bytes ej, inga pengar tillbaka goods cannot be refunded or exchanged
varuhus department store
varuhusinformation store directory [guide]
vattenkran water faucet [tap]
veckodagar weekdays
v.g. ... please ...
v.g. ring på klockan please ring the bell
v.g. torka av fötterna please wipe your feet
v.g. vänta please wait
v.g. vänta bakom spärren please wait behind barrier
vi gör nycklar medan ni väntar keys cut while you wait
vi köper och säljer ... we buy and sell ...
vi talar engelska English spoken
vi tar kreditkort we accept credit cards
vi tar emot mynt coins accepted
vid motorstopp, kontakta ... in case of breakdown, phone/contact ...
vid brandfara ... in the event of fire ...
vik bay
viktig historisk sevärdhet important historical feature
vindbrygga drawbridge
vindsurfa windsurfing
vinter winter
vinter tidtabell winter timetable
visa era registreringspapper show your car registration documents
visa era väskor innan ni går show your bags before leaving
vår spring

vårdcentral doctor's office [surgery]/clinic/general practitioner *(doctor)*
våning floor *(level in building)*
våningshus apartment building
väderkvarn windmill
väderleksrapport weather forecast
väg road
vägarbete roadworks
vägkarta road map
vägren hard shoulder
vägen stängd road closed
väg under byggnad road under construction
välj destination/zon select destination/zone
välkommen! welcome!
vänta på biljetten wait for your ticket
vänta på ton wait for the tone
väntrum waiting room
väst(lig) west(ern)
växlingskontor currency exchange office

Å **åka skridskor** ice-skating
åka vattenskidor waterskiing
ångbåt steamer
åskådarläktare viewing gallery
återbetalning refund
återvändsgata dead end

Ä **ägaren kan inte ta ansvar för skada eller stöld** the owners can accept no responsibility for any damage or theft

Ö **öl** beer
öppet open
öppet 24 timmar 24-hour service
öppet till/på ... open until/on ...
öppettider business hours [opening hours]
öppna här tear here
öre öre *(Swedish currency)*

ostadig vägren soft shoulder *(road)*
öst(ra) east(ern)
övergång för fotgängare pedestrian crossing
övergångsställe zebra crossing
övertäckt marknad covered market
överviktsbagage excess baggage

Numbers

GRAMMAR

Swedish uses a period [full stop] to indicate a decimal point and a space to indicate thousands, e.g., **23.5%** (twenty-three point five percent) and **45 850** (forty-five thousand eight hundred and fifty). When indicating a price, the sign **:-** is put after the number, e.g., **SEK750:-** (seven hundred and fifty kronor).

0	**noll** *nol*		15	**femton** *femton*
1	**ett** *et*		16	**sexton** *sexton*
2	**två** *twah*		17	**sjutton** *sheutton*
3	**tre** *treh*		18	**arton** *arton*
4	**fyra** *fewra*		19	**nitton** *nitton*
5	**fem** *fem*		20	**tjugo** *cheugoo*
6	**sex** *sex*		21	**tjugoett** *cheugoo-et*
7	**sju** *sheu*		22	**tjugotvå** *cheugoo-twah*
8	**åtta** *otta*		23	**tjugotre** *cheugoo-treh*
9	**nio** *neeoo*		24	**tjugofyra** *cheugoo-fewra*
10	**tio** *teeoo*		25	**tjugofem** *cheugoo-fem*
11	**elva** *elva*		26	**tjugosex** *cheugo-sex*
12	**tolv** *tolv*		27	**tjugosju** *cheugoo-sheu*
13	**tretton** *tretton*		28	**tjugoåtta** *cheugoo-otta*
14	**fjorton** *fyoorton*		29	**tjugonio** *cheugoo-neeoo*

30	**trettio** *tretteeoo*	fourth	**fjärde** *fyairdeh*
31	**trettioett** *tretteeoo-et*	fifth	**femte** *femteh*
32	**trettiotvå** *tretteeootwah*	once	**en gång** *en gong*
40	**fyrtio** *furteeoo*	twice	**två gånger** *tvaw gonger*
50	**femtio** *femteeoo*	three times	**tre gånger** *treh gonger*
60	**sextio** *sexteeoo*	a half	**en halv** *en halv*
70	**sjuttio** *sheutteeoo*	half an hour	**en halvtimme** *en halv-timmeh*
80	**åttio** *otteeoo*	half a tank	**en halv tank** *en halv tank*
90	**nittio** *nitteeoo*	half eaten	**halväten** *halv-airten*
100	**hundra** *heundra*	a quarter	**en fjärdedel** *en fyairdeh-dehl*
101	**hundraett** *heundra-et*	a third	**en tredjedel** *en trehdye-dehl*
102	**hundratvå** *heundra-twah*	a pair of ...	**ett par ...** *et paar*
200	**tvåhundra** *twah-heundra*	a dozen ...	**ett dussin ...** *et deussin*
500	**femhundra** *fem-heundra*	1999	**nittonhundra-nittionio** *nitton heundra nitteeoo-neeoo*
1,000	**ett tusen** *et teusen*	the 1990s	**på nittio-talet** *paw nitteeoo-taalet*
10,000	**tiotusen** *teeoo-teusen*	the year 2000	**år tvåtusen** *awr tvaw-teusen*
35,750	**trettiofemtusen-sjuhundrafemtio** *treeteeoo-fem-teusen-sheu-heundra-femteeoo*	2001	**tvåtusenett** *tvaw-teusen-et*
1,000,000	**en miljon** *en milyoon*	the Millennium	**milleniet** *millenee-et*
first	**första** *fursta*		
second	**andra** *andra*		
third	**tredje** *trehdyeh*		

Days Dagar

Monday	**måndag**	_mondag_
Tuesday	**tisdag**	_teesdag_
Wednesday	**onsdag**	_oonsdag_
Thursday	**torsdag**	_tooshdag_
Friday	**fredag**	_frehdag_
Saturday	**lördag**	_lurdag_
Sunday	**söndag**	_surndag_

Months Månader

January	**januari**	_yaneuaari_
February	**februari**	_febreuaari_
March	**mars**	_mush_
April	**april**	_apreel_
May	**maj**	_my_
June	**juni**	_yeunee_
July	**juli**	_yeulee_
August	**augusti**	_aeugeustee_
September	**september**	_september_
October	**oktober**	_oktoober_
November	**november**	_noovember_
December	**december**	_desember_

Dates Datum

It's ...	**Det är ...**	_det air_
July 10	**den tionde juli**	_den teeondeh yeulee_
Tuesday, March 1	**tisdag, den första mars**	_teesdag den fursta mush_
yesterday	**igår**	_ee gawr_
today	**idag**	_ee daag_
tomorrow	**imorgon**	_ee morron_
this .../last ...	**på .../förra ...**	_nesta/furra_
next week	**nästa vecka**	_nesta vecka_
every month/year	**varje månad/år**	_varyeh mawnad/awr_
on [at] the weekend	**i helgen**	_ee hel-yen_

Seasons Årstider

spring	**vår** *vawr*
summer	**sommar** *sommar*
fall [autumn]	**höst** *hurst*
winter	**vinter** *vinter*
in spring	**på våren** *paw vawren*
during the summer	**under sommaren** *eunder sommaren*

Greetings Hälsningsfraser

Happy birthday!	**Gratulerar på födelsedagen!** *grateul<u>eh</u>rar paw <u>fur</u>delse-daagen*
Merry Christmas!	**God Jul!** *good yeul*
Happy New Year!	**Gott Nytt År!** *got newtt awr*
Happy Easter!	**Glad Påsk!** *glaad posk*
Best wishes!	**Varma lyckönskningar!** *varma lewck-<u>urnsk</u>ningar*
Congratulations!	**Varma gratulationer!** *varma grateu-la<u>shoo</u>ner*
Good luck!/All the best!	**Lycka till!** *lewcka til*
Have a good trip!	**Ha en trevlig resa!** *haa en trehvlig rehsa*
Give my regards to …	**Hälsa till …** *helsa til*

Public holidays Allmänna helgdagar

On days before most public holidays, offices, banks, post offices, and stores usually observe shorter working hours.

January 1	**Nyårsdagen**	New Year's Day
January 6	**Trettondagen**	Epiphany
May 1	**Första maj**	May Day
Saturday that falls between June 20 and 26	**Midsommardagen**	Midsummer Day
Saturday that falls between Oct. 31 and Nov. 6	**Allhelgonadagen**	All Saints' Day
December 25	**Juldagen**	Christmas Day
December 26	**Annandag jul**	Boxing Day
Movable dates:	**Långfredagen**	Good Friday
	Påskdagen	Easter Sunday
	Annandag påsk	Easter Monday
	Kristi himmelfärdsdag	Ascension
	Pingstdagen	Whitsunday
	Annandag Pingst	Whitmonday

Time Tid

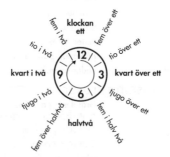

Sweden's official time system uses the 24-hour clock. However, in ordinary conversation, time is generally expressed as shown above, often with the addition of **på morgonen** (in the morning), **på eftermiddagen** (in the afternoon), **på kvällen** (in the evening), and **på natten** (at night).

Excuse me. Can you tell me the time?	**Ursäkta, hur mycket är klockan?** *eurshekta, heur mewcket air klockan*
It's ...	**Klockan är ...** *klockan air*
five past one	**fem över ett** *fem urver et*
ten past two	**tio över två** *teeoo urver tvaw*
a quarter past three	**kvart över tre** *kvart urver treh*
twenty past four	**tjugo över fyra** *cheugoo urver fewra*
twenty-five past five	**fem i halvsex** *fem ee halv-sex*
half past six	**halvsju** *halv-sheu*
twenty-five to seven	**fem över halvsju** *fem urver halv-sheu*
twenty to eight	**tjugo i åtta** *cheugoo ee otta*
a quarter to nine	**kvart i nio** *kvart ee neeoo*
ten to ten	**tio i tio** *teeoo ee teeoo*
five to eleven	**fem i elva** *fem ee elva*
twelve o'clock (noon/midnight)	**klockan tolv (på dagen/på natten)** *klockan tolv (paw daagen/paw nutten)*

at dawn	**i gryningen** *ee grewningen*
in the morning	**på morgonen** *paw morronen*
during the day	**under dagen** *eunder daagen*
before lunch	**innan lunch** *innan leunsh*
after lunch	**efter lunch** *efter leunsh*
in the afternoon	**på eftermiddagen** *paw efter-middaagen*
in the evening	**på kvällen** *paw kvellen*
at night	**på natten** *paw nutten*
I'll be ready in five minutes.	**Jag blir klar om fem minuter.** *yaag bleer klaar om fem mineuter*
He'll be back in a quarter of an hour.	**Han kommer tillbaka om en kvart.** *han kommer tilbaaka om en kvart*
She arrived half an hour ago.	**Hon kom för en halv timme sedan.** *hoonn kom fur en halv timmeh sehdan*
The train leaves at …	**Tåget går klockan …** *tawget gawr klockan*
13:04	**tretton noll fyra** *tretton nol fewra*
00:40	**noll noll fyrtio** *nol nol furteeoo*
The train is ten minutes late/early.	**Tåget är tio minuter för tidigt/försenat.** *tawget air teeoo mineuter fur teedigt/ fursehnat*
It's five minutes fast/slow.	**Den går fem minuter för fort/sakta.** *den gawr fem mineuter fur foort/sakta*
from 9:00 to 5:00	**från nio till sjutton** *frawn neeoo til sheutton*
between 8:00 and 2:00	**mellan åtta och fjorton** *mellan otta ock fyoorton*
I'll be leaving by …	**Jag åker vid klockan …** *yaag awker veed klockan*
Will you be back before …?	**Kommer du tillbaka innan …?** *kommer deu tilbaaka innan*
We'll be here until …	**Vi stannar här tills …** *vee stannar hair tils*

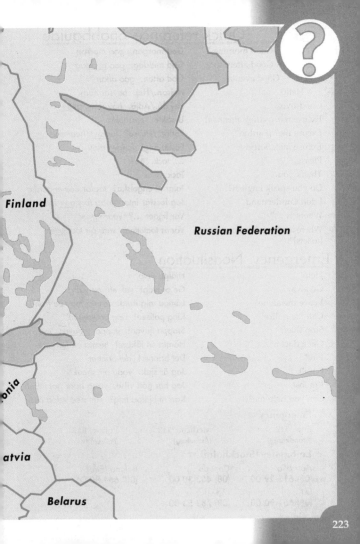

Finland

Russian Federation

onia

atvia

Belarus

Quick reference Snabbguide

Good morning.	**God morgon.** *goo morron*
Good afternoon.	**God middag.** *goo middag*
Good evening.	**God afton.** *goo afton*
Hello.	**Hejsan./Hej.** *haysan/hay*
Good-bye.	**Hej då./Adjö.** *hay daw/ayeur*
Excuse me. (*getting attention*)	**Ursäkta.** *eurshekta*
Excuse me? [Pardon?]	**Förlåt?/Hursa?** *furlawt/heur saa*
Excuse me!/Sorry!	**Förlåt mig!** *furlawt may*
Please.	**..., tack.** *tuck*
Thank you.	**Tack.** *tuck*
Do you speak English?	**Talar ni engelska?** *taalar nee engelska*
I don't understand.	**Jag förstår inte.** *yaag furstawr inteh*
Where is …?	**Var ligger …?** *vaar ligger*
Where are the bathrooms [toilets]?	**Var är toaletten?** *vaar air tooaletten*

Emergency Nödsituation

Help!	**Hjälp!** *yelp*
Go away!	**Ge er iväg!** *yeh ehr ee vairg*
Leave me alone!	**Lämna mig ifred!** *lemna may ee frehd*
Call the police!	**Ring polisen!** *ring pooleesen*
Stop thief!	**Stoppa tjuven!** *stoppa cheuven*
Get a doctor!	**Hämta en läkare!** *hemta en lairkare*
Fire!	**Det brinner!** *det brinner*
I'm ill.	**Jag är sjuk.** *yaag air sheuk*
I'm lost.	**Jag har gått vilse.** *yaag haar got vilseh*
Can you help me?	**Kan ni hjälpa mig?** *kun nee yelpa may*

Emergency ☎

Fire **112**	Medical **112**	Police **112**
(Brandkåren)	(Ambulans)	(Polisen)

Embassies (Stockholm) ☎

Australia	*Canada*	*Ireland [Eire]*
(08) 613 29 00	**(08) 453 30 00**	**(08) 661 80 05**
U.K.	*U.S.*	
(08) 661 90 00	**(08) 783 53 00**	